BARNSTORMING

by
Frank Bacon

BARNSTORMING

by
Frank Bacon

This limited edition was printed in 1987 as a membership premium by the
San Jose Historical Museum Association
635 Phelan Avenue
San Jose, CA 95112

Printed in U.S.A. by
The Rosicrucian Press
76 Notre Dame Avenue
San Jose, CA 95110

Limited first edition, 1987.
Published by the
San Jose Historical Museum Association

FORWORD

When Frank Bacon died in Chicago on November 19, 1922, he was the theatrical sensation of America. *Lightnin'*, the play which he co-authored and in which he starred, had smashed all previous records — playing on Broadway for three years and a day.

Yet Frank remained a hometown boy. And home was San Jose, California. This is where he was raised, where his family remained, and where he longed to return when his barnstorming days were over.

"Barnstorming" is a term often associated with the early days of aviation. Yet the principal meaning of the word, according to Webster, is "to go about [the country] performing plays, giving lectures, or campaign speeches, playing exhibition games, etc. especially in small towns and rural districts."

For most of his adult life Frank Bacon barnstormed throughout California and the western United States, often with his wife, Jennie, at his side. He learned the art of the stage through years of bit parts and in struggling stock companies, all the while crystalizing his talented portrayal of old man characters.

In 1986 we uncovered the manuscript for *Barnstorming* tucked away in a corner of the Museum Archives. It had originally been given to the City's Landmarks Commission by Frank's widow, Jennie, and newspaper columnist Evelyn Wells. Wells had used it, apparently, as the basis for a series of articles on Frank Bacon's life which appeared in the *San Francisco Call & Post* in 1920. Volunteer Patricia Loomis recognized the name "Frank Bacon" as that of the famous actor. Several of us read the manuscript — and were hooked. The warmth and personality of this man, combined with the significance of his contribution to the American theater, made us realize immediately the importance of publishing the manuscript.

We were able to locate the grandchildren and great-grandchildren of Frank and Jennie Bacon, as well as a great-grandniece and nephew. They have been most helpful in providing family photographs, playbills, and other memorabilia to enhance the publication and promotion of the book.

Barnstorming was probably written between 1918 and 1922. Frank had made it to New York by this time, breaking all records on Broadway in his play, *Lightnin'*, and secure in his position as the premier character actor, or rube comedian, on the American stage. It was from this perspective — at the pinnacle of success — that he reviewed the events of his life with humor and warmth.

In 1930, eight years after Bacon's death, the play *Lightnin'* was made into a major motion picture by the Fox Film Company. It was directed by Henry King and starred Will Rogers in the role of Lightnin' Bill Jones, made so famous by Frank Bacon. The film was chosen as one of the top movies of the year by the *New York Times*.

But in the years since his phenomenal success, his death, and the movie, *Lightnin'*, Frank Bacon has largely been forgotten, even in his hometown. It is a pleasure, therefore, to publish this story of his life as he wrote it himself. We have made very few changes in the manuscript; the grammar, people and place names, and expressions, stand as they were written in the early '20s. Some expressions and characterizations might not be generally acceptable today, but must be seen in light of the era in which they were written. A limited number of footnotes have been added to give the reader more information, where available, on people and places associated with the history of the Santa Clara Valley.

In no way is this intended to be a reference book. Please enjoy *Barnstorming* for what it is: the warm and human account of one man's struggles and his eventual contribution to the American stage.

Kathleen Muller, *Editor*

TABLE OF CONTENTS

Frank Bacon in character of Lightnin' Bill Jones.

CHAPTER ONE

WHILE WATCHING MY SHEEP

Imagination was always my lead characteristic.

It made me a happy mendicant on Main Street—a million on Broadway. Now, after half a century, and in the clamor of New York and the third year of my record run in *Lightnin'* imagination returns me to the tumbleweed littered plains of the San Joaquin where I herded sheep as a boy.

On this day in the broad, hot Californian valley my future was bared to me.

I was twelve. Mother always used to say I had the most innocent blue eyes in the world—so innocent they looked kind of scared— and my round face was covered with fluffy down and burned to the shade of leather, and even my mop of curly tow hair was tipped with brown by the sun. Father and my big brother Charley—he was eighteen and father's companion—were out with the horses on the daily hunt for fresh grazing range. Nellie, our old collie, and I, were alone with the gray flocks.

It was hot with the heat of the San Joaquin, that dances wickedly along horizons and sends sharp lines around the youngest eyes. We were camped about twenty-five miles out of Bakersfield. The acrid scent of hot wool rose like steam from the broad backs of the sheep as they quietly nuzzled the barren soil, hunting food.

Our camp was by a little stream, but the water was thick and floated a lathery black scum. I watched the sheep put their noses to the water edge and shrink away. It would have played a stranger destiny with the Bacon family, had father guessed the greasy water his sheep refused to drink was floating millions in oil!

Today, oil derricks stem this desert scene like giant dollar marks against the blazing sky, but then was only waste and the rustling

1

sheep, in 1876. A few great lavender flowers gave vague color to the gray sand—childishly, I imagined them to be a variety of squash blossom, cousin to those in mother's kitchen garden back home in San Jose. But that was small matter to amuse a lad of twelve, and I am telling you my entire healthy young body ached with the agonizing boredom only boyhood can know.

I explored my imagination for amusement—although it had frequently brought me to grief. An old square kerosene can, slung around my neck with a bit of broken hide riata and pounded with two cottonwood sticks, became a drum. I marched. I was an army. Perhaps—for it was only fifty years ago and I have forgotten—I was a parade. However that was, I drummed and marched and shouted military commands at Nellie she refused to obey. Nellie was too faithfully in earnest with life to play. Her entire dog duty lay with the herds. She kept her brown eye on the bellwether and the blue one—Nellie's eyes were not mates—on my maneuvers.

Tarr-att-att-att! Tarr-att-att-att!

"Boom!" I chimed in with adolescent bass, finding the drum disappointing in volume.

Around and around the camp I marched, while the sun slathered in hot strokes over amethyst rims of flat valley land, and far off against the western Coast Range jiggered a blue lake that was mirage. Loneliness and the sheep and the disapproving stare of sober Nellie were all I had around me, but believe me or not, around me in that heated desert stillness, miles deep and violent in applause, was my audience!

I think I was born with the consciousness of one. They say that is the mark of the actor. Yet I have often wondered why such a birth mark was accorded me. At home in San Jose, while three of her "men folk" followed the sheep and my oldest brother, Ed, the photographer, remained with her, my mother marked out her days and lived according to the good old Methodist plan. Mother had been born Lehella Jane McGrew, of a pious Scotch family. "Methodist born, Methodist bred, Methodist till I die."

While on the other side my stern father's line, the Bacons, were from a severely religious family of the south. (Some of them like to trace our ancestry back to the Sir Francis of Shakespeare's day, but I don't mind.)

On both sides my people had ever regarded the theatre as the damned spot on the Christian civilization. Even to attend such a place was as difficult on the morals as dancing on Sunday. Why did I alone, out of this doubly pure lineage, meet my doom as I marched to my make-believe drum?

For something flickered over the sand to me, that at first I took for a vagrant tumbleweed. Now, of course, I realize it was a message from destiny! I forgot I was a parade or an army, forgot the stirring hordes of sheep, for spread out upon the sand was the first theatrical display paper I had ever seen.

What was it lept in my soul to meet the words? Or pounded in my veins at the crude woodcut of a woman who stood immensely in fluffy skirts on the bounding stallions? With sobbing breath I spelled out the miracle:

```
*****************************************************
*                                                   *
*                                                   *
*              IN BAKERSFIELD . . . SOON             *
*          THE MONTGOMERY QUEEN CIRCUS               *
*                                                   *
*****************************************************
```

From destiny, from the unknown, that took all one's breath away and left one feeling curiously trembly inside — like the day you ate soap to get out of going to school! I hid the miracle under the cornmeal sack in the chuck wagon and in a frenzy of excitement beat my drum around the camp again, until father and Charley and the herders came in with the scattered herds.

Even at twelve years I recognized the dramatic value of biding my time. Father, silent and a trifle saddened by struggle, his long face browned and lined by desert wind and sun, settled down before the sage-root fire with a grunt of relief that the day was over. Frenchy, oldest of all the herders and father's "top hand" man, began dexterously juggling bacon in an iron pan, and set corn pone to crisping odorously in the iron "Dutch oven" sunk in the ashes. The others squatted around the open fire balancing tin pans on their knees.

Night settled down with the purple odorlessness of orchids and the running firelight on our faces as we ate seemed the only thing left living in the world. There was the odor of powerful coffee, musky sage and oily wool. There were the movements of men who ate with fingers and jacknives and drank the strong milkless coffee from tin cups. Around us the impassable barriers of silence lay desert-deep.

"Mon Dieu! for why you don't say notting?" exploded Frenchy, sopping the last of his pone in the bacon pan, " 'smatter, you little Frank? You go dumb tonight like the sheeps?"

3

I was strangely still — usually the nuisance and amusement of these men! Still I told nothing of the message and not until the last tin plate was put away and the cigarettes rolled — mine among them! — did I spread my poster on the sand.

"Look!" I told them simply: all drama should be simple, yet how did I know that?

The tall letters, the lady, the horse, pranced together in the firelight. Father understood my nature, even then — Oh, how wise this worn westerner was concerning his youngest son! I saw his tired eyes twinkle as he remarked severely:

"Sonny, how long you been a-planning this?"

"I didn't . . . I jus' found it this afternoon!" I argued indignantly. "Honest, father, the wind blew it down the creek. Oh, father — Charley — do you think . . . ?"

The dignity born with me would not permit my pleading. But the men felt my unvoiced prayer and noisily demanded the holiday. Frenchy, loudest in his Gallic abandon, protested that I be taken to the Montgomery Queen Circus at any sacrifice. Charley, quieter but with sparkling enthusiasm, put in:

"There's no use all fiddelin' around in camp if they's a circus in Bakersfield, pop. Nellie and me can go partners tending camp and the rest of you take it in with Frank."

We went!

Life may in later years have done much that seems unfair, made me lower my shoulders to the bitterness of storms and meet with much of failure, but all cannot overbalance the flaming truth that we did attend the circus of the Montgomery Queen!

Viewed from this sober distance of fifty years and Broadway, that memory is still glowing with the pinkness of colored popcorns and lemonades, with orgies of peanuts and candy and every single one of the side shows. Holidays were rare on the range and father gave me one to remember always. I recall the crowd of us jolting back to camp in the wagon late at night, and my lying drowsily against his bent shoulder, distended, gorged, miserable of body but glorified of soul!

Months after, around the camp fire at evening, I was still imitating the clown. It was foolish work, but anything is fun in camp, and the herders roared uncritically over their cigarettes. There was little enough to laugh over then, in the San Joaquin.

Always we were moving on, following the wide gray herds that were like shadows in spreading storms of dust. At night, in the

4

camp's inadequate tin basin, we labored hopelessly at washing the grime from our drawn faces. The hot winds stiffened even my young and tender skin. Uncomfortable and weary nomads, we wandered over endless heated desert, solaced only by the beauty of the nights as we slept on chilling sand with the moon on our faces.

Many people mention my stillness in crowds, as if I were listening. It isn't that. Desert nights give one something never entirely forgotten nor outlived, an undying restfulness and calm. I have felt it in the clamor of Broadway, and recognized above flaring New York electrics, the faint, familiar stars of California.

Yes, it is wonderful to remember now, but then I did grow tired. When father had taken me from school in San Jose to follow the sheep with him, I swelled with the sense of adventure. Anything, when one is ten and normal, to escape school! But before a month ended lessons seemed all holiday by comparison, and for three interminable years in the long San Joaquin valley that sinks deep into the interior of California, we moved constantly to new ranges. Every day was as yesterday. Every camp was the same, fronting empty desert, mirage, tumbling vistas of yellowed weed.

Yet there was adventure in California then!

There was the bandit Tiburcio Vasquez, a Spanish-Californian son of old Monterey on the Coast, famous for his love affairs, his limpid playing of the guitar and sonnet-making, and his cruel banditry. Vasquez had been outlawed at seventeen and was hanged a few years later. California hunted and dreaded him. Nighttimes, around the campfire, the men told of new robberies by Vasquez and his insane daring and I, a tow-headed child huddled under my blanket, played the role of the great bandit chief in my dreams. I never told father of this ambition to become a bandit like Vasquez — to be anything not desert and sheep and monotony! I knew father would not understand such a yearning, particularly after his historic meeting with the hot-blooded Tiburcio.

Father had driven to Bakersfield that day with the chuck wagon to get provisions. He knew posses were scouring the San Joaquin trails for Vasquez, who had robbed, pillaged and murdered from Los Angeles to San Jose, and was reported hiding on the Coast Range with Rosario, his most beloved woman, who deserted her husband to live in hiding with Vasquez. The almost indecipherable road to Bakersfield was soft with dust, and clouds of gray dust spun from the wagon wheels as father drove, hoping to reach the town before night.

5

Two Mexicans came galloping towards him, riding, father always said, the best California ponies he had ever seen. There was one, alert and easy, who acted as leader and ordered father in fair English to throw up his hands. Hands in air, father leaped from the wagon as ordered, and was instantly lariated and flung face to the soft ground, exactly as the vaquero ropes a calf.

Father didn't so much mind their taking the chuck money in their easy process through his pockets, but he did feel badly listening to their soft pleasure over the fine silver watch Grandfather Bacon had given him when he left Kentucky and came west. Few live long in California without learning a little Spanish and as they counted the spoil, father, face drowned in the sand and miserable, caught twice the word "muerte" and guessed he was to die.

But Tiburcio Vasquez spoke to father again:

"¿Tiene Ud. una esposa? . . . Have you a wife?"

"A wife and six children in San Jose," reported father, unhappily.

Now San Jose was birthplace of the woman Rosario, and Vasquez loved her with a madness that was later to cost him his life. Now he unloosed the riata on my father's hands, and said to him in a sensible tone while the other Mexicans clamored softly in their own tongue for father's death:

"Lie here until we are across the arroyo, or life is not sweet for you, Senor!"

"Muerte . . ." the smaller man was repeating angrily, but Tiburcio Vasquez turned with the manner of a grandee and snarled, "¡No! Vamos!"

When their horses' thudding feet were fainter on the sand, father got up and drove on to Bakersfield.

The sheriff of Bakersfield heard his story and a possee returned over the trail ahead of our chuck wagon, for the face of Tiburcio Vasquez was known through all California and they knew he was the man. But Vasquez was vanished from the San Joaquin, and not until years later was he captured and brought in to San Jose, our home, and the county seat of Santa Clara County. We were living in San Jose then and father went to the old jail to examine the plunder. He identified his silver watch. Today, that watch is mine.

Although Vasquez had been positively identified as the plunderer of the highways, the Santa Clara County sheriff asked father to identify him. In the dark dungeon without windows father held a long conversation with his bandit of the desert. When the under-sheriff happened to be looking out of the barred doorway, Tiburcio Vasquez begged father in a low voice not to testify at the trial.

Father did not act as witness at that famous proceeding, recalling perhaps how his life had been spared on the road to Bakersfield, but there were many others to take his place on the stand. In the old Plaza before the City Hall in San Jose, on a day in 1875, Tiburcio Vasquez was hanged.

This is all the adventure I recall in the three years of sun and sand in the San Joaquin. The years dragged slowly, yet when they ended it seemed as if only the week before I had left mother in San Jose. The days came when the dusty gray herds were winding homeward. We climbed the mounting green range of the Coast chain, past the Pacheco where Fremont had marched his men before the American flag crossed the California lines, over the Diablos and toward Mount Hamilton. Trees were smaller, and manzanita appeared on the mountain sides, and toyon bushes that in winter flamed with berries. Boy-wise, I ate the sweet dust of the manzanita berries and grubbed in the hard earth for soap root to carry to mother; California women used it for washing their hair.

Over us Mount Hamilton loomed with a royal greenness, innocent then of the pearly domes that are now Lick Observatory. Back of Mount Hamilton, about forty miles above the city of San Jose, father put his herds to pasture and drove the wagon down the steep mountain side.

Home lay under our feet, the widest, flattest, most glorious of valleys, called by the traveler and poet and writer, Bayard Taylor, one of the three beautiful valleys of earth. Always, to me, that valley is home! It lay green and gold in the sunlight, drenched with the sweetness of fruit blossoms. At the north Alviso Bay glittered and ran like quicksilver into San Francisco Bay, and beyond lay San Francisco and the Pacific Ocean I had never seen although it was but forty miles from San Jose.

The wagon rattled down Santa Clara street, that once had been part of the old Alameda that led to Mission Santa Clara three miles away. Father Junipero Serra, barefooted and suffering founder of our western missions, unlocker of the gate to the Golden West, had walked it a hundred years before.

"Home" was the little house near Santa Clara street, just at the edge of San Jose. The prim little flowerbeds in the small yard, the pepper tree with ruby berries, the ruffled curtains at the windows, had not changed. I had left that home when a child of ten. I had spent three vital birthdays among the flocks and was now thirteen, but did not know I had changed. I was tall and awkward with the ungainly approach to Manhood, my face was covered with down and my yellow, curly head had burned to a dull tow.

I didn't wait to drive into the yard with father and Charley. I had to see mother, that moment, alone. I was her youngest son, she could never dream how I had missed her. Panting, ahead of the others, I raced around the house to the kitchen door.

Mother was there! Through the screen door I could watch her as with deft, certain strokes she tossed biscuit dough to feathery lightness on the floured end of the kitchen table. The oilcloth was turned back, and of a brown color, like mother's firm, bared arms.

She was singing. A hundred times I had listened to her crooning this favorite Methodist hymn, but now the words seemed so beautiful they brought tears to my throat:

"Bear me away on your snowy white wings,
To my immortal Home . . ."

The fragile, sweet voice quavered slightly with reverence for the meaning of the song. Mother was turning from the table to the roaring cook stove when I knocked at the screen door. She whirled briskly upon me, standing with floury arms raised away from the checked brown apron with the bib.

Ah, when last did I see a checked brown apron — with a bib!

"What is it?" she demanded gently, but with no recognition.

She did not know her boy! I stood outside the screen, a pathetically dusty little figure in overalls, dazed by her coldness. My lip quivered.

"I'm — Frank!" I murmured.

She had me through the door, her floured arms around me, had my slight figure close to the checkered bib, while both of us wept. Through my tears I kissed her, patting her thin cheeks awkwardly, and half ashamed putting my lips to the gray streaks that had not been in the soft brown hair before we left with the sheep. Life had not been easily lived, for mother.

If only she might have waited! I think of that often, looking around at what largess life has given me, and the little luxuries and

8

Frank Bacon at age 3.

An adolescent Frank Bacon. Portrait taken at Wright's Gallery, 284 Santa Clara Street, San Jose.

Bacon family and friends photographed at Capitola in July 1880. Pictured from left to right: Frank Bacon, Netta Jefferds, Annie Bacon Keesling, Helen Bacon, Lehella Jane Bacon (Frank's mother), Harrison Gruell, Mary Doughty, and Lyddall Bacon (Frank's father).

places and people mother would have loved. For she appreciated all things, in her grave, sweet fashion. She was a woman of rare dignity.

Father might tumble from his paternal pedestal at times to quarrel with his three growing sons, but mother never failed her gentleness by a word. She was my ideal of womankind, and I know whatever good has entered my life, whatever I have done, is mother's work. She was brave, she was the pillar that upheld our family life, and yet things were to be still harder for her while I resented it with the helpless bitterness of a child.

I was to feel this young fury fiercely that year after we returned from San Joaquin, while life went harder with the Bacon family and I could not do my share.

Father sold the last of the sheep. They had been a troublesome investment. He settled down at home, but it was a long time before life in San Jose seemed to readjust itself for him. He bought a small woodyard across the street from our house at last and sat there in its tiny makeshift office week after week in moods of hopelessness. Perhaps he had grown used to the undemanding life of the desert.

It was then that strange people began making themselves at home in our house — a school-teacher with ruffled lace around her thin throat, a man who informed me he was a lawyer and teased me with questions, a man who locked himself into the little room off the porch to mother's despair, for he was an inventor and she hourly expected him to " blow up the house." Mother explained to me, rather sadly, that these people were boarders. It was a new word to me.

Mother was working very hard. Every morning she was up at five, and every morning we had flaky hot biscuits on the table. We had them again every evening, southern fashion, and they made her famous in San Jose. She seemed to toss them together just anyway, but it was an old southern recipe of her grandmother's she followed, and a magic one. Her biscuits — I have eaten in cities famous for food, New Orleans, San Francisco, and never met biscuits like hers — they were flakily, deliciously white in a crust of golden lusciousness, and you ate them southern fashion, splitting them while hot and drenching them with golden butter.

Reluctantly, school entered my life again. And with school — Uncle Morris!

Uncle Morris appeared magically in our house one day and proved not to be a boarder. Mother explained he was her brother and

9

our uncle, and had come on a visit from our old home in Marysville in Northern California, where her sister lived and where I had been born in 1864. From the first moment I was entranced by this strange, delightful relative. He was lanky and tall, he moved with a slowness that astonished me, and under his chin from ear to ear went a fascinating fringe of stiff whiskers.

Of the many droll characters that were, years later, to resolve into my "Lightnin' Bill" Jones, Uncle Morris was the first.

His long career was unblemished by a single day of work. He was without chick or child. He visited one relative for a few months, then wandered on to the next. He was a spinner of amazing yarns. Open mouthed, I drank down all his tales. They were all of his great achievements. Nothing could be mentioned he hadn't seen, or done, or said. It was difficult to doubt Uncle Morris, he seemed to take it so for granted you believed in him.

I never saw his gallant laziness ruffled. He never grew angry. His stalling became my wicked delight, watching him when in a corner, if anyone doubted his yarns, gracefully tacking off to another subject. And he had a genius for getting out of anything.

"Now, Morris, get me in some wood. This oven's cooling off", mother, hard-ridden by the day's work, would order rather sharply, and Uncle Morris would start with unhurried grace for the woodshed.

"Come along, Frank," he would invite me on the way. "Load me up and start me back — see that I get home all right."

I would follow, lured by the commaraderie of his southern drawl, and once in the woodshed I loaded his arms for him. "Huh!" he'd remark teasingly, after that. "Bet you can't carry half as much."

Then I would be wrathful at this reflection on my strength, and pile up herculean armfulls of the splintery redwood and carry them to the kitchen woodbox, and puff mightily and grow damply pink in the countenance, while Uncle Morris, with no trace of professional jealousy cheered me through the entire job! Long after, perhaps, it would occur to me how delightfully I had been hoaxed.

After a month or so of visiting us, Uncle Morris wandered back to his sister's home in Marysville. But he would be back, oh, yes, Uncle Morris would always be back. And, I, and all our family, would welcome his gallant, whimsical, lackadaisical self. His naive dignity stayed with me, and at home and in the schoolyard I imitated Uncle Morris. Poor Uncle Morris! I wonder if it ever occurred to him he was a character, doomed to appear on earth again long after he had left it — "without much trouble, even as he had loved" — incarnate, as "Lightnin' Bill" Jones of California, Nevada, and Broadway!

Uncle Morris was one member of the family who sympathized with my struggles at school. I had returned to lessons eagerly enough after three years vacation. I was honestly, if rather vaguely, anxious to learn something. Anything, to help mother.

I found myself in the classroom of the Santa Clara street school, sunburned, awkward, tall for my years, studying with boys far smaller than myself. I was even taller than the teacher. My brain quivered over the simple division sums I had mastered and forgotten years before. Every day at four I came home and tried to hide the small but bitter humiliations of the day from mother. It is difficult to be a martyr at thirteen.

"Say, if you think I'm going on with old school . . ." I burst out bitterly one morning, when she came upstairs to call me early and found the patchwork and counterpane scattered over with pages of homework I had failed to master the night before. "Mother, what's the use! Schooling ain't — isn't so much. I'm most as tall as Charley and I want to work. I want to help out. I want to learn a trade."

"Well, Frank, if you think . . ."

Mother hesitated, looking so anxiously sweet my heart seemed breaking with hers. I was her youngest son — she had dreamed such things for me! Yet mother never interfered with the lives of her sons; perhaps that is why we were all eager to succeed in her eyes.

"I wanted things different for you, son, but . . . if your father is willing . . ."

CHAPTER TWO

WHITE TURKEYS AND BURNT CORK

Watching my three little granddaughters playing about me, somehow, I pity them. Science has given much to their young hands — speech from around the world that answers to a knob the youngest may turn, the wisdom of Einsteins and Edisons, machines that speed through cloudways to the Poles.

Yet, they will never see "Uncle Tom's Cabin!"

Not as I saw Uncle Tom, black, despised and glorified, at the old Brohaska Opera House[1] in San Jose when I was a lad of fourteen.

I think I wore even mother's calm morale to a thin edge, begging to go. Across the street from our house father's woodyard was thriving sadly and there was little extra change in the Bacon pockets, these lean years.

"And besides," explained mother, almost impatiently, "you went to a play-house only a few months ago."

Her sweet mouth tightened with the strength of her Puritan disapproval. She feared the loose influence she felt surrounded the "playhouse" life, and my other treat had not been lightly won. That had been the Royal Marionettes, my first show and a great disappointment. Goodness knows what I expected to see! But the little stage people of painted wood who danced to strings had not been real, not as real, say, as the pictures conjured by Jennie Weidman when she recited. So I had yet to see my first play.

Perhaps I didn't deserve to go. I was not a shining figure in family affairs. I was not attending school, nor was I working. I idled away my days with older boys, waiting the time when my big brother Ed, who was re-toucher in Wright's Photography Gallery[2] on Santa Clara Street, could take me into the gallery as his apprentice. Also, I smoked cigarettes, having learned the trick in the sheep camps.

12

Perhaps it was to distract my mind, that mother gleaned for me, from the household funds she kept in a handleless cup on the upper pantry shelf, the price of a matinee ticket to "Uncle Tom's Cabin."

You cannot know how I felt that afternoon, unless in your soul is born the lure of the tinsel world! I sat in the very first row of the gallery, and for days my jaw ached from its long tense rest on the ledge before me. By straining forward and keeping my mouth well opened, I missed no word or movement of the little people below. I forgot my bag of peanuts, forgot reality. There were plenty of acts and every ending was a cruel awakening. Each time the lights came on I sat blinking at the worn curtain in a state of dazed and miserable recognition that life was real and earnest. But the curtain would rise upon more wonderful scenes, and I would be complete again.

I guess that was the worst "Uncle Tom's Cabin" ever presented, with the possible exception of some I was later to present with my own company. Yet never again shall I see acting so inspiring. Eliza crossed the ice and I was with her, the hounds — courtesy San Jose pound! — foaming at my heels. The lawyer Marks strutted on — I felt myself aching under the weight of the enormous umbrella he carried. "I'm a lawyer, my name is Marks!" In that early version of the American classic, Marks had a few love scenes with Miss Ophelia, the acid maiden aunt. Simon Legree cracked his slave whip and I actually thought of waiting out on Santa Clara steeet later and punishing him — I didn't know exactly how. Poor Uncle Tom! No tears shed for him were ever more heart-rending than mine, and as for Little Eva, who was stout and rather elderly for that angelic child, she became the symbol of all my future dreamings long before she was hoisted to that ethereal plane several feet above the wings, rather jerkily, on a very visible rope.

I was home in time for dinner, but with no appetite for the sweet pork imbedded in southern baked beans and sugary ham that night. Later, while mother washed the dishes and we were alone in the kitchen, I told her the story of the play. I played Uncle Tom. I was Uncle Tom! — lashed to the door leading into the pantry, groveling of body but unmutilated of soul, until my tears drowned out the story.

"Sonny! My land, but you mustn't take on so!" exclaimed mother, staring at me across the steaming dishpan on the table. "Here, put away this platter for me and don't get so excited about things, — my stars, I never saw such a boy!"

While I stood on a chair to reach the upper shelf mother handed me the plates and told me the history of the Civil War. Like a statue, I stood there entranced, and even she forgot the dish water and let it grow tepidly gray, lost in her story of a nation that warred upon itself.

"The trouble between North and South began way back in the 'fifties," she said. "Your father's folks and my folks lived in Kentucky, and his folks always kept slaves, but we were always with the North in thinking every man had his right to be free. We wouldn't keep slaves for that reason. My folks moved West in '52 and . . . your father came after us."

Was there a blush on her thinning cheek? I wondered then, as mother turned her sweet face from me — from a part of her life I was not to know for many years, of a strangely true romance clean as the winds that swept across the early west. My father, tired and bent and growing grandiose with years, as though vanity tried to recompense itself for failure — I could not imagine his braving the perils of prairie life and Indian warriors, for the girl who was mother!

"By coming west our folks missed the Civil War, but your father lost two brothers in the fighting," said mother. "He and all his sisters had been nursed by an old black mammy in Kentucky, but he was all for wanting the slaves free, just as we were. And Harriet Beecher Stowe wrote "Uncle Tom's Cabin" and I read it and cried, although I was only a girl, and southern born . . ."

Listening to her story of Civil War, I felt the gooseflesh laving my hands and arms. Now it was I who marched through Georgia with Sherman, heard the stir of righteous anger in a bugle call that was heard across "the beauty of the lilies,"— it was I who thrilled to "Just Before the Battle, Mother," met imprisonment, despair and hunger, and died to save Uncle Tom!

Today, the old battered army hat of faded blue I wear in "Lightnin'," never fails to touch me with the hurt of those years of war. I feel as if I lived through '63. Around that hat goes the gilt cord that marks the wearer an inmate of an Old Soldier's Home. I have loved these places, hunted them out always, in my travels. I feel as if I belonged there with old comrades as I sense the oldness and the ache of the place. And yet, I was born in the year that marked the end of the Civil War.

Mother's voice ran thrillingly over the story while I, accomplishing a silent running commentary of great deeds, finished wiping the dishes.

14

Well, Uncle Tom was one of two adventures that colored the bewildering months after leaving school and before starting to work, and they were to influence all my after years. The other was so queer and personal I can't believe now it actually happened. And yet, I can't imagine living unless it had!

This was attending one of the monthly entertainments of the Good Templar Society.

I admit that doesn't sound like much of a thriller to normal youngsters. Usually the Good Templar meeting bored me to the point of murder. Mother was a leading spirit in the movement. Perhaps it is because she so dreaded liquor in any form that I have never taken a drink. Not from prudishness, only a memory of her horror of alcohol. King Alcohol was a living and dreadful demon to mother, for all good women to march upon and demolish, in the name of Good Templars. I was fairly dragged to one of their entertainments, and there it was I first heard little Jennie Weidman recite.

I was reciting too, that night!

Mother had sent me for a few lessons from Miss Ida Benfey, the dramatics teacher. Later Miss Benfey deserted San Jose for the east and became well known as a dramatic reader. My sister Emma was attending her elocution classes in a cloud of starchy ruffles and importance, and as I was as crazy about learning to "speak pieces" as Emma was, mother sent me at last.

With the fruition of these brief studies I appeared before the Temperance Society. That evening I wore one of my earliest pair of long trousers, miserably tight according to the fashion of the '80's, and I retained upon my head with supreme dignity, my very small black felt hat. With a passionate sincerity peculiar, I believe, to fourteen years, I stood upon the platform and declaimed the recitation Miss Benfey had taught me, with gestures:

"The White Turkey is dead!
The White Turkey is dead!
How the news through the barnyard went flying!
Of a mother bereft,
Two small turkeys were left,
And a case for assistance was crying. . . ."

Please, don't laugh at me, now, for I was pouring all the pathos of my life into the epic of that lost mother turkey, all the drama that was native to me, all Miss Benfey had taught. And with a little stab of

15

misery, even now, I remember "taking my bow," and, glancing down the rows of good applauding ladies, I saw that dreadful little Jennie Weidman, in one of her famous attacks of giggles.

I couldn't imagine why her aunt, Miss Emmy Jeffery, had brought that child to a temperance entertainment. Jennie was then — I never was any hand at guessing women's ages — just nine. I knew her well — by sight. While helping father in his woodyard I had seen her stroll impudently by, always with her arms entwined with those of one of her four intimate girl friends, and always giggling. Directly after my recitation, her name was called, and she stepped forward, trying to suppress the smile on her face that was fresh and sweet as a pansy's.

That smile left me in a sore fury. It hadn't occurred to me I was funny.

"But I just broke my neck to get to one of my girl friends who knew you and tell her how funny you looked, Frank," years after, with the same refreshing lack of tact that marked her youth, Jennie often told me.

There was nothing funny about her reciting. Her "piece," as we called them in those days, was "Corporal John," the sad ballad of a one-armed organ grinder, written by a Mr. Dunlap of San Jose.

"And he grinds, and grinds, and grinds . . ."

Jennie declaimed the words slowly, standing before us in Miss Benfey's most approved fashion, for she was also taking elocution lessons and was a star pupil. She wore that night, she now explains, a very best dress made over from Auntie Em's old salmon grenadine, banded with narrow black velvet, with three pleatings around the little skirt and a little jacket, and her brown hair had been curled most especially for the occasion, in rag curlers, for three days!

I drank in every syllable of the mournful grinder's song and thought it too pathetic! So did the Good Temperance ladies. I saw them putting neat little white lace hankies to their eyes. And Jennie Weidman, aged nine, could do that to people! While I was — funny.

That was the hour I resolved to some day show Jennie Weidman! It has taken me half a century to do it. No, for Jennie, somehow, always believed in me. No matter what others were thinking — what they said. Even that night, although she had laughed at me, she stung me with her sincerity. Then began a faith the years have never lost, in clear womanly brown eyes and a sweetness only strengthened by time.

16

For many years now, Jennie Weidman had been "Mother" to me, and to our children, and to theirs. And yet — she hasn't changed. She has always been the mischievous spirit that danced ahead of me in my 'teens and symbolized all my dreams of a career, for Jeannie, the years were to tell us, was also stage-bound. And all the dreams a boy of fourteen may possess were for the stage.

The idea broke over my head before I knew its meaning. Sam W. Piercy[3] brought down the storm by playing San Jose. Piercy's name means little enough these days, even to San Jose, yet he was Californian born, his people lived in San Jose, he was a brilliant and handsome young actor — our idol come home! Imagine what his coming meant to me! Imagine what it was to learn that Sam Piercy needed Supers for his first night in San Jose!

I had more leisure than talent, and was the first person outside Brohaska's Opera House that morning. Not another person showed up until eleven. By that time I was wrecked emotionally and whatever genius I had was wilted with suspense. Even now it is astonishing to remember that I was hired!

Not a part requiring deep emotional talent. I was given no "try-out," no chance to declaim upon a real stage my one recitation pertaining to a defunct turkey. No, I was merely hired, to go on with a mob of other "supes," well back stage, and "mutter angrily." I was merely one mutter in the mob. For this I would be permitted to go out front, afterward, and view the rest of the performance. That was all my reward, and entirely too much honor, at that.

I told mother I was making my first appearance on any stage. I had to. For until I was twenty and started "keeping company" with Jennie Weidman, the "Mother," of later years, my own mother always sat up for me. No matter how tired she was after the cooking and mending and cleaning, mother sat up in the parlor reading her New Testament and saw every one of her chicks safely to roost. So it was fearfully, yet with a certain pride, I informed mother that I had not lived in vain but was going on the stage.

Remember, mother was devoutly Methodist. But also, she had, without knowing it, a great respect for personal ideals. She fought back the objections I knew were hers. Yet I do remember her saying:

"Frank, actors as a rule are vain and worldly — they wander from town to town with no home ties — people flatter and spoil them — but," and her dear eyes seemed to peer into the future, "if you ever do go on the stage, don't let any one flatter you — and keep to yourself."

17

Flattery! I received little enough at the solitary rehearsal of the "mob scene." The stage manager, perspiring and unpoetic in a shirt that seemed alien to laundries, yelled at me because I had unfortunately attracted his attention. He referred to me in a manner my early training considered impolite and I, unused to the severe criticism of stage life, passed through the rehearsal as through an ordeal.

Opening night was worse.

Seven o'clock found me crowded into a small, unventilated "supes" dressing room with a dozen other young San Jose fellows. In a corner was piled our allotment of preposterous pink tights, faded and shapeless, and other raiment of a period that never existed off the boards. I sat down on a box in another corner to stare at my tights. There is a trick about getting into tights, as every real actor knows. But these defied all trickery. They bulged in the most startling places. I slid into them at last without hope. They came under my arm pits.

As I tied them there I was suddenly paralyzed by the horrible thought that they might come down. Someone gave me safety pins — lifesavers of our profession. I fairly nailed the pink horrors into position. I donned my ballooning coat and jerkin and faced a cracked mirror and greasepaint for the first time. That was a miraculous experience, slapping into a strange make-up, crowding on the greasepaint and seeing my face disappear under a profusion of pink lumps! Only, these were the days before theatrical cold cream, and vaseline was used. There was no liner, either in blues and browns, only heavy powder was used, and black grease for beading the lashes. More make-up was used in those days, but it was less real. It had not yet become one of the finer crafts of the stage.

At last I took my turn before the half-length mirror, fascinated and pleased out of all proportion. My physique, quilted in the faded tights, left much to be desired by lovers of art. But the other supers looked no better than I. A wilted herd, we waited outside the wings. I heard laughter and applause out front, from a San Jose that welcomed home its talented son.

The perspiration poured through the make-up on my face, I put my hand to my forehead and encountered vaseline — remembered. Our cue came. I had forgotten it. Some one pushed me. A blinding flare of lights rose in a half circle before me, there were cries and angry mutterings from other throats — and mine! — and Sam Piercy was addressing us with a composed elegance, and without turning his face from the audience.

Then, I cannot express it, but I experienced the footlights! It must be something like a conversion, or a man finding home after long years of wandering. Suddenly I was serene and confident as Piercy — I, in my ridiculous tights, standing as if plastered against the back drop, I hid in the mob. I felt ridiculous. But, oh, divinely happy!

Later, when the supers were permitted out front to see the rest of the show, I hung around back stage. I hated leaving the tawdry enchantment of the life behind the wings. I knew a couple of the fellows shifting scenes. In those days such fellows were called "Glories," and they worked the scenes without pay, just to see the show. This was long before the organization of the Theatrical Mechanics Association.

"Coming around to see the "Marble Heart" tomorrow night, Frank?" one of the "Glories" asked me. "They say it's Piercy's best part."

"I haven't the money," I admitted.

"Come anyway," he invited, shouldering a wing. I'll tuck you away in the flies."

So I was in the theatre on the second night, and sitting in a sort of hammock made of ropes, far overhead in the flies, I saw Sam Piercy play "The Marble Heart." For me, time, place and reason faded away. I was Raphael, the poor sculptor but magnificent lover, underneath me on the stage. Marco came, and she was very beautiful; I loved her with Raphael's love, but she deserted him for his wealthier rival and I longed to kill her with my own hands. And these hands bit the ropes I clung to as I looked down upon lonely Raphael, saw him chiseling the white marble that held his soul, heard him singing the song the mournful, godlike Byron sang under Italian skies:

"Maid of Athens, ere we part
Give, oh, give me back my heart!
Or, since that has left my breast,
Keep it now, and take the rest."

The words broke in his strong white throat. He flung the chisel to the floor, buried his face in his hands — wept! Far overhead I was weeping too, — Sam Piercy didn't know that. Poor fellow, he was just beginning a glorious young career. A few years later he died of smallpox.

I wanted to act like Piercy. The way he talked and sang and moved haunted me night and day. Now I knew I had to be an actor.

It was startling to learn that my destiny was settled, but, suddenly, I had a job and a career. I was to be a photographer.

"Frank might have made a good photographer," Wilbur Wright says of me now in San Jose. "But he had every kind of business to attend to except work."

Wright knows. I was entered into his service, in the Wright Photographic Gallery on Santa Clara Street in San Jose. Wright wasn't much more than a youngster himself, but he had working for him my brother Ed, and John Tressider — a jolly young Englishman, later married to my sister Helen.

I was started on printing photos. But I had many friends, and they interfered with my professional career. Sam Howes and his dog were always dropping in to see me, and all the other fellows I knew. They thought I might be lonesome. They offered to help watch the prints. Often, Wright entered to find me warbling in close harmony with the other boys while the visages of glassy-eyed San Joseans faded from view in the developing tank.

"If we only had a few more boys in here!" Wright would growl sarcastically.

But we kept on with our singing for now we had organized a quartette that must have cost Wright half his trade. We sang on the flat roof of the old building where I was supposed to print the plates. Once we imitated a Salvation Army meeting and had crowds gathered on the sidewalk below waiting for the testimonials. Below, in the stuffy old gallery, graced with the weird iron head rests and the marvelous backgrounds of the period — the favorite a rustic church with a gate for the subject to lean upon — was born my barnstorming career.

I said one day out of pure inspiration:

"Say, let's get up a minstrel show!"

The idea went over with a crush. We only started the thing to kill time, and I'm just beginning to realize how lucky we were that time alone was killed. Mr. McLaughlin,[4] who owned a bank in San Jose — perhaps I had better say *The Bank*, for this was long ago, let us have a room in his building two evenings a week. We held our first rehearsal immediately.

We practiced in our usual suits and faces, as solemn a group of young owls as ever gathered with bones and tambourines. Influence, my friends, won me the position of right end man, opposite Howard Hill.

20

Louis Lieber, J. H. Titcombe, and Frank Bacon. Photographed c. 1875 by Wilbur Wright.

Studio portrait of Jane (Jennie) Weidman taken at Bacon Bros. Studio, 58 South First Street, San Jose.

Golden hours, every week, we wasted upon those foolish evenings. We raked through every old joke book for jests. We even made up some of our own. Our rehearsals were interrupted by our laughter.

We had many songs, as everyone wanted to sing as loudly and often as possible. Elmer Chase,[5] who has a lot to say now about the Apricot Industry in San Jose, had two favorite selections, "Rocked in the Cradle of the Deep," and "Thy Sentinel Am I." The rest of us didn't think these ballads went very well with blackface and a huge red tie, but Elmer always was a sentimental sort of minstrel.

We worked hard. We worked harder at keeping the minstrelsy a secret. Not that we weren't proud of our efforts, but we knew the comic trend of the journalists of San Jose. Particularly Hugh De Lacy.[6] Hughie is in the sheriff's office now, but then he wrote for the *Item,* and gave me the first press notice I had ever received. The *Item* editorial room was directly under Wright's Gallery, and Hughie heard me singing as I worked and wrote a squib about it.

Somehow the news of our practice got about, for one night four more boys walked in on us. We knew them. They were the quartet from the University of the Pacific,[7] the old Methodist College on the outskirts of San Jose. Joyously, we welcomed in their voices. And after them came the Parkman Boys, and they had the best band in San Jose just then, and wanted to join our show!

Now with so much talent, we had to show it. But where?

We couldn't face the ridicule of our home town. And as we were poor but honest lads, most of the boys, like myself, learning trades, we would have to pay our own expenses to wherever we went, and back. Therefore, we could not go far from home.

"Gilroy!" suggested Louis Lieber,[8] who always had comical ideas. Gilroy is about thirty miles below San Jose and not noted for its liveliness. But we agreed upon Gilroy.

"Now we have to select an advance man to go on ahead, put up the stickers, and everything," said the oldest of the Parkman boys.

To my astonishment, they were all looking at me.

They could not have found a worse advance agent. I doubt if I had ever heard the expression before. My objection was overruled, was hissed down. I WAS the advance agent.

The trip would cost me at least three dollars. That was a large financial undertaking and I had an awful time scraping so much cash together. And a still worse time explaining to Wilbur Wright just why I would not grace his photographic halls the following day. He gave me the holiday at last. Mother loaned me three dollars. I was ready for my march upon Gilroy, that would end in victory, or disgrace.

It was the year of the Cleveland-Blaine campaign. A Democratic excursion was running south next day — would pass through Gilroy. I took advantage of that excursion, and saved two dollars!

I admit it was not honorable. I have never whipped up an interest in politics and the tariff issue meant nothing to me. And anyway, I've always been a dyed-in-the-wool Republican, perhaps because of this very trip. I huddled down in a seat with my roll of minstrel billings, and listened in a dazed way to the chanting of the merry politicians:

"Cleveland, Cleveland, don't be afraid,
Tariff reform is not free trade."

I'll bet it was the first time a minstrel advance man was ever carried to his destiny by a Democratic excursion.

The thirty miles slipped by, at times too long, at times far too short for my relaxing courage. I hadn't the faintest idea how to storm Gilroy.

Yet, I found little enough of Gilroy to storm. A single street, two quiet, small hotels, country life stirring sleepily along the boardwalks and around the post office, and beyond, green country that held cattle and grain. I stood upon the station platform staring down the single street. I hadn't the faintest idea how I was to prepare for the advance of the minstrels.

That hour began my barnstorming career.

CHAPTER THREE

WHERE BLUFF IS MIGHTY

Victor Bassignano, looking exactly as the manager of a small town theatre should, sat in the little wooden office of the only theatre in Gilroy.

His door stood open. I didn't knock. I walked in with the supreme insolence one acquires at eighteen. Under my arm was the wad of one-sheet advertising the Valentine Printing Company had struck off for us. It meant much hard scraping of pennies on the part of the minstrels.

"I'm advance man for the greatest show on earth," I bubbled, trying to follow Elmer Chase's advice to act in a "dapper" fashion.

"Wassanamea your show?" smote Bassignano.

That was a right hook to the jaw. None of the minstrels had dreamed we needed a name. I stared at Bassignano—he looked friendly enough. The straw of last despair floated through my mind and I grasped at it—at something Louie Lieber had said jokingly when he saw me off on my journey from the San Jose depot: "Go on and win, Frank, the big twelve will follow..."

THE BIG TWELVE!

The words came to mind just as I spoke them. There were twelve minstrels, not including the band boys. I couldn't understand why the name didn't impress the manager as it had me. He only dusted off his table with the side of his hand and looked suspicious.

"Never heard of 'em," he commented flatly.

That was not the surprise to me it might have been had I ever heard of them myself. However, I appeared astounded and grieved. I assured Bassignano the Big Twelve had stormed and startled America. His next question was murderous!

"Where's the Big Twelve playing now?"

23

"Salt Lake!" I answered — inspired.

My hands were wet, gripping the bills printed with so much sacrifice on our parts. They seemed pitiful now, as I guessed the Salt Lake answer was wrong. Bassignano grinned.

"Then — why do you want to play Gilroy before San Francisco?" he demanded.

Numb with the weight of his dismissal, I was again alone on the one street in Gilroy.

Along the board sidewalks sat those wise men of every town who toil not and only spin amazingly of the yarn that wearieth. These watched me with the profound suspicion of men who grow old with their town. Behind me Victor Bassignano slammed the door of his theatre — the only theatre in Gilroy! My ignorance had locked its doors to the Big Twelve!

Every town like Gilroy has its hall where lodges meet, where entertainments were held, and where the local belle's coming out party is given. I met the owner of this hall. I rented it from him for a single night. There was no vulgar talk of percentages, receipts, or such patter that marks the salesman. In supremely happy ignorance I closed the deal, and started out for the town expressman.

The expressman sat on the veranda of William's Hotel staring across the street with philosophical repose. Around him lounged his cronies — men whose opinions ruled Gilroy. I walked between the tilted chairs to him.

"Say, I'm advance man for the Big Twelve Minstrels — playing here Saturday night. Bring our traps up to the hotel for us?"

Every man present was listening. The expressman spat out into the dusty street — he enjoyed the distinction of spitting farther than any man in town — and demanded without respect:

"How many trunks ye got, sonny?"

In my rage of insulted youth, in the presence of these wise ones of Gilroy, how could I bare the truth of our one small property trunk? Therefore I looked down upon that expressman as one from a great height and answered distinctly:

"We have twenty-six trunks!"

I tell you, that even galvanized those men of wisdom. They stopped chewing tobacco out of respect and the expressman said with sudden reverence:

"Whew — biggest load ever came to Gilroy, Mister. Guess I'll have to get out the big truck."

"Beyond doubt," said I.

I left them on the veranda in a profound discussion as to the portent and content of twenty-six trunks. I knew I could trust them to act as real advance agents through the town, while I hunted up the Gilroy sign painter. In the interests of art, he advanced me a bucket of paste and a brush, and I marched upon the main street with my paper.

Our printer had been generous. I papered Gilroy to a turn, out of our bounty of signs, until every fence, telegraph pole and barn reeked with the news that the Big Twelve Minstrels were on their way to the little town.

No one had ever told me pasting up bills was strenuous toil. Late that evening, with the sensation of a dislocated spine and a neck crooked from staring upward, I caught that midnight Democratic excursion train to San Jose.

But I reported to the gallery on time — or almost — next day. Louie Lieber was the first minstrel to drop in. All day long, until Wright yearned to throw us all from the gallery window, the boys straggled in to help watch prints and learn the details of Gilroy. My advance tactics were praised, my neck, aching still from the bill posting, received sympathy. We were all nervous before the day ended. We, the Big Twelve from Salt Lake City! That was violent swank, and all of us in our 'teens, and from San Jose! Elmer Chase made dark references as to the law concerning imposters. The rest of that week was gloomy, yet electrical with hope.

On Saturday I was returning to Gilroy, this time with the other boys as a member of the minstrel cast. I've said before one thing made us distinctive in minstrel lines — each of us paid our own fares! Now to many the train was a novelty, to all it was cruel expense. Including the Parkman Band, there were eighteen members of the Big Twelve.

Remember, this was forty years ago, and stage coaches still plied the country roads and an omnibus was not an object for a museum. There was one of those monster vehicles in a livery stable in San Jose, that looked large enough and worn enough to have carried the Gold Rush across the plains in '49. The dear old thing was called the Mayflower. It needed axle grease, paint and new fringe to replace the mangy festoons of string that garnished its top. But it was warranted not to spring a "one hoss shay" act upon its inmates, and we dickered its owner down to a nominal cost that was far, far cheaper than riding by train.

25

The Mayflower held sixteen. Saturday morning, early, sixteen minstrels clambored up its rickety steps. The band boys carried their brass instruments. The drum was sandwiched in somehow. Every boy carried a small lunch to eat along the road. The entire outfit resembled the sophomores first annual picnic, not a respectable minstrel troupe.

"Now don't start cutting up any shindigs," I warned them uneasily before starting. "And whatever happens — don't let anyone in Gilroy get a sight of the Mayflower. They'll think we're queer enough without this old "bus.""

The minstrels promised to act with dignity, but I knew what their word was worth, and nervously watched the Mayflower lumbering down First Street. Louie Lieber, young Stephenson and I went to the depot. We were going by train, I, because I had been advance agent, Louie, because he had a real occupation as a sign painter's apprentice and could afford the luxury, and Stephenson because he worked in the Southern Pacific depot and had been given a pass. How Louie and I envied him.

We rode in dignity and at Coyote went sailing past the Mayflower. Above the roar of the train we heard their cries as they recognized our faces and saluted in deafening chorus. My worst fears came true, for dignity had been forgotten at the City limits and the minstrels were rocking the valley with happiness. One was hanging upside down by his knees from the mouldy top. One was riding on the top, in a pose like Washington's, crossing the Delaware. The startled horses trotted to the wild music of the Parkman band.

"They'll never get to Gilroy." I said, desperately.

But they did get there. They didn't appear in town with that ridiculous omnibus — they didn't dare. They left it a mile outside of town, staked out the horses, and walked the rest of the way into Gilroy. Their mysterious appearance, hours after any train's arrival, must have seemed miraculous to the natives.

We had planned to meet them at two o'clock that afternoon in the Williams Hotel. At two, the minstrels were there.

"Sure, I'll put up your sign for you," said Williams, the proprietor, in a very friendly way.

After he had gone to the trouble of putting up the big sign Louie had painted, prominently, in the hotel lobby, we moved down the street to the Southern Pacific Hotel. Yes, we did — thanked Williams gratefully and moved out to another hotel! The numbest-brained

26

ham actor knows better, knows that a company should be scattered over a town, that one actor in a lobby is a better ad than six in a theatre. But our band of eighteen settled down in the other hotel and began preparing for the big parade.

The parade is as much a part of a minstrel show as the burnt cork. Our cork hadn't arrived. Somebody tapped me on the shoulder. It was my admirer, the expressman.

"Guess those trunks are down at the dee-po now," he suggested.

"I presume they are," I said, with dignity and a failing heart.

He had rented an extra team of horses and brought out the big town truck. I rode with him to the depot, balancing on the stilted seat while all the cronies of the wooden sidewalk watched us with a healthy respect. At the depot, on the rickety platform, was the one small trunk. Crowning it, was our little can of burnt cork.

"Where in heck's them twenty-six trunks?" gasped the expressman.

"They must have been lost coming from Salt Lake!" I exclaimed desperately. "This is terrible . . . I'll sue the Southern Pacific. . . ."

Solemnly, pompously, we rode back to the hotel, the four heavy-footed horses dragging the great dray, and, lost in its vastness — the small trunk, the black can.

Gilroy never did know what became of the other trunks.

Within the hour our faces were glossed with black. Wide collars and queer ties — most of them manufactured by our mothers — made our customary suits into minstrel costumes. Several wore ancient coats found in attics at home, and absurd hats. The Parkman boys tuned their instruments and we strutted out to the street. In a blur of noise, we were off.

Howard Hill led the parade. I came somewhere off-side, pounding a drum for lack of higher musical accomplishment. Down the single Gilroy street swung the Greatest Minstrels on Earth — the Parkmans, Johnny Bowman, Jimmy Pembroko, Billy Athens, John Tressider, Louie Lieber, W. P. Codingtron, Jimmy Hatch — all the others of "that old gang of mine," gee, somehow it hurts to remember! The funniest things seem mournful, the silliest songs are plaintive, after years pass.

Every man loves to get into some character not his own, loves to parade. Only one dark cloud covered the minstrels that day. For our minstrel treasurer was not parading with us. He was a San Jose boy but he happened to be living in Gilroy just then and we couldn't risk

27

having him recognized. How he begged to be allowed to parade! But we locked him up in the hotel and paraded without him.

We marched down the street and back again and I was enjoying one of the fullest moments of my life when the world turned upside down for me — standing on the sidewalk with a huge grin of recognition on his face was Johnny Owens, the County Clerk, from San Jose!

He knew me — knew half the boys in the parade. My vanity fled, and a tragic minstrel that was I skulked past him. Then — Owens winked at me. Like a flash the world righted again, and I winked back, knowing the secret of the dark horses of Minstrelsy were safe with Owens.

The air was sultry. Our make-ups were hot and melting like butter on our faces. The street was treeless, and yet for two hours we paraded. Forty years ago that single Gilroy street was not a long one, and I hate to think how many times we marched up it and down again. Only youth could stand such a marathon. The music was aching in our ears, but the Parkman boys played their repertoire over and over again, the minstrels rattled bones and tambourines, we hooped and sang and shouted jests to the lean crowds along the sidewalks, and through it all I pounded blissfully on my drum. When we stopped at last before the hotel, we weren't tired. Gilroy might have wearied of us, but we were fresh as daisies. Grouped before the porch, we played on, before what was then a large crowd in Gilroy — perhaps as many as twelve people. At last the smallest boy went home for supper. The minstrels were alone.

Eat! I suppose we did — I know boys well enough to assure you we ate, yet in the excitement of the day even that important ceremony is forgotten. But we hurried to the hall I had rented.

Eight o'clock came at last, and we lifted our skimpy curtain. We faced Gilroy — more of Gilroy than we had dared hope to see!

Elmer Chase — no burnt cork could mar his dignity! —stepped close to the footlights, that were candles, behind reflectors. In his powerful, sonorous bass he sang his favorites, "Thy Sentinel Am I," and "Rocked in the Cradle of the Deep." His voice sank at the end no lower than our conceit.

"Frank, it's up to you . . ." he muttered hollowly after announcing, for Elmer was also interlocutor — that Mister Frank Bacon would now sing that humorous ditty, "Allee Samee 'Melican Man."

I rose into what seemed to be the frost belt. My voice quavered and died in an ocean of frozen silence. Perspiration filtered through

28

my black complexion as I struggled to be humorous. The comical Chinese number climaxed. There was not a clap.

Inexperienced as I was, I knew something was wrong. I retired to my right end of the bench and toiled to bring the minstreling back to a normal temperature. The stories we ourselves had roared over in practising over the Bank, now seemed pathetic. Our singing became suddenly off-key. We came to one pitiful gag, no one but myself had ever thought it funny, and I had swiped it from Billy Rice of the Haverly Minstrels. It was one of my faults to see something funny where nobody else could. But this joke ran as follows and we told it drearily, using local names:

I said, "I was out rowing the other day with my girl. Her engagement ring dropped into the water. Just then along came a big whale. I killed him with the oar. When we cut him open what'd you suppose we found inside?"

Chase, solemnly, "I don't know. What did you find inside?"

I: "The Constable, shaking dice with the Postmaster."

Just as we began on this intelligent jest, I remembered that in the day's excitement I had forgotten to learn the Constable's name! Only one Gilroy name came into my head — I had noticed it on a saloon window while parading — it was Giannani. When I had to answer, I said:

"Giannani, the popular saloon man, shaking dice with the postmaster."

We couldn't understand the deafening applause that followed. It was our first. We couldn't even understand it later, when we learned the Postmaster was a woman!

Finally, gratefully, we saw the curtain fall. But that night was a victory. For the three of us who had to travel home by train had made expenses, and we had cleared enough to pay for the hiring of the Mayflower, waiting a mile outside of town. We arrived home in San Jose not far ahead of the dawn that gilds Mount Hamilton. In the gray light the burnt cork smudges on our countenances showed like shadows, for we knew nothing of the art of removing make-up and most of us wore the marks of minstrelsy for many days.

Glory dies hard, and fast, in youth. For the *Gilroy Advocate* came out with what might be called a "notice" and it was copied happily by the two papers, the *Mercury* and *Item*, in San Jose.

Declared the *Advocate*;

"With a furious blast of trumpets and a considerable spread of printer's ink, the "Big Twelve Minstrels" were ushered into Gilroy.

In one respect they were like a comet — where they came from and whence they are going no one knows. We have learned that some of the boys attend the University of the Pacific; for that reason we draw the mantle of charity over the performance."

One by one the boys came drifting up to Wright's gallery to share in the gloom. No, not all the boys. Not the four from the University of the Pacific. That strict old Methodist school had taken firm charge of her erring sons, and the quartette had been obliged to give solemn pledge never again to take part in any manner of theatricals.

Grief doesn't last, at eighteen. Within a week Louie Lieber and I were plotting that the soul of the Big Twelve go marching on. Now we turned our faces toward the written word. We would present drama!

There were plenty of thumb-stained play books to be had at the second-hand store on First Street and we bought all we could afford. A little group of us met at one another's homes and rehearsed, and rented the cheapest hall to present our play. Our first — at least the first play I appeared in — was "The Quiet Family." That show is very vague in my mind, for my part was small and my applause no greater than in Gilroy. But our second presentation is stamped upon my soul. That was "Above the Clouds."

From "Above the Clouds", to *Lightnin'!* I seemed to be an aerial figure dramatically. This play was pretentious. There was a brand new theatre in San Jose and we decided to "make it." This was the "California,"[9] on Second Street. It was modern and fine and far outclassed Brohaska's. We rented it and gave our show for the benefit of the Good Templars. Mother was pleased with that! Anything to help prohibition along.

I had a light comedy role and that night I first tasted the strong wine of applause. From that night, our little group was wild with ambition. Particularly Louie Lieber, for he had more talent than any of the rest. He was apprenticed to Rinaldo, the sign painter, but now he determined to break his apprenticeship and go to New York, to the stage!

"Vell, let him go," said Rinaldo, upon hearing this. "Blenty other sign painters in the country."

So Louie was to go to New York. There was fever in my blood now as I whiled away the long hours at photographic work. Louie was going to New York — I was remaining in San Jose. The cruelty of

30

passing my life at work I hated oppressed my boyish soul. Yet, with ardent enthusiasm, I started work on the farewell benefit for Louie Lieber.

The '80's was the golden age of benefits. Louie's was a farce fittingly called "Nerve." His failed him — he was home and resigned to sign painting within a few months. Broadway denied Louie as his employer had prophesied, and today he is happily at home with his signs on Second Street.

"Anything to eat," as Louie might say.

"Nerve," called for quite a small group of people and we soon had them together. All but one. That was a part calling for "a pert and positive maid."

"I don't know any girl like that,"said Louie, hopelessly.

"I do," I put in. "Jennie Weidman — she's just a kid but she can recite — takes lessons from Miss Benfey. Friend of my sister's. . . ."

Louie and I walked down Santa Clara street to Jennie's house. We found it tucked away at 59 Santa Teresa Street, across the way from the beautiful old Convent of Notre Dame. The wee bit of a home gave no prophesy of future friendliness to me. Yet the day was to come when I could call that little house by the convent walls, "home."

Jennie came to the door. She had a tooth ache. Her round childish face was wound around with a hot towel. She recognized me, blushed and smiled, and that smile upon her aching face was painful to view.

Jennie was fifteen now. She wasn't pretty. But her eyes were brown and set far apart and were always blazing with interest. It was her pert vivacious way that made you feel like laughing with Jennie. She wore a white ruffled "all-over" apron tied with a big bow behind and didn't in the least resemble the Little Eva of my earlier dreams.

"Oh," I gasped, foolishly, "Allow me to present Mr. Lieber."

"Allow me to present Mr. Bacon!" echoed the quick-witted Louie.

Neither of us had ever been introduced to Jennie. We sounded like a couple of chorus men out of "Pinafore" and I saw Jennie's smile widen until it was lost behind the folded towel. Anyway, she was still young enough to giggle deliciously.

"Excuse me for having a tooth ache," she said, resentfully. "Won't you come in — my aunts are home."

The moment I faced Aunt Mary in the little parlor, I felt that worthy woman regarded me with a natural and deep distrust. Auntie

31

Em regarded me closely — I fared no better with her. Well, I was to prove worthy of this suspicion. Only Jennie watched me with candid trust while we made our request of the aunts that their little ward be allowed to play the maid role in "Nerve." Jennie, veiled in her towel, fell into a demure mood and seemed to notice none of us. Later, she admitted she had noticed my eyes — thought they were kind!

The aunts agreed, and Jennie was to play the "pert and positive maid." And it was at Louie's farewell benefit we learned little Jennie Weidman could act.

Louie went to New York, while I remained in San Jose to plod through the gallery work I hated, with my heart turned toward Broadway. Praise came to me slowly after long work with the amateur shows. But to Jennie it came with the suddenness of a summer storm.

"Our Jennie," the papers were calling her long before Louie Lieber, disillusioned and resigned to sign-painting, returned from New York. She was called the leading elocutionist of San Jose and . . . (pardon the interruption, folks, but Jennie is at my elbow now) me, a faded clipping from her old blue scrap book, reads:

"Frank is always perfect in his lines, his voice is magnificent, he is good in every part he attempts and is justly recognized as the leading male amateur of this city . . ."

So reads an old San Jose clipping, but I earned that notice only after long work among the amateurs. Now my life had become a round from routine to glamor — from the photograph gallery to our small rehearsals and plays. And all through these years, mother dominated me as if she were my own soul. Mother seemed to regard me as the baby of the family, although Emma was younger than I. Perhaps it was because I had been away from her so long in childhood, while following the sheep, that she watched over me with greater care as if to atone.

In the sternness of her great faith, mother tried to turn my thoughts from the stage. Now I understand and love her more for it, but her judgment seemed harsh to me, when my great chance came.

"There's a letter for you. From New York. Frank, it's written on a typewriter. I didn't know you knew anyone in New York," chattered my little sister Emma, meeting me in the yard at noontime. She was just returning to afternoon school. I was home from the gallery for lunch.

The rest of the family were still around the table. Father had my letter propped against his glass of water and was studying the typed address as if it were in ancient Sanskrit and he a student of languages. It was typical of our household that while father sat at the head of the table, mother did the actual serving.

"Frank," spoke my father, with the air of conferring a degree, "Here is a letter for you."

I read it, while the blood rushed to my face and drained again. It was the first typewritten letter I had seen and the great, miraculous chance I had hungered for was packed in its tidy lines:

Mr. Frank Bacon
North 3rd Street,
San Jose,
California.

Dear Sir: —

You have been very highly recommended by Hugh Delacy of your city and our mutual friend. He has told me that you will meet with quick success on the stage if given a chance. As I was in your position at one time in the same town and appealed to the same friend to help me gain my ambition, if you desire to accept a part I will give you in a play and if you will be in New York by the first of August, I will be glad to engage you.

Yours truly,
John W. Dunne[10]

P.S. Will it be necessary for me to advance your fare East?

From John Dunne, who had married the soubrette, Patti Rosa, and later, after her death, was to marry the popular Mary Marble! He was a San Josean and a great manager in my eyes — it was a miracle!

Hugh De Lacy, my friend of the *Item* had written him in my behalf.

"No, Frank," said mother, gently.

I faced my family. They were my jury, but mother was judge. And she was dominant, as always. She could not see me cast into what was to her that vast shame — the stage.

That afternoon, I returned to the gallery with Ed. All my ambition was sunk beneath despair. New York might blaze and glitter, but not for me. My life seemed ended. What was there left to look forward to?

That question would be answered along with the others, by little Jennie Weidman!

CHAPTER FOUR

"AND THIS IS WISDOM"

Monotony!

There was little in San Jose to interest a boy hungry for Broadway. But every show that played San Francisco, played San Jose for a night. They played all week, Fair Week. I didn't miss a show.

I nearly always found the money to go and if I couldn't, Mother would unearth some small treasure from her housekeeping money. On such nights in the old California Theatre I atoned for the dull, hated routine of the photograph gallery. Sam Piercy was always to remain my hero among actors, but others came to dim his colors in my memory.

There was Frederick Warde, playing with Kate Forsythe in that grand old drama of North and South, "Lynwood." He left me chilled with awe. So this was acting! This was before Warde's fine career in Shakespearean drama.

Yes, things happened in San Jose, even if it was only a one night stand. Grismer and Phoebe Davies came to town with their companies once a season to play straight through Fair Week — I was in the gallery every night, alone and spellbound.

William A. Brady, the powerful manager who was later to be equally famous as the father of the beautiful Alice — didn't I once see him play Fernando in "Monte Cristo?" "Monte Cristo!" — there will never be another play like that for young and ardent souls, not another such hero rising on the crags through the lather of rock salt flung up for foam, to stand bleeding but unconquered there and cry, "The World is mine!"

A thousand times I rehearsed that line before my mirror at home, but quietly, in terror of family ears. Don't laugh. I'll bet not

34

one of you but has carried some dramatic instinct before your confessor, the mirror.

Stagemad! I tell you I lived the stage in the years between eighteen and twenty. George P. Webster came to town to star in several plays. Some kind friend introduced me to him behind the scenes. Webster was just starting out for a walk. He must have read the sincerity in my voice when I spoke of his acting, for he was flattered and asked me to walk with him.

"Come along and show me San Jose," he said.

San Jose was smaller then. We strolled out First Street toward Alviso — it was an honor to walk beside his swinging cane. I was afraid Jennie Weidman would not learn of this, unless I told her myself. The walk was short, for Webster had to get back for a "bite" before the evening show, but he talked easily the patter of his beloved world. Each word was leaven to my soul. I told him, and it was hard work, somehow, that I wanted to desert photography and go on the stage.

"Don't be rash," he said in a rather annoyed way. "Live it down, boy, and you'll thank me. You're stage-struck, that's all."

Critically, he surveyed me, a spare, eager lad of eighteen. I did not impress him.

"So many try," he added, kindly, "but for the thousands that go in — just one comes out ahead."

How could I know how the years, in passing, would bring this critical hero of mine to playing leads in a company owned by Frank Bacon?

I might have been more grateful for Webster's advice then. But I only felt lonely and misunderstood. Like an indignant child, I consoled myself by promising to show George Webster some day! And I didn't go back-stage again while he was playing San Jose.

I felt I was getting even with him, with everyone who refused to believe in me, when I landed my first role!

Mrs. Neimyher came to town with an operetta, "The Triumph of Love." She made all the arrangements herself and was finally ready to produce the thing. I had the leading role!

I'll never know why she gave it to me. But I was the Duke of Burgundy. I received five dollars for the performance. I wore tights, a hauberk, a mustache! I sang!

Almost viciously in the midst of my triumph, as I trod the boards that night, I reflected that at last I was showing 'em! All of them, from the star Webster to little Jennie Weidman. Yes, I was strangely interested in winning the praise of that self-sufficient young lady. She had her own career as an elocutionist and everyone believed in Jennie. But I — I wasn't even a good photographer. And bad as I was at that art, I was no better as the Duke of Burgundy. The papers, even that edited by my friend Hugh, drew the curtain of unrecognition across my performance. My triumph was ignored. All mother's gentle advice against not heeding wordly flattery was wasted.

After that, comes a sort of pained silence in my life. The gallery work must go on, but I was always burning with hope. Oh, yes, William Sheridan, the tragedian, came to town! His opening performance was "Ingomar," and his Parthenia was Luie Davenport, who was also his wife. She was beautiful, but I scarcely noticed her, lost as I was in the genius he put into that barbaric role. The next night he played King Louis the Eleventh, and if I had been roused by his Ingomar, I was electrified by his Louis! The crafty, sinister old king lives with me today — next to Booth's Hamlet. I've discussed Sheridan with many actors through the years and they always concede he was one of the greatest of tragedians.

After that the months went pounding past with the empty dullness of a dream and I grew fearfully restless. Every manager who brought a company to San Jose was interviewed by me, only to send me from the theatre with the old trite dismissal of the stage:

"Leave your name and address — if we need anyone . . ."

Life was routine. I was tired of Wright's Photograph Gallery. I had never been interested in photography. Now I felt myself dreading the morning that returned me to work. I tried to hide from mother my boyish restlessness, but she felt it keenly and tried to help me. Hadn't her life been hard? Hadn't things gone badly with the Bacons ever since the family came west? Life would brighten for us — it had to! Father, never a man of business, felt that the business of the wood yard was improving. One by one the boarders were disappearing from our family circle. And one day Ed came home with a staggering plan.

"You know that little photograph gallery at 58 South First Street, Frank? It's failing — I can buy it for a song. If I only had enough saved to make the first payment — but I lack $175 . . ."

I had one of my rare moments of business ability.

"I'll have my bunch give me a benefit!" I burst out with as much excitement as I ever cared to show. "Louie Leiber and that crowd —

36

they'll love to give a play and maybe I'll get some money from it. Then you and I will be partners, Ed."

"But you aren't interested much in photography," said Ed, slowly.

"I would be if we owned the gallery," I promised recklessly, with the sureness of the actor who falls in with any situation. Already, I saw myself as a real proprietor, wearing a flowing black tie.

My interest in photography was given a sudden boom. Wilbur Wright was astounded at my new passion for learning every detail of the trade. I learned more that next day than in all the months I'd been there as apprentice.

"Frank, you'll be a photographer yet!" he promised generously.

I had just persuaded a doting mother to have three poses, instead of one, of her squalling offspring. I heard Wright's praise and appreciated it, but even then a warning voice was repeating sadly, "Heaven forbid!"

One by one, that day, my boy friends came into the gallery. One by one, I told them my inspired plan. They were delighted to give me a benefit — anything for the sake of a play! We began rummaging over our supply of play books. After much argument we selected, "Hiranda, or, the Boat Man of Cuba."

We rented Brohaska's Opera House for an evening — it was cheaper than the California. We took a collection for the printer, and blazed the announcement on gaudy sheets through San Jose:

GRAND COMPLIMENTARY BENEFIT
FOR THE
RISING YOUNG ACTOR
MR. FRANK BACON

After the performance, after our friends had clapped their last from the crowded rows and out front the janitor was slamming up the seats, I breathlessly counted up the spoil. I had two hundred and fifty dollars!

I've made much money out of *Lightnin'*, but it's a small amount compared to that two hundred and fifty. I had never had a twenty dollar gold piece in all my life. Now I had — handfuls. I turned the entire fortune over to Ed. Louie Lieber went to work painting our sign.

★★★

BACON BROTHERS, PHOTOGRAPHERS

★★★

The boys — my friends who had made this new state of dignity possible, were impressed. They switched their attentions from Wright's gallery to ours. It was impressive to be a man of affairs, to find myself consulted on all matters pertaining to the gallery. Wealth had won me respect, as it always will. I put on dignity and the stiffest small hat to be found in San Jose. It was the final note in elegance. With firmness I learned to pose brides and grooms so as not to insult either side of their families. Families always expect so much in the matter of bridal photographs!

But through all my work another thought was glowing of the great parts I longed to do and the words I yearned to utter on the stage.

It was about this time that I played first in Eugene T. Sawyer's[11] play, "Loyal Hearts." That was my biggest amateur triumph. Gene was, and is, an author living in San Jose. He has written hundreds of books of the school — "and another redskin bit the dust." The truth is, Gene is known to literature as the justly famous "Nick Carter."

Gene was great at selecting raw stage material. The first girl he chose to play the lead in "Loyal Hearts," was Nellie Calhoun. This little San Jose amateur became the greatest of the little group that began their careers from my home town. She went east, then to London, became a famous star, played before royalty, and is now Princess Lazarovich. A few years later, Jennie was to play for Gene the role first taken by Nellie Calhoun. We would play together — "Loyal Hearts." But she was not in our first performance — she was still a child.

Only a child, but someone else recognized her ability. She was now a delicious sixteen and was given a part in "Robert Emmett." It was to be produced on St. Patrick's Day, with Jennie the only non-Catholic in the show. Jennie had many Catholic friends. In the Notre Dame College across the street from her home she had first recited "Miss Flora McFlimsey of Madison Square, who had so many clothes she didn't know what to wear." And behind those walls she was to adore Sister Mary Joseph with a sincerity that was to influence all her days.

Jennie's rehearsals in the "Robert Emmett" production became the maddening mystery to the rest of the amateurs. We were wild to know what was going on. I don't pretend not to be curious. I know I was then. I had to know what Jennie was doing.

38

They rehearsed in secret. Some of the amateurs — and I was always among them — prowled around their hall nightly to try and get a peep at the rehearsing.

"One night at rehearsal there was a fearful scandal in the company," Jennie reports to me now. "We heard that two amateurs were hiding in the gallery!"

Amateur! — it was a word to be spoken as if referring to a species of fiend. We were not popular when other work was going on. Anyway, we weren't hiding in the gallery that night. We didn't get a glimpse of rehearsals.

It was on the very last night the director told Jennie and the others that two amateurs would be permitted inside the hall and behind the scenes on opening night, to help them make up. These two "leading amateurs" appeared with their make-up boxes. Mr. Louie Lieber! Mr. Frank Bacon!

"I'll never forget the look Jennie gave me!

"I was never so astonished,"says Jennie. ". . . or so mad," but I don't believe that. She seemed rather pleased. Of course, I made her up. I'd threatened Louie with instant death if he asked for the privilege. What had we gone to all this trouble for, if I did not make-up Jennie for the show?

She was looking adorable in the tight-fitting little Irish outfit, and I went to great pains in the art of using powder and vaseline. Her cheeks were flushed under the carmine. I remember her asking me to powder her arms — and I thinking she was rather forward. Finally I was frantically searching my box, and Louie his. We had brought no grease paint for the lashes!

We made up their eyes at last with show blacking out of a tin box. It was guaranteed waterproof, and I can testify Jennie's didn't come off for weeks.

"You look so sort of nice in that costume," I found myself telling her between acts. "Why don't you come up to my gallery and let me take some poses?"

I added, hastily, that the pictures would be complimentary. Jennie promised.

She appeared a few days later in the little gallery and under her arm was her costume and with her was a girl friend. I was astonished — I hadn't counted on the friend. Jennie was demure and delicious, and I posed her in every recognizable attitude. It took an astonishingly long time to adjust the iron clamp behind her ears.

"I'll have them ready for you Wednesday," I promised, with what I intended to be a meaning look.

On Wednesday I wore a brand new "string" necktie for the occasion. Morning passed. The necktie wilted with suspense. Afternoon came, and with it — Jennie's girl friend.

"Jennie went up to visit friends in San Francisco, — she asked me to call for her pictures,"explained the other girl.

I couldn't keep from muttering:

"Since the pictures are complimentary — she MIGHT have come herself."

Perhaps that is why it came about that Jennie posed often for me, in the gallery on South First. Particularly after we founded the "California Dramatic Club."

Another boy and I started it. All my interest in theatricals fired again. For was not Jennie our leading lady!

She was not a bit overwhelmed by the honor. Our first presentation was " The Ticket of Leave Man," and a sensation in friendly San Jose. Jennie played Sam Willoughby, the boy. I thought her the sweetest thing I'd ever seen on any stage. I played opposite her as the heavy, Jim Dalton. And somehow, playing with one another in that show, first our names were linked together, then our hearts.

That play gave the amateurs the courage we needed. We shot forward with our ambitions in a series of benefits. I must admit it was seldom anyone was actually benefitted. That was the excuse — the play was the thing. But we gave benefits with unbridled glee. I'd had a benefit. Jennie was to be given testimonial, called "Bread Upon the Waters."

I poured all the art and energy I had into this production. It had to be perfect, because it was Jennie's. Not only did I act, but I was dramatic and business manager. We rehearsed frequently. The rehearsals, like all amateur affairs, were long and difficult and broken into by argument.

One night I found myself watching our youthful leading lady with an almost painful interest. I tried not to — that was the night I decided to take her home.

"But another boy is taking me home. He always does," explained Jennie.

"That's all right, he said I could take you home tonight," I replied without a tremor of conscience.

We walked to her home on Santa Teresa Street, down under the convent walls. Jennie was just sixteen and I was twenty. We found

40

ourselves talking hurriedly together. There was so much to be talked over. We hadn't known we had so much in common. Our words flamed at mention of the stage. Yes, we both had it — bad.

After that, I always took Jennie home. And I called upon her every night, for a year.

The rehearsals for "Bread Upon the Waters" were interrupted for a night by the circus coming to town. It wasn't often the circus came to San Jose. I invited Jennie. She couldn't get out evenings, often, except to rehearsals or something like that. But Auntie Em said she could go, and I called off rehearsing for the night in my capacity of manager.

It was at the circus we learned what good companions we really were. A circus brings out all the kid in a person's nature. We loved all of it, the acrobats and animals and tinsel and blare, we lived through all of it as if our life were all circus days. Somehow, we always would be able to feel ourselves part of things — that is what has kept us happy through thirty odd years.

"You know, this was really your treat," I told Jennie on the way home.

For some reason I always found myself telling Jennie everything. Now she was puzzled.

"I didn't have enough money to take us to the circus, so I borrowed two dollars from the reserved seat sale. It's your benefit money. So the treat's on you."

Another girl might be angry over a confession like that. Jennie always drew the nicest deductions from my rankest failures.

"Frank, you're a wonderful manager!" was all she said.

Jennie had a real offer before long. The Grand Army of the Republic wanted her to play the leading part in "The Color Guard." This play was produced every year in San Jose by the two posts, John Dix and Phil Sheridan. Members of the two posts were used in the soldier scenes, with groups of Civil War Veterans singing, "Tenting Tonight," and "Just Before the Battle, Mother." This year it was to be a big affair and two professional comedians from San Francisco had been hired.

They offered to pay Jennie in actual coin!

"Ask $25 for two performances and the matinee," I advised in the capacity of Jennie's manager.

She had made me promise always to act as her manager, in the certain event that she became a star!

41

There was one member of the G.A.R. who wanted to play the lead opposite Jennie. When I learned that, I changed my mind about the $25. The thought of someone else putting their arm around Jennie, even in a stage scene, was too much to bear. As her manager, I gave Jennie final orders.

"Tell the Grand Army that you will reduce your salary, and play the three shows for $15," I said. "On condition that you are allowed to play me in the opposite part."

The Grand Army was astonished and we were both afraid Jennie would lose the part entirely — and the salary. Old Colonel Bennett went to call on her in Santa Teresa street with two other members of the post. Jennie could be strong minded when she chose. Now she held out, at any sacrifice, for her favorite amateur leading man — Frank Bacon.

"Then — we will give him the part," said the Colonel at last, reluctantly.

There was no telephone then, and the moment they left Jennie was out of the house and flying down Santa Clara street to the gallery, to tell me our side had won!

So it was no strange veteran who put a manly arm around Jennie in the stirring love scenes of "The Color Guard." Among those impressed by the realism of our acting was one of the hired comedians. His name was Fred Mackley. He told me that he had not only written a play but had found a backer for it.

"It's going to be produced first in San Francisco," he said. "Then we'll take it on the road. I'll make Miss Weidman and yourself leading man and lady!"

The name of that play was "The Blacksmith's Vow."

We couldn't believe it. We told no one. But we talked by the hour, in secret, of becoming leading man and lady together. There was one cloud across this faultless heaven of delight, for how were we ever to confess to our families that destiny had opened and taken us in? Jennie's aunts were scandalized by any mention of the professional stage. Amateur work was sinful enough. The Jeffreys were as firm on this matter as the Bacons.

So we kept the secret between us, and it was one of many we had together.

But one day while I was posing a family group of scandalous proportions, a hack drove up to the door of Bacon Brothers' studio. Think of it — a hack! Something like having a procession of Rolls

42

Royces arrive, these days. In came Mr. Mackley, himself, and a San Francisco business man he introduced to me as the promised backer of "The Blacksmith' s Vow."

As Jennie's manager, I made her promise as well as my own. Before the two men left we were promised to go to San Francisco, on the stage, on the road. Pledged to glory! Now let the assembled Jeffreys and Bacons burn us at the stake, for Jennie and I were to be leading man and lady — together.

Jennie, in favor of excitement and secrecy, came to the gallery to be photographed as a leading lady. I was to have some pictures also, as leading man. These would be used for publicity, we believed, with "The Blacksmith's Vow."

But even Ed, who took my pictures for me, did not dream what worldly use we planned for them. He just thought I was up to some more of my nonsense, I suppose, when I insisted upon posing on our fanciest balustrade, in an overcoat and derby kindly loaned by the retoucher. My curly hair was parted in the center and I carried a cane. For the dramatic effect I put on a pleased, bright expression. After that, I posed Jennie.

Jennie was also in borrowed plumes. Three huge red ostrich plumes were on her large picture hat, and around its crown went a glittering band of small horseshoes. Heaven knows where she borrowed such an affair. Her small figure was squeezed into the popular "hour glass mold". The brocaded basque, the astonishing hat, and the red parasol — all were borrowed.

Jennie likewise posed leaning at an elegant and precarious angle over the balustrade.

Both our families thought the pictures lovely. They didn't dream of the base use we planned for them. And they never did learn. For the backer, very wisely, changed his mind about "The Blacksmith's Vow." The play fell through. Another bubble broken — Jennie and I would not be leading man and lady together, after all.

We recovered from this blow to take part in our biggest amateur work in San Jose. This was Gene Sawyer's second production of "Loyal Hearts." I told you Nellie Calhoun had played in it first. This time, Gene gave her part to Jennie. So we played leads together after all, for I was John Bushnell, U.S.A., and that was as fine a role as I ever played.

We planned another production after that, "Among the Breakers." Perhaps I selected that play for its title, for it fitted the fortunes of the Bacon Brothers just then. Our little gallery had been weighted down with mortgage when we bought it. That mortgage ate up all we made. Otherwise, we had worked hard and done well enough. But the mortgage was always at our heels.

Someone wanted to buy the gallery. It looked like a wonderful chance to escape the mortgage. But we would have to look for something else.

"We could buy a big tent and tour the state as traveling photographers," suggested Ed, earnest with enthusiasm. "I'll do the taking. You do the talking as outside man. Will you do it, Frank?"

A thousand thoughts hit me at once.

"Wait," I said, constrainedly.

That night I took Jennie home from rehearsal, as usual. We were not definitely engaged. We were simply in love. I used to walk to her little gateway with her, then she would walk back to the corner again with me. Under the poplars in front of the big Kenny house on the corner we would kiss goodbye again. Then, I'd walk back to the gate with her, for another goodbye. But this night there was no laughter on our lips.

"I can't leave you in San Jose and go over the state with Ed," I said. "I know we're only kids, but Jennie . . ."

She promised.

CHAPTER FIVE

"EVER THE WIDE WORLD OVER, LASS"

This happened on a warm evening in July, under the poplars of Santa Teresa Street. Jennie had been eighteen the March before. I was twenty-one. We had been "going together" a year.

Now we had to face our families. Both of us shivered over the ordeal. Marriage would mean escape from this tyranny of family love, to both of us. It meant realizing our ideals, escaping from the Puritan dread of the stage life we loved. It meant that someday, somehow, we would try to go on the stage.

"You tell Auntie Em!" coaxed Jennie.

I did. I told the aunts on Saturday night and Jennie and I were married Sunday a week later. During that week Auntie Em did not speak to my promised bride.

"I'd like to pay a Chinese highbinder ten dollars to kill him," Aunt Mary remarked flatteringly of her nephew-to-be. Aunt Mary favored an admirer of Jennie's who lived in San Francisco. He was more genteel, she said, and much more likely to get on in the world.

My family was equally cheerful. Mother said little, but her eyes were red and I know she was pitying Jennie with all her tender heart. I had shown no signs of being able to support a wife.

"And why," said father grandly, when I broke the news to him, "did you not let me know in time? I would have bought you a gift!"

But the worst troubles must be faced bravely, so the two families got together to prepare for the wedding. We wanted a quiet ceremony, and goodness knows, our families didn't care to make a social event of it.

"Among the Breakers" was produced Saturday night. None of our friends who played with us dreamed we were engaged. Foremost

45

among the well-packed rows we spied our friend Hugh De Lacy. He was there to report the show. In his paper on Monday, we read:

"Frank Bacon as Larry and Jennie Weidman as Biddy Bean made up a dish of Bacon and Beans unexcelled anywhere."

But by that time, Jennie and I were married.

Sunday was the 25th of July, 1885.

On that day was a stirring in the little brown house by the convent walls of Notre Dame. The Bacons arrived in a large family group. There were father and mother and Emma in their best go-to-meeting clothes, and my brother Ed and his young wife and Charley and his wife — my eldest sister Annie was kept away by a visit from the stork — and Aunt Kate Decker, father's pet sister from Kentucky, was a guest of honor. I wore a suit with a cutaway coat. It was a great bargain — Hobson[12] the tailor had made it for someone who didn't take it after all, and I got it for a mere $25!

Mother supplied the ice cream. Mother always supplied the ice cream for all events, particularly Methodist socials. She had always made me turn the crank. Well, I had churned my last on the old family freezer.

Quite a crowd of us were squeezed into the little house waiting for the minister. Jennie's grandmother, Susan Jeffery, was there, eighty-seven years old and had never been inside a theatre! The Jefferys were pioneers as my people had been. William Jeffery, Jennie's uncle, had been a miner in Cornwall and the Gold Rush carried him to Grass Valley in 1850. Then he came down to the big New Almaden quicksilver mines near San Jose. He used to have a livery stable on Santa Clara Street, among the adobes that were the heart of a San Jose that was built under Spanish rule. Jennie, who came to the town from a small Pennsylvania town at the age of eight, used to see the Mexican women smoking in the adobe doorways and fancy herself in the infernal regions.

Jennie's and mine were the lightest hearts at the wedding. The Jefferys and Bacons were inclined to gloom. I recognized Jennie's wedding gown. It was the dress she had made to wear in "The Color Guard." Aunt Mary explained she had made it out of an old one of hers, and it was of white grenadine trimmed with Spanish lace.

"What ceremony do you want?" asked the minister, the Reverend D. E. Bushnell arriving late.

"What ceremonies have you?" I demanded.

46

It seemed the ceremony without the ring was shortest so we chose it. But we had a beautiful ring — I'd paid five dollars for it. I'd only had twenty dollars to begin with. Ten went to the minister. That left us with five dollars to give meaning to the solemn words — "and I all my worldly goods to thee endow." No, that doesn't sound right, but remember, this happened thirty years ago. Anyway, I slipped the gold band that symbolized eternity over her finger the minute after we had finished saying "yes" to everything the Reverend D. E. Bushnell asked us.

To us, it seemed the most beautiful sort of a wedding, although Auntie Em sighed whenever she looked at Jennie, and mother's kind face was tenderer than usual with what seemed to be pity. But we had roast chicken bursting with stuffing and lots of other things, and afterward mother's ice cream and the big wedding cake Aunt Mary had baked herself and piled high with white frosting until it looked like Mount Hamilton at Christmas time.

"Where did you go on your honeymoon, Gram?" one of our smallest granddaughters asked a few week ago.

"To Santa Clara," said Jennie, referring to the mission town three miles away, "on the street car."

This isn't kind of Jennie. Perhaps I did take her for a ride to Santa Clara, but it wasn't for the sake of the honeymoon and she knew it. Our honeymoon path led through a forest of trouble but there was always sunlight breaking through the trees.

By six o'clock that evening, with the little house in order and the gold band conspicuously on her small hand, Jennie was rocking away on the front porch in an old willow chair. She wore a starchy white house dress and we might have been married twenty years for any excitement the little house revealed. It was over, we were man and wife, and surely no marriage began under more clouded skies.

Three days later, on Wednesday, we took to the trail.

Ed had bought the tent and wagon. There might come a time when the stage would loom again before Jennie and me. But now we must follow the way the camera pointed. Ed drove the wagon to Vallejo. We followed like Arab lovers.

If we had hunted California through for the unluckiest spot to settle in just then, we would have selected Vallejo.

And yet the little town on the upper edge of San Pablo Bay would be remembered by us as our honeymoon town with a sadness rainbowed with mirth.

47

Hard times were upon Vallejo. It was the year of Cleveland's first administration — the first break in twenty-four years of Republicanism. The shadow of panic quivered over political America. The Navy Yards at Vallejo were closed and they had been the sole support of the little town. Along the salt-odorous streets idle men talked in ominous, despairing groups, and in the rows of houses their wives and children were hungry. There was no talk of trade unionism in the '80's. Only — despair.

It was July, but a freak of temperature was upon the bay and all the few weeks we were in Vallejo it rained or threatened to rain. Down the short street that led to the black landing the gutters ran like rivers. The wooden sidewalks were soft to our steps and warped with rain. On the corners at nighttime the Salvation Army, then in its infancy, sang to groups of sullen and jobless men.

Still, Vallejo with its memories of poverty and rain is one of my beautiful California towns, one of the places I shall visit again with Jennie — someday.

We came into town like gypsies. Ed arrived driving the wagon, and upon the wagon were our cameras and developing tanks and boxes of dry plate, and covering it all was our folded tent. Jennie and I made the short trip by train.

Our tent was pitched on a damp and empty street corner. Ed had his cheerless quarters in the tent. It was divided by a curtain. In front of the curtain was the "Studio." Behind were our household goods — a coal oil stove that smoked vilely, a rickety kitchen table that "walloped" as we sat around it to eat, and the scantiest set of pans and dishes ever possessed by bride and groom.

Jennie — she was the light of the tent, those days. She and I found a little furnished room in the home of a news agent, but we spent our days with Ed. There was never a gayer bride as she fussed over the wretched stove that seemed ever at the point of blowing up and ending all our careers. "Better a dinner of herbs where love is" — that expression came home to us then, although I was barely of age, and Jennie was still like a child.

Before the curtain Ed lay in wait with his camera. Outside the tent I exhausted my power of oratory upon the passersby. But the weeks passed and no customers came into Bacon Brothers' Photographic Tent. There was no money in Vallejo. There was no money in the tent.

Portrait of Edmond Bacon, brother of Frank.

Jennie Weidman Bacon in her wedding gown, 1885. Photograph taken at Bacon Bros. Studio, 58 South First Street, San Jose.

The damp canvas sagged over our heads like gloom. The gypsy meals grew slimmer. As each day ended Jennie and I were glad to leave the tent to Ed and return to our rented room.

We couldn't help loving Vallejo. We learned to pronounce the word correctly, Val-yay-ho, after that great Spanish-Californian family whose descendants still live there. Under our doorway lay San Pablo Bay and anchored there was the powerful warship Wauchusetts. I photographed it. Evenings her band played on the Wauchusetts' deck and hand-in-hand Jennie and I sat on the porch of the Agent's home, listening. "Sweet Dreamland Faces" was the favorite waltz of the battleship's band. It was the song Kipling loved and made famous as the most sentimental of all waltzes. We hummed the words as the music swung over the black water:

"Sweet dreamland faces
Passing to and fro,
Bring back to memory
Days of long ago,
Murmuring gently
Through a mist of pain,
Hope on, dear loved one,
We shall meet again . . ."

The Agent's wife regarded us with the pity of a mother. She felt we were lost babes in the wood without enough intelligence to be mournful concerning our future. That was before she found out Jennie could recite. Overnight, the junior edition of the Bacon family found they were prominent in church and social circles of Vallejo. Especially Jennie.

We always went with the landlady and her husband. He felt his wife didn't appreciate him. Jennie and I certainly did. It was the sort of appreciation one has for a magnificent joke.

He handled a newspaper route for the *San Francisco Chronicle*. The entire weight of writing, editing and publishing that paper rested upon his shoulders.

"I'll have to be over in San Francisco tommorrow — Mike needs me," he would say, referring to Mike De Young, who owns the *Chronicle*. "Mike has a big deal on — he can't do a thing without getting my advice."

He was always being "called over" to San Francisco. He never left Vallejo.

49

He and my Uncle Morris were the two originals of my character "Lightnin' Bill" Jones. There were others that added flavor to the character, but these men were the first to expose to me the swagger and pretense most of us possess, but most of us are able to suppress.

He went with us one night to a Lodge social, carrying the large basket that contained our contribution to the refreshment booth. There, as often, he partook too often of the cheering cup, greatly to the resentment of his wife. We started for home, he carrying the empty basket. He talked — talked with weighty dignity concerning everything under the sun. His speech grew vague at times. At last he flung out his unbasketed arm in this Parthian stroke:

"Civilization! Naturalization! Education! It's all the same!"

"Shut up!" said his wife.

He did.

Yes, we enjoyed Vallejo but our successes there were all of a social order. The tent grew drearier. Everywhere the same answer drifted through the streets: No money!

"We'll have to get out of here," said Ed.

We had wasted six weeks in Vallejo. No, the time was not wasted, for we had made friends there who would be ours for a lifetime. Ed talked to men who came from the northern counties and learned that there lay virgin territory for photographers. I don't know why he decided upon Napa.

Again we folded our tent like the Arabs. We piled our sadly few dishes and the tripod and oil stove aboard the wagon, and left Vallejo and the bay for tumbling hills.

The pioneer spirit was upon Bacon Brothers, photographers, and as for Jennie, she was a born soldier of fortune.

We went into a valley that seems to me the loveliest in California after the Santa Clara, and that means the world. But instead of prune trees, were vineyards that mounted over miraculous hills to the very base of Mount St. Helena. Legend from the early days named that mountain for the Russian princess, Helen, who came to Napa Valley in the '30s when California was claimed by Russia. Robert Louis Stevenson had lived upon that mountain in a deserted mining cabin, not so many years before our coming. There the great master had written his clear little western classic, *Silverado Squatters*.

As poor in goods but as rich in adventure as Stevenson had been before us, we set up our tent on a street corner in Napa. The little pioneer town wore a quiet and homelike air after crowded, hungry

50

Vallejo. For two weeks we waited in the tent. It might have borne a small-pox warning. For not a soul came near us.

"No one wants to have a picture taken — in a tent!" I told Ed, with some vague idea of the psychology of salesmanship flickering in my mind long before the phrase was invented. "People don't recognize value unless its wrapped for them in fancy parcels. We can't get people into a tent — we need a gallery."

It bled our fortunes dry to rent a gallery. Only, we called it a studio. It was an empty room in a nice new building on Main Street and if you doubt my word you can drive up to Napa some day and look at it. Any of the old timers can show it to you. Also you have my permission to look through the old files of the *Napa Daily Register*. In the edition of January 12, 1886, is our first advertisement:

****

BACON BROTHERS, PHOTOGRAPHERS
MAIN STREET, NORTH OF FIRST, NAPA CITY

Examine our display of beautiful and artistic results in the ART SCIENCE OF PHOTOGRAPHY. Our cases contain shadow effects of many of Napa's most prominent and familiar faces, as evidence of our Ability. Novelties and the latest styles introduced as fast as they become known. Bacon Brothers have, do and will excell.

Because they can.

****

This reads as though we were flooded with orders. Bumkum, my dear friends! Customers were scarcer with us than orders for winter flannels in the South Sea Islands. The citizens of Napa evidently did not think their features worth handing down to posterity. But in spite of this, we were having a beautiful time!

We met, right away, everyone in Napa who was interested in theatricals. We never got far away from that interest. I was soon up to my ears in burnt cork — nothing on earth could have prevented my joining the Acme Minstrels. This was made up of men and boys of Napa, most of them hard-working fellows. Some worked in stores and some on their farms and some in the tannery. But they were all ready to miss sleep for a chance to rattle the bones.

When we could afford it, the Acme Minstrels performed at the Levenseller Opera House on Main street. When we were low in funds and pride we played up in an old barn loft and charged less admission and gave even better performances. I remember in one show being on the bones and singing "No Likee Boycott," as One Lung — also acting as one of the "Four Doves." That night William Parker sang his riotous song, "The Blushing Bride." This was a take-off on Sarah Althea Hill Terry, who, claiming to have been the secret wife of the popular Senator Sharon, was rocking California to the depths with scandal.

It was all child's play compared with what I longed to do. Ed and I had our poor but proud little business but I couldn't forget my hopes for a stage career. Neither could Jennie, although hers was silenced for the time by the new weight of household affairs. But it seemed part of my life was missing. Something wasn't living that should be alive. The minstrel nonsense was just a form of incense offered up to the life I craved.

The Acme crowd were ambitious. We received flattering, if foolish, comment from the country papers. We played beyond the friendly limits of Napa. We even played at Yountville.

Near Yountville village, under heavy foliage, lies the Veterans Home.

Under the shadowy trees old warriors of the blue and gray refought in memory their battles of the Civil War — Vicksburg, Chattanooga, Shiloh. Lincoln lived on among the broken regiments that had been disbanded long ago, and he was a man to be blessed in Yankee diction or reviled, perhaps in the purring dialect of the south. Lee and Grant still had loyal followers there, and the name of Clinton Fisk was well remembered. Jeff Davis was spat upon and John Brown re-hanged in effigy, at the Home.

At the sunset gun the worn battlers marched to their quarters — brave, spent figures against trees and sunlight.

It was like a place I had always known. I was young, but I found my comrades there. Perhaps because father and mother had felt so keenly the years of the Civil War, although both had been in California, and my boyish years had been stirred by their memories. Perhaps because of the tired romance of the Home. Perhaps because of the old comrades and the stories they told me.

Why, even the spirit of "Lightnin' " Bill was to be found there — I met him one evening in his quarters after the sunset gun. In the cell-like room, over his army cot, were pinned dozens of small card pictures of actresses.

52

Without him, the world would have gone clean to smack, long ago!

"I could have stopped the Civil War," he informed me.

I begged him to explain.

"I was walking with General Grant," he said. "All of a sudden General Lee went riding by on a white charger. I was going to shoot him. Grant begged me not to. 'Grant', sez I, 'It will stop the war if I kill him'. 'That's the point', sez Grant. So me and Grant let him live. That's how I come not to stop the war."

It was this conversation later grew into my play, "Me and Grant."

The old comrade swept his single arm toward the pictures of the actresses.

"Yes, and I knew every blame one of them, too!" he added, belligerently.

He was as much a delight to me as was old Wall Kennedy, known throughout Napa as "Old Bill." Bill was town janitor. He always referred to himself as "Street Commissioner." Without him, the United States would long before have lain in ruins.

"Working hard, Old Bill?" I asked one morning on my way to the studio.

Bill paused in his labor of pushing a flat broom across Main Street.

"Nope. Ain't nuthin' to the time I druv a swarm of bees acrost the plains," said he. "And I never lost a single bee!"

At noontime I told this to Jennie. She didn't think it particularly funny. But years later President Wilson was to ask for the *Lightnin'* script, just to get the answer Old Bill gave me that morning in Napa, thirty years before. Wilson had heard it on our opening night, in Washington. He carried it to the Peace Conference as the cream of American humor.

As months passed we knew that this gallery was also a failure. But bills, crowding down upon our heads, held us in Napa. "Foss" became a devil-name to conjure with in family affairs. Foss was the wholesale photographic supply man in San Francisco. Through the months we fought to get at least even with the Foss bill. Always, always, we found ourselves short of dry plates and with no money to send for deposit. And with no deposit, there were no dry plates. Even now to hear of anyone named Foss strikes me like a chill. It was years before the last Foss bill reached me in my travels, and I knew my slate was clean.

53

That was why we clung to the studio, dreaming that luck would veer our way. Jennie courageously matched her wits against the eternal wolf, three times a day. Ed would sit for hours adding up our bills in a disbelieving sort of way. Nothing happened.

Then word came from San Jose.

Mother was dead.

It didn't seem possible at first — doesn't now, after these many years. But it cast a shadow over our small affairs that was never to completely drift away. It aged all of us. Ed went hurriedly to San Jose. He did not return. Father needed a strong, kindly grip and Ed would remain with him. The Bacon family seemed shattered, with mother gone.

And Jennie — even her courage broke at last. She wasn't much more than a child herself and we had learned there would be a new member in the Bacon family. And we had been doing so sadly in the little Main Street studio! Jennie left me at last. I begged her to go back to Aunt Mary and Aunt Em in San Jose where there were more comforts of life, until the baby came. And after Jennie left, I was alone in Napa.

I had youth and more energy than anyone has ever given me credit for, but I'll admit those were lonely days. There is no drama to sitting in a deserted studio trying to look brightly expectant in case some customer should chance in.

Then Fanny Wood came to Napa.

The idea of one of my favorite stage heroines coming to town revived me mightily. The bigger companies didn't play up there, often. I haunted the lobby of the Palace Hotel, that magnificent two story structure that still widens its arms to guests arriving in Napa. There I could watch my heroes and heroines in the flesh — even have the pleasure of glimpsing them in the small dining room, devouring country dinners. In those days companies brought their own portable scenery and oil lamps and all the rest, and played wherever they found space to hang their back drops. And no company carried supers but culled the extra players from whatever talent they found in the visited towns. I was beginning to hanker after a job as "supe" at perhaps a salary of fifty cents a night — for the sight of such aggregate talent excited me beyond words — when something happened.

Frank Wright, the leading man, received a telegram. All Napa was talking over its contents within the hour. No invention will ever equal the speed of news in Napa. Wright's mother had died suddenly. He left town on the next train.

The editor of the *Napa Reporter*, Dwight Hackett, hurried to the manager of the Wood Company to get all particulars for the press. Dwight was a good friend of mine.

"Logan Paul can take Wright's place," said the manager, in such depths of anguish as only a manager can know. "But who under the high heavens can take Paul's?"

They were two hundred miles from a booking agency.

"I know just the man!" crowed Hackett. "He's in Napa, an amateur but, say — he can act rings around any actor in your company."

The manager must have been desperate, for he sent for me. I wiped my stained hands dry of the developing fluid, locked the studio door and sauntered up Main Street to the Opera House. My many disappointments had trained me never to seem eager. I believed firmly in dignity.

CHAPTER SIX

AND I STAND, A FAILURE

That was how I came to make my first professional appearance in "The Streets of New York," presented in Levenseller's little brick Opera House on Main Street in Napa, California.

Mine was a comic character part, Dan Puffy. The manager handed me the script for my part. I had to learn the lines before evening.

I have always been tarnation slow on lines. And now I had only a day for "making" the part. Enough to bring tears to the eyes of the strongest actor. But I brushed all thoughts of failure away and set to work "cramming" the lines.

Napa is a forgiving town. It overlooked all the blunders I must have made on that nerve-racking night. The town papers practically neglected every member of the company except Fanny Wood and myself. The star and the supe received the "big play." And our friendly local critics scarcely mentioned one young genius who had the role of my father in "The Streets of New York." For David Warfield was as unknown then as the plays that were to carry him to glory—"The Return of Peter Grimm," "The Music Master," and "The Auctioneer." Yet I remember how electrical he was in his part and how I played the better for his acting opposite mine.

That magic night was a rift in the blue. It closed again on the Fanny Wood Company, the tarnished scenery, the enchanted craft of the stage. How I wished the manager would recognize something in me that might make good and offer to take me away from Napa! But the company left on an early train—left me again in the studio that was hollow with poverty.

Time ambled through a few more weeks of chaotic trouble, of Foss' debts and wondering how Jennie was faring in San Jose. Then

56

the Cotton and Birch Minstrels came to Napa. And how I did love a minstrel show! Could I afford it? Can a man afford to eat! Why, it would have been criminal extravagance for me not to have gone to the Cotton and Birch Minstrel show! They brought all the excitement to Napa the Big Twelve had hoped to bring to Gilroy, when I had been a youth with not a care to my heart! And yet, that had only been three years before!

Boyton's Drug Store carried the reserved seat sale. That was where I bought my modest ticket. The magic slip was a sesame to one perfect evening. That night I forgot the studio and the debts and worry in minstrelsy. How I loved it! I stored away all the jokes, laughed endlessly over the funny songs, longed to be up there on the stage far out of the reach of debtors, playing with the grotesque kings of blackface.

I mention Boynton's, the drug store and trading post for Napa news. In the rear of the store was the Western Union. Also, all important telephone messages for anyone in town were telephoned to Boynton. All messages met in the drug store and Boynton scribbled them up on the slate behind the counter, known as the "bulletin board." The folk of Napa drifted into the store on any pretense or none to read the slate and all the town affairs.

While I was shaking my sides, Boynton received a message for me at the drug store. He had no idea where I might be, so wrote it up on the slate for all to read. All did — with the exception of myself. I left the minstrel show for my furnished room and sleep, and awoke in the same innocence. Only on my way down Main street to open the studio for the day — a useless rite — did I learn the news.

"Good morning, papa," said my friends as I met them.

At first I thought they were joking for the title was new in my ears. Then I met the wife of the man who kept the big general store and she appeared to think my blank ignorance almost scandalous.

"My goodness, haven't you heard?" she demanded. "Why, it's up on the bulletin board . . ."

It was. I stood before the slate meekly reading the message all Napa had read before me:

"Frank Bacon's wife has a little girl."

I was the last person in town to know that Bessie Bacon had arrived on earth, to follow the barnstorming lives of young parents destined to wander in the wind's path. And I had a sad half hour, later, trying to explain this ignorance to Jennie, always after to be

57

known as "mother." She was deeply wounded in not getting an instant rapturous answer to her wire.

I went into a fever of preparation for her homecoming with our child! The housekeeping room was a doll's place, when you considered there were three of us now. Jennie was to have a real home if I had to work in the tannery! At last I found a wee little house on the edge of the small town that would just hold three. It was furnished, but even my man's eye saw it was a barren sort of furnishment. Things didn't look complete. Finally I discovered what was missing.

A carpet.

Jennie should have a carpet upon her return to Napa! I went down to the second hand store on Main Street that was my principal "hang-out." A friend of mine owned the store. It was a sort of club, for the town characters dropped in through the day to talk over town affairs, and "Old Bill", the street commissioner, was often to be found there giving air to his views. The second hand store was the stamping ground for theorism in Napa.

It was there I purchased — on time — a small carpet. My preparations were complete. Now I could proudly meet Jennie at the depot and walk with her to our new home. And to my dismay it was I who carried into this home a ridiculous little living object I couldn't believe was my daughter, Bessie.

I say I was dismayed, because I had to carry the baby. It was a new sensation. Also, the baby worried me at first. She appeared to have inherited a trait from my Uncle Morris — she was always asleep. But "Mother," who was gayer and sweeter than ever, simply laughed and tried to take up life in Napa where she had left it.

But life in Napa wasn't the same as before. For now there were three of us and this new member of the Bacon family couldn't live gypsy style and be satisfied with only the cruder comforts of life. No, for now there were small garments everywhere and always in a state of washing and drying, and a small tub to be filled with heated water and talcum to be bought . . . Life was suddenly responsible and complicated. What had been gypsy fun for two, when faced by three became — poverty!

Never more for us the vagabond lightness of soul. Life demanded we face it fairly and not laugh at it behind the mask of youth. We were parents.

Jennie had energy for two. One day, in spite of caring for Bessie and our little home, she developed an idea of business.

"I'm going to do it! I will!" she declared, mysteriously.

And she did — just like the little red hen in the fable. Jennie found a few boys and girls in Napa interested in elocution, and she gave lessons! She saved twenty dollars and that did not go into the slender but deadly stream of bill-paying. That was for a rainy day and there were many in our lives.

Still there was amusement enough. There was the colored lady next door who made up songs and sang them to little Bessie. It was the day of the popular ditty: "Go tell the Jersey Georgie Lily, the sights will knock her silly, Climbing up the golden stairs. . . ."

This kindly woman would rock Bessie in her arms while Jennie labored with the elocution, and in crooning southern dialect her version of the song would reach our ears:

> "Oh, little Bessie Bacon,
> She had 'er picture taken,
> Climbin' up the Gall-ry Stairs,
> Mister Brewer stood behin'
> And 'er papa was no kin',
> Climbin' up the Gall-ry Stairs."

Then, there was Bessie's buggy.

Jennie, it seems, had long suppressed a desire for a baby carriage. For Saturday night was gala night in Napa, when everyone paraded Main Street in their choicest finery. And then would be seen the proud parents of the town behind buggies that streamed with ribbons of pink or blue — according to the fashion of the day and the sex of the offspring. But we! — we had no buggy.

And that, it seems, had been iron to Jennie's motherhood. When on Saturday nights we joined the promenade before the drug store and past the Bacon Studio, we argued as to which should carry our child. That was the way I stumbled upon Jennie's passion to own a baby buggy of our own.

Next day I arrived home for lunch. I was pushing a buggy.

It was a perfectly new buggy, even if I had bought it at my stamping ground, the second hand store. It was valued at $7.50 and little had I been able to afford such a luxury. But I bought it, as I did everything else, on time. And I never will forget the woe on Jennie's face when she saw me coming through the gate.

It seemed her dreams had treasured a magnificent vision of wicker and pink satin with a fine high top that pulled down and embroidered coverlets and miniature cuddly blankets and elegant

59

yards of fancy ribbon and . . . This was of wicker, to be sure, but the stringy weave was so far apart it didn't look safe and around the limp top of the thing ran a woolen fringe that resembled a frayed rope.

I had thought it quite handsome until I saw Jennie's face.

"I - I think it's beautiful!" gasped the poor child and hunted the house over for a piece of pink ribbon — or maybe it was blue, I never can remember which is for girls.

And she washed and ironed that ribbon, which had seen much service but was still very good, and ran it through the market-basket weave of the object I had pushed home so hopefully, and next Saturday night the Bacons appeared on Main Street and I was pushing little Bessie's buggy!

But the studio seemed to grow more deserted through the days and the Foss bills grew larger in our eyes. But I'll say this for Jennie's managing — we never missed a meal. The pantry might be fearfully empty but Jennie would stand before it with a frown on her face and conjure a meal out of the air. Only a good housewife can understand the trick.

But winter came and with it the first bitter hardship we had known.

Our baby awoke us one night in a terrible attack of croup. Then we knew what terror meant, while Bessie fought for breath — for life — shrouded in under her little blanket with the tea kettle steaming close to her face to give warm air to the swollen lungs. The homely cure saved the little one, but Jennie and I had learned what sickness could mean when it came with poverty. And when morning came and we knew the danger was over, Jennie went to pieces for the first time. She couldn't stand this life! She wanted home!

"Then we'll go home," I promised her.

To return to San Jose would be a slap in the face of the family. They were depending upon my staying with the Napa studio, that belonged not to me alone, but to Ed as well. And Ed was with father. I would be returning to a scourging of the family scorn.

I sold our studio for one hundred dollars that I never was able to collect, and took a chattel mortage. The twenty dollars Jennie had saved teaching elocution I had to commandeer to carry us home and pay the freight on what little furniture we had. We went from Napa to San Francisco by boat, because that was the cheapest way, and were two solid days making the short trip home.

Along the peninsula the prune trees were in blossom and Santa Clara Valley was laid level with the foaming gray-rose of the flowers.

It was gala at least for our homecoming. We did not go to my home. We took our baby to the little house on Santa Teresa street and in the small parlor where we had married, the aunts put up an extra bed for us. There we unpacked our scant luggage and looked about to whatever luck might come.

My family came to see us and most of them were cold with wrath. I had sold the studio, the only hope of the Bacons. It was hard to forgive our desertion of Napa.

"Yes . . . but we were starving there!" flamed Jennie in answer — always the little spitfire and able to hold her own.

I said nothing. There was nothing to be said. I was back as a guest in my wife's home, I had no work, and a debt hung over my head it would take years to pay.

This was the time father said reproachfully:

"So you sold the studio, Frank! And I behind you with thousands!"

Poor dad. His future then was no brighter than mine. His outlook and fortunes were sad, yet at times he flashed pitiably into grandeur. There was nothing in his home to interest him but he moped there, missing the wife who had been his strength through the years, missing the woodyard that had passed from his weakening hands. A friend's influence secured the job of janitor at the Reed street school. That revived father's faith in life. He knew every child. He guarded their destinies to and from the schoolyard. He was gentle and affectionate by nature and his heart broke, years later, when old age led him out of his janitor work. He never recovered from that blow.

It was then, for I had by that time a steady job and a little money, that I bought him "Grant's Reminiscences." The sensational volumes on the war were just out and I bought them — on the installment plan — for father's birthday. After that father ceased living beyond 1865. Every morning while Emma made the biscuits for their breakfast in the old homey kitchen, father sat at the table and read and reviewed for the poor girl the violent scenes of the Civil War.

The work I had found — rather, that had found me, was as startling a change from any of my previous jobs as most work has been to me. I was always finding it necessary to change my entire mode of life to suit my new means of livelihood. This time, I became a solicitor.

I'd sworn quits on photography forever. But with a wife and child to support, I could not choose my next calling. Before real

61

trouble, all dreams of the stage faded like sunlight behind a cloud. No time for dreaming. I needed work.

I was nearly desperate when I met Steve De Lacy[6] on First street one afternoon.

He was my friend Hughie's brother, a fiery little southerner who carried himself bravely upon his glossy high heeled boots and wore a ferocious goatee. He had just started out upon its long career that redoubtable little newspaper, the San Jose Times. Now Steve saw I was despondent and tapped me brightly on the center button of my vest.

"Frank," said he, "why don't you solicit ads for the Times?"

So the Times and I started out together, but my start was one of many. I was accustomed to meeting people. My "approach" was easy, and I could make friends. But I couldn't sell them my wares, whether it was a morning paper at fifty cents a month or my own talent. I had certainly made a brilliant failure at wheedling the residents of Vallejo, San Jose and Napa into being photographed. So I had sore doubts as to my ability to get new advertising matter in the columns of the Times. But not Jennie.

"Nonsense! Of course you can get ads," she said, indignantly. "Go to all the big stores — you know everyone in San Jose. Because it means a steady income for us . . ."

She looked down at the growing baby in her arms and I knew then my destiny lay in soliciting ads. It did mean a steady income. I went to work next day for the Times.

I received ten dollars a week, and a commission!

For the first time since we had married we had money enough for our living expenses. We continued to make our home with the aunts. Bessie was like the third child in the family to Auntie Em and Aunt Mary, who never would believe Jennie and I were grown. Then came the wonderful day when my talent for ad-getting was recognized.

The Mercury was the leading paper in the Santa Clara valley. And now it wanted me to solicit ads!

That was too great an honor to refuse. Overnight I achieved success, recognition, respect from the two families and fifteen dollars a week.

"At last!" said the relatives, enthusiastically, but a little dubiously, for I had fooled them before. "Frank seems to have settled down."

I felt settled. One does, after living next door neighbor to actual hunger and then being swamped with the grand largess of sixty dollars a month! On sixty dollars, said we, anyone can support his family. There was much I could do with sixty dollars — more than I've been able to do since, I can tell you! Aside from contributing our share of the expenses in the little house on Santa Teresa street, I paid faithfully a monthly deposit on the Napa gallery debt.

Also, the day came when we were putting by a neat little nest egg from that same sixty dollars! Remember this was in the later '80s, and a grocer's heart then was as full as the ladies skirts were voluminous and a vegetable man called twice a week to leave a fortune in fresh green provender in exchange for five cents.

For one untroubled year I stayed with the *Mercury*, and there was peace and prosperity at home.

You will notice my career runs in cycles of a single year. I didn't seem able to stick anywhere, or with anything longer than that. At each year's ending luck veered for better or worse. This time, it was for worse.

On a warm day that summer I went from store to store in Mountain View soliciting ads. That was a town of perhaps eight hundred people and twenty-five saloons and is perhaps fifteen miles from San Jose. Aside from saloons, Mountain View appeared to consist principally of waving fields of hay.

There were few ads to be claimed from Mountain View. For that matter, there were few to be found anywhere. For summer is the evil time for a newspaper. The subscribers leave town for vacation, circulation falls off and the ads, that are blood and brawn to a paper, fall away.

I had a horse and buggy for these trips and had criss-crossed the valley until I could draw a map of it now, blindfolded.

"Anyway, what we need is a paper of our own in Mountain View. We'd advertise in that," said one storekeeper after refusing a *Mercury* ad.

His refusal was like a message. Perhaps because the heat made me discontented and restless — anyway, it seemed a direct hunch. Of course, what Mountain View needed was a paper!

I wonder what conceit stirred me into believing myself the one chosen to bless Mountain View with its newspaper! However, upon that conceit I founded the *Register*.

This was the first paper published in Mountain View, a weekly, and yet not so weak, for it still is being published there. Charley Shortridge[13] encouraged me. Charley — brother of Samuel, our Senator from California — was the editor and proprietor of the *Mercury*. He had a passion for amateur theatricals and had been a pioneer of the art in San Jose. When I stopped soliciting ads for him to branch out as a newspaper owner myself, Charley paved my way with the type foundry people in San Francisco. He urged them to take a sporting chance, and sell me a press.

All one needed to found a paper, I thought, was a hand press and unlimited nerve. I had plenty of nerve left, at twenty-four, although I had met with more discouragement than most men of eighty. I hopefully canvassed my family for funds. They doubted my new venture, yet were delighted to find me still willing to venture. Aunt Mary dug up two hundred dollars from somewhere. Horace Keesling,[14] my brother-in-law, secured my note at the bank for another $250.

I tracked the peninsula over like a frenzied rabbit, hunting ads. I simply wrung them from my friends for anything that could be advertised. At last I had seven hundred dollars worth of ads. But it had meant deep rustling on my part.

Then the press arrived in Mountain View — an impressive monster of wheels and levers. The man who hauled it from the station in an old hay wagon took his pay out in advertising. The foundry people had kindly paid the freight. It was a magnificent beginning.

And John McNaught[15] wrote my first editorial for me, just to give the *Register* the finest sort of a start. Later he wrote editorials for Joseph Pulitzer on the *New York Evening World*. At this time he was editor on the *Mercury* with Charley Shortridge and later went with him to *San Francisco Morning Call*. But I had known McNaught when he worked in a lumber yard in San Jose, a mysterious sort of fellow with a sensitive, brilliant mind. He created a line I was later to use in my play, "Hills of California:"

"California! — where the oak lives on for a thousand years and the poppy blooms for a day!"

I solicited all the advertising, — also I set up the type, wrote most of the paper and ran off every sheet myself on that old style Washington hand press. And that was no mean job!

One dubious old farmer blocked the door of my office after I had handed him his copy of the first edition.

"Think ye'll ever get it out again?" he remarked.

Whatever role in life I played that was new, Jennie was always opposite me, playing leads. Now that I was an editor — Jennie was editress. She wrote our snappiest editorials on local and national topics, covered — what we might politely term "Society," and learned to set type. She bravely faced subscribers and urged them to keep on with the *Register* at least one more month! In her spare moments, Jennie cared for our little home, boarded the printers, and mothered all of us.

Hard work never dimmed our love for the footlights. Within the month we knew every amateur prospect in Mountain View. Before long we were playing in my old favorite, "Above the Clouds." And also, in the drama that had first stirred my soul with the unquenchable fire, "Uncle Tom's Cabin."

Perhaps it was our frenzied efforts toward art that persuaded Mountain View it needed an opera house. Lenzen[16] of San Jose — he has an avenue named for him there — was the architect, and my old companion, Louie Lieber, won the contract for painting the curtain. When I saw that curtain I firmly expected to be run out of town. For Louie, the most frivolous sign painter that ever blocked a letter, had painted a lifelike head of Shakespeare on one end, and Bacon on the other. Only, I was the Bacon!

None of the villagers guessed that sacrilege had been done their curtain. Louie's reputation as an artist was saved. Or, maybe, it was gone forever, as no one suspected I was the original. The curtain burned in the fire of '06, I believe.

Years later the Bacon family would return to this Opera House as professionals, in "The Hills of California."

I've told you my life runs in cycles of years. At the year's end I was ready to leave Mountain View. Oh, but during that time I made my first and last appearance as a political figure. I, as assemblyman for Mountain View — until they voted.

There was one sad interruption to this year. Jennie went home to San Jose — little Dixie was born. Seven months and sixteen days later, on December 8, 1888, from the little home on Santa Teresa street, that had known all our small happinesses and tragedies, our little girl was buried. For a time the world was ended.

Came January, and with the new year I realized the *Register* had outgrown its creator. I could not renew my old advertising contracts. Most of them had been made on friendship only, with friends in San Jose. But no business runs on sentiment and I could not blame my friends for refusing their ads to the little weekly at Mountain View. Someone more perservering than I offered to buy the *Register*.

I sold.

It was a happy release. I returned to San Jose, yet I was never to forget Mountain View. Years later I bought there the orchard where I hope to spend my final days — Baconia.

Seems as if life was forever forcing me back into something I'd turned my back upon! Hadn't I sworn off newspapers? Hadn't I vowed never to return to Napa, where I had been half-hungry with a worthless gallery on my hands? I broke both pledges that new year of 1889. I found myself again a newspaperman, and in Napa!

I had cleared just enough money from the *Register* sale to buy an interest in Napa's faithful old daily, the *Reporter*. I believed in this venture, but then, I believed in all of them. Yet there must have been the sanity of doubt left in my mind, for Jennie did not go north with me this time but remained with little Bessie and the aunts in San Jose.

Was I always to turn back to what I had outgrown, doing my best with the old, anxious for the new?

I had thought myself too big for a weekly. I found a daily too big for me. There was nothing else. I did not remain long in Napa. I sold my share in the *Reporter* and like an enchanted person doomed to wander in a circle forever, went back to San Jose.

Just in time to welcome to earth our youngest child and only son, Lloyd Bacon! Our three children were born in San Jose, I am glad of that.

I had a son now, as well as my wife and the most beautiful small daughter in the world. And not a chance ahead that might mean bread to them. I had learned but one lesson through these bitter years of young manhood. It had spelled ruin to those I love. It was failure.

Would it always be that?

CHAPTER SEVEN

WE ARE BARNSTORMERS

The newspaper game grips men.

There is something in its swift-moving world makes escape difficult into quieter fields. I know it had me twice after I turned from it. And yet, it was never galley and proof I wanted, but the footlights. I was in the most spirited game in the world, but I never forgot the stage.

Again I found myself a newspaper man, in Mayfield. I hadn't intended it. But third time's a charm, they say, and this was my third attempt as a newspaperman.

Stanford University must take the blame for my third fall. The University was just being built. I was present when the corner stone was being laid. Mayfield was the nearest village to the great tract of university land. Everyone thought that of course Mayfield would be the college town. That gave me my bravest idea. I would found Mayfield's first newspaper! I would grow up with the town, be a prominent citizen, a successful man at last, and wind up President of the Mayfield Boosters!

Another of the smoke dreams that drifted...

Jennie and I drove up from San Jose with a horse and buggy. While she waited patiently outside of homes and stores, I interviewed the citizens of tiny Mayfield. They encouraged my idea — it was no risk of theirs! We drove on, a couple of miles over El Camino Real, the old King's Highway of early Spanish California that leads to San Francisco. Several miles beyond Mayfield, on the River San Francisquito, was the white, forbidding mansion of the Stanfords.

Jane Stanford agreed to see me. The widow of the great railroad man lived alone in the big house that was burdened with memories of her dead husband and son. In the ornate drawing room I faced a

67

stout, apathetic woman with lonely eyes. Her full face drooped with lines of grief. But she listened with deep interest.

"If the Mayfield people support your paper, it will help the town," she agreed, heavily. "I want to see Mayfield grow. I'm supporting the kindergarten there, myself."

Jane Stanford would do anything to strengthen the memory of her dead boy in the heart of California. She found her check book and to my astonishment, wrote out a check payable to me.

"That's for the new paper," said she.

Somehow, she learned that Jennie had been waiting outside all this time, in the buggy. Mrs. Stanford sent a servant to bring Jennie in and show us her enormous house. It was like a museum. The high-ceiling rooms were crowned with treasure she and Leland Stanford and Leland, Junior, had brought from every part of the world. Rare examples of extravagance were shown beside cheap little souvenir knickknacks. Many of these things now are in the University Museum. She had many intimate treasures that had been her son's, including his bicycle with two tiny wheels and one huge one.

Out of doors, under the wide oaks, stood Leland's toy railroad, just big enough for a boy to ride on. It was an imitation of the Southern Pacific line Stanford had helped to build, that brought the east to California. And guarding the great house, a revered member of the household, was the beloved old Newfoundland that had been a puppy when Leland was a child.

Mrs. Stanford's check made first payment on another Washington hand press. Harry Beever, a chap I had known in the old days in San Jose, joined me now to assist in the work. Within the week we had cut the first edition of Mayfield's first paper, the *Alta*.

The *Alta* never came up to its name, which is Spanish for lofty. For Mayfield did not grow. Opportunity knocked on the village doors, but they were swinging doors. Yes, that is true of virtuous Mayfield, for she has had a past and it was her ruin. The University opened, and found Mayfield with eight or ten saloons. She refused local option — she would not abolish her bars! And a college town must not be moist. Therefore, the town of Palo Alto arose at the very gates of Stanford, while Mayfield and her saloons were snubbed forever by higher education.

Often, I couldn't even pay my own board. I was alone in Mayfield, Jennie remaining in San Jose where life was less precarious. Brewer ran the office while I "covered" the entire Mayfield beat —

which was small enough — wrote the news and the staid Republican editorials, and tried to find something amusing in the situation.

One old man of the vanished race of "tramp printer" worked for me at the *Alta*. These were gay, homeless fellows and usually heavy drinkers. They were drifters. They worked their way through the newspaper cycle from one coast to the other. They grew old before the presses, or perhaps they died in startling ways of drink, and a few of them wrenched their way from galley to an editorial desk. Many of our great newspaper men were printers. This fellow, like many another, was brilliantly educated. The drunker he got, the better he could recite poetry. He never wrote a line yet I maintain he was a poet.

"What a trivial name for a sheet — the *Alta!*" he would point out to me with shriveling contempt. "Call it the Hesperian Star! Something classical. Something poetical. You're too practical."

He would fling himself out of the place to get another bottle of "dago red" — a cheap vintage the Italian farmers made from the small California grape.

It seemed he couldn't stay longer than three weeks on any paper. He was back with me several times in the few months I owned the *Alta*. He worked just long enough to acquire several suits of underwear and a shirt or two, but when the highway called, he gave them away magnificently and vanished. No luggage to hamper his stride of Pegasus!

It was good to have him amble back into the *Alta* office again. I didn't know it then, but his personality was just another I was saving for the bag of tricks that would be Lightnin' Bill Jones of Broadway.

The months passed drearily as milestones, pointing out that the *Alta* was a failure. It was not even paying my living expenses. I was not able to make payments on the Washington press, and there was the family in San Jose to consider. Along came a man with an offer to buy. It was vanity on his part to think he could control the wavering sheet, but he was a stranger and I took him in. I offered him the newspaper for $400.

He came back with an offer of $300. That was a fair offer. Only — he failed to show any money. There was much dickering between us. Finally I took his note for $50.

I think I made the best of the sale, for he was to take over the rest of the debt to the American Type Company. I don't know if they ever persuaded him to pay for the press, but I know I never persuaded him to pay me my $50. And at that, I still insist he got the worst end of the bargain.

Speaking of charms, the *Alta* was my third newspaper — and last.

I went back to San Jose and the happy security of $15 a week. For my Alma Mater, the *Mercury*, opened its arms to me and I crept into them again gratefully, as a solicitor. Better to fatten as a hireling than starve as a publisher!

Comfortable days were the reward of the Bacons. There is a sense of security in any sort of steady job. And sixty dollars a month, as we managed, was enough for anyone. When we could afford it, Jennie and I saw every show that came to San Jose. When we couldn't afford it, we went anyway. In gallery seats, with complete understanding of one another and the play, we could be deliciously happy and guilty together.

One morning, Aunt Mary, who had a passion for reading the papers aloud, announced the news of Edwin Booth's coming to town.

Jennie and I looked at one another. I think both our hearts stopped. We had to see him! But the tickets were four dollars each. Eight dollars for two — enough to support us for . . . but we had to see Booth.

We saw Booth, in Hamlet. I'll never know how mother got along without the eight dollars in her household affairs that week. Remember, she was running the entire house on fifteen dollars. Years later we would refer back to this criminal extravagance as "our eight dollar investment."

For we saw Hamlet, and nothing on the stage would ever mean so much to me! It was my one great lesson in Art. I noticed how the other actors bellowed their lines. They seemed afraid they would not be noticed. I thought that correct — it was the fashion to bellow, it was the only sort of acting I had seen.

But when Booth gave the Shakespearian advice to the players, it was the voice of his own philosophy of acting:

> *Speak the speech, I pray you, as I pronounce it to you,*
> *trippingly upon the tongue; but if you mouth it, as*
> *many of our players do, I had as lief the Town Crier*
> *spoke my lines.*

This is the law unto the actor of the modern day, but I wonder if Booth was not the first to glean its true meaning, out of all those who had mouthed Hamlet before him?

In spite of his quiet air, or because of it, he was the one vital figure on that stage. When my chance came, I promised myself I would not yell my lines like other actors, but speak quietly, as men talk in real life, and as Booth acted.

And that chance came.

Our relatives thought it most unfortunate. Perhaps it was, for surely we had enough to make us happy, with Lloyd the very heartiest baby boy on earth, and Bessie the most beautiful child, and our adequate fortune of fifteen dollars a week to shield the little brown house on Santa Teresa street. I flung all this security to the winds again, for my chance.

It came from a stock company that played San Jose with Mrs. E. Buckley. The offer was flattering except as to salary. They offered both Jennie and myself places in the cast. How were we to know the company was on the rocks, and hiring local talent in a desperate attempt to save carfare for professional actors and also in the hope that we might draw a few extra dollars from our friends in San Jose! We did not question such kindness of the gods, for the play was the thing — and we played.

From both sides of the family rose cries of horror. Aunt Mary was grief stricken, Auntie Em prostrated and father sputtering with rage. In spite of all this, we saw our names upon the programs with greedy pride.

We made our professional debut on Monday, December 1st, 1889, in old Horticultural Hall. At this time it had been renamed ''The People's Theatre.'' It stood in barn-like immensity on San Fernando Street near Market Street and had been built for the State Democratic convention hall. Years later, it was to be known as the Garden Theatre.

''At last — we're off for Broadway,'' thought we.

But it was a thirty year trip.

On our first night the gloomy, cavernous hall was almost full. The faithful *Mercury* and the friendly *Item* reviewed us hopefully.

''A large audience, mostly made up of the friends of Mr. and Mrs. Bacon, gave the two a hearty reception,'' declared one reporter.

But there are limits to friendship. One night was enough for our closest acquaintances, and while the second night was poor, the third was painful. The ''local favorites'' lost their reputation as drawing cards. But for three weeks we played to a miserably empty hall, and Jennie and I, at least, were perfectly pleased with the situation.

During that period, by all but threatening the manager's life, I managed to wring from him a joint salary for the two of us, of three dollars a week.

I knew something was wrong with the show. I didn't believe it was Jennie and me. But the controversy ended only when the company closed, and closed its back upon San Jose, and us.

The enchanted door had slammed again. But this time I had tasted blood. I should have returned to the *Mercury*. But I dreaded returning to the horse and buggy and ad soliciting. No, I would stay with the boards until I died of starvation and my relatives and Jennie's died for shame.

"Jennie, I'm going to be a manager!" I said.

"Frank," she said, "That will be wonderful."

No one else agreed with Jennie.

But Jennie faced the family for me, defending my throwing over the fifteen dollar *Mercury* wage, and cheered me through an awful period while I borrowed the rent money for a single month's possession of the Convention Hall Theatre.

I have told you that this scene of our debut was cheerless as a barn and very like one. But the rent was low. I began hunting a show for my opening week.

The William Russell Repertoire Company was at liberty. To be truthful, it usually was at liberty. But it was touring around the small towns just then and I secured it as my opener.

William Russell himself came to San Jose in advance of the show. He came up to "my" theatre to talk over final arrangements and saw in two minutes that I was green as spinach the way mother cooks it with a dash of soda. As for my impression of him, it was as deep as if I realized he was a man who was to mark all my days.

"Pop" Russell was not a theatrical type. He looked like a prosperous coal merchant. He was portly and florid, and his red mustache bristled and curled at the ends. Two things he was never without, his stiff bowler and his watch chain with links that could have leashed a bulldog. The chain could not have been gold, because he always wore it — even after his last cufflink had gone to "Uncle's."

Every "coast defender" as we call the western players, knew him as "Pop"! He was gruff and bluffed like a gambler — he believed firmly in the Russell honesty. He was incapable of being discouraged. He had always handled very good stock players, and previous to this had managed Minnie and Essie Tittle, sisters of Charlotte Tittle, who were prominent players around the northwest in the '80s.

"Miss Hattie Ross tells me you're quite an actor yourself," he said, shrewdly.

Hattie Ross was his leading lady. Once she had set type on the *San Jose Mercury* when we were "leading amateurs."

"Maybe you could play the leading juvenile while we're here," he suggested.

That would save transportation for him. It seemed a brilliant scheme to me.

"Come on home to lunch with me," I invited instantly.

In the little Santa Teresa street home Jennie hurriedly enlarged the noon meal to meet the large demands of the visiting manager. Russell instantly enlarged his offer. He would let the two of us play! And then Bessie came running in to lunch — only we called it dinner then — and put half a rosebud hand into her mouth at sight of the stranger. Bessie was tiny and grave and very fair, and her face had the immaculate, sparkling sweetness of a flower.

"A promising beauty there, Bacon," said Russell, staring at the child.

At that, of course Bessie had to recite for the nice man.

"I had a little doggie
That used to sit and beg. . . ."

Every nursery rhyme her mother had taught her, Bessie recited with an impressive infantile air, while Russell became tremendous with enthusiasm.

"I've got to have Bessie for the show!" he declared, dramatically. "And you too, Bacon — and your wife — the three of you —"

It was the turning point in our lives, and blindly, blindly we rushed around its corner. We thought fame waited at the turn.

No young dreamers have met with stranger despair.

There was no time to regret that Lloyd was still a baby, too young to join us. Auntie Em took care of him. Jennie and I rehearsed with the other members of the Russell company on the stage of "my" theatre. Pop had selected for opening that old and pleasing play, "My Geraldine," by Dion Boucciault.

Russell had a lively company. Little Bessie was to play the child in the first act, Jennie played the child grownup "fourteen years later", and Hattie Ross, as leading lady, finished the play.

73

I gave Jennie the candy privilege of the house. She found two small boys to sell candy between acts and looked gleefully forward to a small fortune in this first business adventure of hers.

Opening night was pretentious. Out in the barnlike front we recognized with extreme delight, rows and rows of our faithful friends. In fact, Jennie and I were always being carried over some crisis by our friends. We were naturally as sociable as Airedales. We liked knowing most everybody, and sharing our good times and bad. We always will. That's why, wherever we are, whether in a single housekeeping room or in the Parlor-Suite, we've always maintained a real home! Jennie is that sort of a woman. She was that sort of a girl.

But no circle of acquaintances can reach to endless limits. And after the first night in Horticultural Hall, the friendly rows melted to a cheerless vista of empty chairs. San Jose had never been noted for generous playgoing.

Before my month's lease expired I knew that a manager was one of the many things I had proven I was not — even to faithful Jennie's satisfaction. And it was always difficult to convince Jennie I couldn't do anything I wanted to do. But I had cleared less money with my theatre than she had selling candy in it. Jennie had made seventeen dollars. She hoarded it like a little miser. That was for clothes — the rarest luxury in her life. Jennie was looking forward to blowing the entire fortune in one mad orgy of new dresses and hats. One could have quite an orgy of any sort with seventeen dollars in those days.

On one Saturday night I found myself with just enough money to pay off the stage hands. Of course the actors were left to whistle for theirs, but they were used to the precariousness of life with Pop Russell. There was little enough money in the rows "out front" that night. But every cent of it was needed and I waited in a sort of aching panic for the curtain to go up. Instead, a frosty agent from the gas and electric company came behind the scenes. He wanted money.

"But I tell you I haven't any," I pleaded. "If you'll only wait till we count the money after the show . . ."

"Pay me now", he ordered mercilessly, "or the lights go off for the night."

We couldn't see that skimpy, precious audience walk out. We couldn't play in total darkness. Poor Jennie had her treasure with her and she had to dig down into the old Grouch Bag and pay the bill.

"There's your old fifteen five!" she wailed viciously, counting it out for him in "chicken feed."

74

Not much of a bill, but just enough to break her little bank. Seeing her bravely tuck away the shrunken bag convinced me that I was never suited to manage a theatre. Yes, but what was my role in life? What had I found that was mine?

Acting, I thought. Something told me I could not fail at that. Pop Russell had the same idea, yet when the play ended and he prepared to take his company out of San Jose, it was not my acting that drew his critical eye, but little Bessie's.

"I'll take the little girl . . . you and your wife, too, of course," he offered, not flatteringly. "What do you say to forty dollars a week for the three of you?"

I didn't hear the rest. Already, I was hunting Jennie to tell her. We had been praying Pop would offer to take us with him, since the very first day he came to San Jose. And forty a week was a flood of money to us. We would play the small towns near San Jose, and truly, they were not so very far from Broadway!

"If you had only married that nice boy from San Francisco," Aunt Mary regretted sadly to Jennie.

This city rival never would have submitted to dragging his young wife around the country, play-acting! And while Jennie's folk regretted lost chances and future woes, the Bacons in one solid Methodist phalanx sat down upon my hopes. To them it was next door to being a patent medicine dealer and travelling around the counties like the King of Pain or Great Ferdon, with bottled exhibits of horrible animal growths and two heathen contortionists on ladders. No, it was certainly not respectable.

But we went.

This was the crisis of what had been a full year. In twelve months I had turned from newspaper advertising to publishing my own paper, then to managing a theatre and now — to acting. I felt I had run the gamut and was at peace with my world, when I helped Jennie and Bessie aboard the train at the San Jose depot. We were crossing the mountains to Santa Cruz.

And this was the almighty road promised us! The one cruel grief was leaving our baby boy. He cooed happily in Auntie Em's arms as we departed.

The next time we would see our son he was to turn his innocent face away, thinking us strangers!

We left behind us a frigid line-up of Jeffrey aunts and Bacon disapproval. With Pop Russell and Hattie and George Hernandes, the comedian, and all the others, we left San Jose on our great adventure. And all the three of us had in the world were our light hearts and one small, aged tin trunk — "Jennie's tin box," as Pop would always call this wardrobe sarcastically. But this seemed the fulfillment of all our dreaming. For we were bound for the road's end at last, with a real company of honest-to-goodness actors!

This was in springtime of the good year 1890.

Santa Cruz is a small seaport town below San Francisco. Jennie and I had not seen Santa Cruz, although it was only a two hour ride from San Jose, over the low mountains of the Coast Range where the giant redwoods stand ankle-deep in frothy fern, and down to the lapis lazuli blue of the Pacific.

We had the shivering thrill that agitated us down to our very toes, of getting off a train and walking up a main street, as actors! The troupe scattered for policy's sake through the small summer hotels — boarding houses they were, rather. I saw Jennie and Bessie tucked away for the night in a small room filtered with clean salt air, and went out to see the town with the boys. This was part of the game. We were to be seen in public as much as possible, always very conspicuous, — yet exclusive — very elegant, and slightly bored. That helped sell tickets.

There was little enough to see. The sandy streets were edged with summer cottages and small hotels, and the fanciest hotel was the Pope House. The old Phelan estate fronted the long beach and when fashionable San Francisco came down to visit there would be yacht regattas and streaming pennants and gay lanterns and the lilt of the polka. But the town was silent. There was no Casino then to strew the beach with gaiety.

Perhaps we did not promenade enough in Santa Cruz. For the tickets did not sell as we had hoped at the little box office window of Knight's Opera House. But we appreciated that Opera House. We had never seen such a grand theatre. It had a Green Room — think of it! — such as Jennie and I had read about but never seen. There were photographs of famous actors on its walls. There was an ingrain carpet. And the stage curtain was a weighty affair that should be in a California museum.

It was a privilege to play in a theatre like that.

With delicious baby industry, little Bessie toiled through her parts, being "fed" her lines by Jennie who was always hidden someplace on stage or off. Jennie continued to play the ingenue. Perhaps that is why Jennie has always seemed like one of the kids to me, for she was playing girlish roles after I worked into old man

76

parts. She seemed so much nearer Bessie's age than mine, that Bessie herself, upon growing older, refused to call her mother anything but "Jane."

The third night in Santa Cruz we found ourselves playing to a small audience that was colder than the winds coming up the sandy street from the sea. We counted the small pile of box office money gloomily.

"Might just as well check out," said Pop, staring thoughtfully at the pile.

As suddenly as we had come into Santa Cruz, we left the next morning. We were in San Francisco that night and Pop marched us right over to Oakland.

We were not to play "the big town," as Coast Defenders lovingly called San Francisco. That is a dream seldom realized by the stock players of the west. But we did look forward to playing Oakland, at least!

I noticed when we were on the ferry boat crossing the bay, that several members of the company were missing. We had been a small company in the beginning. Now, we were short.

They had deserted in San Francisco. I might have recognized the danger sign. But I was too new to the game to realize the meaning of this desertion — also, I was busy trying to memorize all the new parts Pop had given me. Memorizing is a job that takes all my attention.

To our astonishment, we did not stop in Oakland. We were not to play this desirable substitute for San Francisco. Instead, Pop led us sternly on to the small town of Martinez, on the bay. It was the out trail for us now, the flying jumps, the short stops and the small towns.

We were dazed, but at last we knew the truth. We were out in the "paloosa" counties bound to nowhere and Pop's conscience was acting as guide. He alone could lead us through the unknown.

We were barnstormers!

CHAPTER EIGHT

AS IT WAS WITH THE PIONEERS

Few enough were left of the William Russell Repertoire Company. But Pop did the best with those of us left to him. He cut down his plays to suit his remaining players, had most of us playing at least two parts a night, and took us on a drive through the smaller towns of Northern California.

One night was plenty for most towns. Every evening we put on a different play. That was severe training for me, to whom every new part was an ordeal. Desperately we tried to keep up with our dismaying new roles, coaching one another and teaching little Bessie her simple lines. Still, it was like a game to us. We didn't mind.

It is like a dream to remember — these small towns we played, these memories of Main Streets in Springtime. There was always a Main Street. There was always the Opera House. And, a figure of destiny in my travels, there was always an "Old Bill" to be talked to — the delight and despair of every town. I had seen him first as Uncle Morris in San Jose, and in Vallejo and Napa — now I found he was everywhere. He became my familiar friend. In new towns, I looked for him on hotel verandas or on the whittled benches of the inevitable California "Plaza". I found myself treasuring the wise words and quaint mannerisms of these Bill Jonses of the trail.

It was then my code found me first: Go to the young for inspiration, to the old to be informed! The soul of old California was in these men and the bravery of the pioneers in their tales. Many had known my mother's people in the year they came west under covered wagons. Now, Jennie and I were pioneering..."

Slaves to a timetable, we worked our way by rail into the gold counties. We wound our route between hills uprooted in the mad scramble for fortune that gave California to the world, in '49.

We were playing around the golden heart of the state in a time when every town and village still had its many '49ers, men of a race that is passing now.

We played Auburn.

Not far away, John Marshall found the first gold nugget and started the great Rush — to die years later in poverty. Now the gold counties were deserted, their towns haunted by the ghost of fortune. So, although I did not suspect it, was the Russell Company. Our first salary day came around, but no salary. Still, we didn't understand. We were so very green . . . of an enchanted greenness.

Russell took me into his confidence and importantly figured up expenses for the three Bacons. He deducted that sum from our salary and told me how much he owed us.

"I will reimburse you in a day or so," he explained importantly.

"That will be fine," said I, happily.

"— a day or so," catchword of the boards! Days became weeks and still we were without money to send home to San Jose, to provide for our little son. Not that we worried a single moment! Greater artists had suffered worse. And I could see for myself that Pop Russell was fighting in these deserted counties.

And also, the counties we played meant much to me. We traveled to north and west of Sacramento, the state capitol, in barren, lonely legend-ridden country known as the Northern and Southern mines. We played Placerville, Nevada City, Carson — we played Marysville!

I had not forgotten Marysville. I can never forget that town on the wide, rich, beautiful valley land below the Buttes, between Sacramento and the volcano Mount Lassen. Yet I left it when a very small boy, when the family moved to San Jose.

Six miles out of Marysville, in January, 1864, I had been newly added to the Bacon family. It was a large family when I joined it. There were Ed, Charley, Annie and Helen. Later, my little sister Emma's name would be placed at the bottom of the impressively long list in the clasped family Bible. I had an old letter written by mother in this year, referring to me as, "the dearest, sweetest boy, and his name is Frank."

And it was at Marysville I had first been tainted by what my stern parents termed original sin. The old town recalled it to me, and I told Jennie the story and laughed wryly at a memory that had once been dreadful. When I was six and playing behind the sheepherder's house on the family ranch, I found a grimy copy of the Police Gazette.

Mother, coming around the corner of the cabin with a pail of eggs in her hand, found me hunched over the wretched periodical. To her it was almost too humiliating a stain on the family purity to be reported to father. But she found her courage and told him, as a dutiful wife should, and I spent the rest of the day profitably learning the Psalms.

"Young women who go about showing their — their limbs!" snorted father, glaring down sidewise at the bright pink pages, and I can feel the scorn of his Puritan lip as it pulled down. He burned that magazine in the kitchen stove as if its sacrifice were a rite of purification which might save my tender soul. It didn't. Years passed before I would lay eyes upon another Police Gazette, which proves it is not always environment that makes the man.

The circle had swept around since that day of shame and the penetential Psalms, and brought me again to Marysville — an actor!

I played roles that would have made my grandfather's hair rise in virtuous horror. And yet they were innocent parts, for drama was innocent in the '90s. Being an actor was sin enough, however, in the eyes of grandfather McGrew.

Dear old soul, I thought of him often during the two days stay Pop Russell's company made in Marysville. It was on his ranch, near town, I had spent my earliest childhood. He died years before our playing there, in our home in San Jose. I remembered him as a white headed, bent pioneer of eighty three years, who sat all day long upright in a rocker and chanted Methodist hymns. They were the only light in his darkness.

Yet even stern grandfather's soul had played its full drama of love.

There were many who remembered grandfather in Marysville. There were others in Nevada City, another "ghost town" of the Gold Rush that was not completely dead. We played "My Geraldine" there, I believe, and before the show I went around town looking up pioneers and recalling all I could of grandfather's venture westward. Pioneers form a network across California. Know one and you know them all, and the story of the state as well.

It was just outside of Nevada City, at Fort McDowell, that grandfather John McGrew had halted his train of covered wagons in the year 1852. It had been a six months trip across the plains from Frankfort, Kentucky. This was three years after the start of the gold excitement, and as Bill Jones was to put it later in *Lightnin'*, "The excitement was still on."

John McGrew was a forbidding Scotsman and a "Shouting Methodist." He came west for the health of his invalid wife, who stood the half year trip on a bed in a jolting wagon drawn by yoked oxen, only to pass away after one month in California. He worshipped her.

The family erected a tent outside of Grass Valley and started a sort of pioneer boarding house for miners. The McGrew girls were the cooks and waited on the long rough tables. They were the only single girls in the wagon train, and let me tell you that single girls were rarer than orchids in '52, when men were still sending their shirts as far as China to be laundered, and one group of miners held a dance around the cast-off hoop skirt some woman had forgotten. These girls knew a popularity and regard granted to few women. They were Levise and Leffina and Emma, who later married Judge Heacock of the Superior Court in San Francisco, and Lehella Jane, who would later be my mother.

When the family came into Grass Valley, they had been met by Will McGrew, the oldest son, who had ridden on horseback to California ahead of them. Will had done well in the new state and was already a Judge in Sacramento. The youngest son, Morris, had ridden a horse alongside the wagon that held his sick mother. These were the six children left from a family of twelve.

This youngest son was my famous Uncle Morris. I don't know how he ever found enough energy to ride to California. I'll bet one of the girls backed the horse against the wagon for him mornings, so he could climb on. He atoned for that one blemish of industry on his career by never exhausting another breath in work. Let others scramble for the heavy nuggets that meant mansions in San Francisco, tours in Europe, pacers with lengthy pedigrees! Not Uncle Morris!

The McGrews were hard at work, not far from the place where Jennie and little Bessie and I would be playing forty years later, when a new wagon train arrived, several weeks behind theirs. Among the single riders was Lyddall Bacon of Kentucky.

That was Father.

I cannot imagine my stern, struggling father ever having flung the east away to follow a wagon train where rode the girl he loved. I cannot imagine that meeting on the harsh new California soil, nor the quiet, conscientious mother I knew, rushing with open arms to

81

meet him, crying with happiness because he had dared to follow. But that is what Lehella Jane McGrew did, in ' 52.

They would be married at once. There was little time to be spent in marrying, for the valley was thick with tents and lean-tos and men still swarmed there with picks and shovels, and father was the first to give the stirring cry in that new cavalcade, "Boys, I've struck color!"

Even Uncle Morris had a nice gravely claim staked out in the creek bed. But no tales of $100,000 nuggets could stir his leisurely blood. Uncle Morris, men told me in Nevada City with much smiling, even after forty years, lounged around camp and related yarns of the mythological nuggets he found of great circumference and richness, that like the fish of his later stories, always got away.

Each day was golden. Like hunted animals, the men dug and flung out gravel into running sluices and watched it burst into yellow in the homemade wooden "cradles." This was before hydraulic mining and every ounce of the precious dirt was lifted by hand. But father gave up one of his golden days to make a trip to Sacramento. There he purchased a new suit. It was to be his wedding suit. He packed it neatly in the chest in his tent corner, not to look at it again until his wedding day.

By this time, mother's sister Emma had made up her mind to marry young Heacock of the same wagon train — he was the one I mentioned as the San Francisco judge of later years. It would be a double wedding and the entire party would leave early on the trip to Sacramento.

On that morning father opened the cedar chest. His suit, the glossy fancy shirt and the glittering boots, were gone.

"I seen Morris riding off towards Sacramento last night," one of the boarders volunteered. "Said he was startin' early so's not to miss the wedding. And he was all got up in a new suit . . ."

This was father's introduction to the gentle whims of his new brother-in-law.

Father was married in his working clothes, with the miner's blue checked shirt and the pants tucked into thick boots. Through the solemn double ceremony, he found time to glare at the magnificently clad and resplendent Morris, who beamed upon the scene in his sweet, gentle way and made the entire occasion, as he did every-thing — his!

During this same year, Jennie's uncle was also shaking a mining pan in Grass Valley. Her folk and mine, strangely enough, had pioneered together in this country we were storming with Pop Russell. We also, forty years after, were pioneers.

Ours were the hardships of constant travel, the tight airless rooms of country hotels, careless cooking and no money of our own. Pop held the purse strings. Just like the '49ers, we were trying to wring a living from these gold towns that had aged so quietly.

Placerville is the heart of the gold country in northern California. It is the gateway to the "southern mines." Joaquin Murieta, the famous bandit of old California, who sprang to terrible prominence in the '50s, had made his headquarters there. When my people and Jennie's were in Grass Valley, he was pursuing his reign of terror, with men organized from the Oregon to the Mexican line. In 1854 he was shot down from a racing stallion near Bakersfield, not far from the place where I herded sheep as a boy.

At Placerville we met with the first warning. I did not realize the danger.

"Guess we'll get off the railroad," said Pop.

To me, that merely meant the added adventure of playing old towns sleepy with legend. To the older and wiser actors it meant the first note of disaster. They knew the danger of storming off a railroad line. But Pop mentioned Nevada and Jennie and I felt like explorers. I had never been off California soil, nor had Jennie since she was a child.

At Placerville, then, we left the rails behind, to beat our way in horse-drawn stages toward the Nevada line.

I was sent on ahead as trailbreaker. Russell hired a wagon for me, and we piled aboard all our scant scenery and baggage and posters. I was to drive on ahead to Georgetown, about forty miles away. I would drown that struggling village under paper announcements and wait the arrival of the company, two days after.

That last night in Placerville, I played in "Lynwood" — also in a shabby property Confederate uniform. Not much sleep had been mine when the wagon driver knocked next morning early on my door. It was 3:30 in a chilly summer dawn. I said good-bye to Jennie, and while she snuggled back under the warm covers beside the slumbering Bessie, I crept noiselessly out of the hotel, feeling very sleepy and abused.

Before the veranda an immense haywagon was waiting, piled with our property. Four heavy horses were harnessed and waiting, and even they seemed sleepy. I sympathized with them. It made me doubt I was really an actor, getting up at such an hour.

The driver wasn't sleepy. Neither was he awake. He had maintained the same state of coma for forty years, but he knew those mountain roads. He was another Bill Jones, who had grown elderly with Placerville and taken on the grayness and the peace of the trails. We crawled up the trails and down their narrow, deadly loneliness like a wee group of ants toiling monotonously.

Great clouds of dust announced our passing. Within these clouds, in un-Jovian discomfort, we jolted, choked, coughed and drove.

Poppies gilded the hills. Not the great golden ones that enwealth the Santa Clara valley, for these blossoms grew smaller and paler as we climbed higher in the Sierras. There was endless dry lacework of fern, and the glossy-leaved madrone, and the small manzanita. Everywhere in the hills were staring dark mouths that were tunnels, vacated by discouraged miners, long ago.

"Feller owned that there coyote hole jumped another feller's," explained my driver, leisurely crunching down the brake. "Wait along the line here a spell and I'll show ye the oak we hung him on."

He regaled me with tales of the "coyote holes." Every deserted claim had its inhabitant, for him. He knew the names of dead men who had worked them hopefully, in his or his father's time. He told me stories of the fierce, unguarded '50s, of Joaquin Murieta and his mad four hundred who lathered California with red death and banditry, of Three-Fingered Jack, his lieutenant who tore out human hearts, of dangerous old-time gamblers with black felt hats pulled low over the eyes, who flung down their lives with their cards.

Through the lurid pictures his drawling yarns gave me, we jolted miserably on. The hills might be romantic, but not this equipage hired by the Russell Repertoire Company. The dust caked into mud on our hot faces. At times the tales seemed turning into lullabyes and I forgot the discomfort in sleep. I would jerk awake again just in time to keep from pitching off the high, swaying seat.

"Aren't we nearly to Georgetown?" I demanded crossly for the hundredth time. "How much farther?"

He jerked the horses to rest on a hillrise and spat reflectively into the thirsty fern.

"Oh, just a hill, a hollow and an eyesight," he replied.

A classic answer. I have put that line into many a part through the years.

Georgetown proved to be a modest settlement flavored still with pioneer struggle. The place was one of Russell's discoveries. Pop

84

discovered more towns then Baedaker. He knew the name of every cranny with a name on the western coast. He arrived two days later with the rest of the company. We played Georgetown with little enthusiasm. That little was more than the town gave us. We left early next morning.

That week we crossed the California-Nevada Line.

All this was done by stage, and we played every town as we went. Staging over the line meant much to Jennie and me. We were incurably romantic, I am afraid, and with a feeling of adventure we deserted the only state we had ever known. How soon the time would come when between our tears we would yearn again for California!

Over roads dry and soft with dust we came into the small Nevada towns near the line, with Carson City the first to be played. The days were longer and hotter now. It was summer. The night before the Fourth of July, we drove into Virginia City.

We had played the towns of gold — this was the city of silver. It also was desolate, although untold fortune had been dragged from it twenty years before. Piles of ramshackle houses climbed the steep hillsides to the mouths of the mines that had made this city famous in the silver 'Sixties'. These years were to Nevada as the forties to California. Millions had been combed from the deserted hills. Mackey, Flood and Fair, great triumvirate of western millionaires, had made their wealth in these Bonanza Mines. Mark Twain had begun his writing career as a journalist in Virginia City, before going to the *San Francisco Call*. Men had fought and died here at the drop of a hat.

Our rooms were in the old International Hotel. It had been a palace in Mark Twain's day. Now we had practically to ourselves the great shell of a building, with the old-fashioned feather beds and the big flowery water pitcher in every room. Across the street was the famed Orndorff and McGee saloon. The Hotel mounted the hill, so that the back door opened into the third floor! I believe the old International had the first elevator in the west.

We played next night — Fourth of July. On that gala night the sleeping town wakened into the old life of the sixties. We took in a few extra dollars that night, and Pop was majestic with the weight of so much wealth. But did we see a dollar of it? Over Pop's dead body! Only for us the glory of extras lines — which really meant extra work — as Pop cut down our parts to fit our shrinking company. An actor's deserting simply meant more lines for the rest of us, so we didn't mind.

85

The days were warm and comfortless and the dust of the alkali-ridden Carson Valley was still dry on our skins. The romance of our life returned only when evening came, when in our small echoing stable of a hall we donned the crude make-up and the piecemeal costumes and played before the stuttering oil lamps. The play — that was all we had, and we gave it our souls.

Sunday came to find us lingering on in Virginia City. We did not play Sundays. This would be a free day on my hands, and I decided to put it to work.

I needed money. Every actor in the company needed money. Pop held the money bag with the grip of a drowning swimmer and never doled us a dollar for spending money. The bills he paid himself — when he could. If not, the hotel sent the bill on to the next town where we were pretty certain to make good. But the trifling small luxuries, such as a bag of candy for Bessie or a yard of ribbon for Jennie — where was the money for these! I couldn't even buy a sack of tobacco. We were traveling as blindly as a troupe of day-old kittens, with our expenses paid and nothing more.

But I did know how ads were solicited. Had I not learned the advertising game while on the *San Jose Mercury?* George Hernandez, the comedian, offered to lend me his services for the Sunday. Together we worked out a special program and solicited ads for it through Virginia City. Nearly every merchant in the quiet town "came through." Sometimes they wanted to advertise but lacked the ready cash.

"Pay us in trade," was my answer to that.

That was how George and I happened to return to the International Hotel bending under the weight of goods we had taken in exchange for ads. We had candy from the confectioner's on the main corner. We had boxes of crackers and other edibles we could eat while traveling. We had shoes! And I even had a beautiful pink celluloid powder box for Jennie — the thing lay around the house for years.

Our only expense was the printer, and he was reasonable. George and I cleared ten dollars each from that day's work. Pop was staggered. I gave him no chance to borrow this precious ten dollars. I went instantly to the Post Office and wrote out a money order for the full impressive amount. I mailed it to the Aunts in San Jose, and pride warmed me like wine. This was the first money I had been able to send home.

Also, it was the last.

But I wasn't the only member of the company to whom Virginia City proved a bonanza.

"Props" fell into fortune there. He was our property man, a big, good-natured German, exceedingly fond of the ladies and the butt of all our jokes.

Fortune first sighted Props while he was dancing at the big town ball that followed our performance the night of the Fourth. Jennie had to stay in our room at the International to watch over the sleeping Bessie after the show, but everyone else in Virginia City that night — the cowboys from Carson Valley, the miners from the hills, the townspeople and the distinguished visiting actors! — were all at the dance. We met everyone. We danced with everyone. One of the grocers nudged me.

"Watch your property man!" he whispered with a grin. "He's danced every single dance with Plasters!"

The beaming German lad was careening around the hall with a woman in a low-necked, full-skirted evening dress, garnished with miles of what Jennie calls "edging." They passed us in the latest dance step, know as the "hop waltz." Sure enough, peeping over the edge of her dress in the back was the square end of a porous plaster. The grocer informed me she always wore them and was thereby known through the countryside as "Plasters."

Plasters was a widow. Next day Props was seen driving her around Virginia City. Only, it was her team of spanking bays he drove. She didn't look so promising under the glaring July sunlight. I knew Props thoroughly and could see he was bored. But when he helped her out of the buggy before her home, she dropped her purse. It opened. A cache of twenty dollar gold pieces bit the dust.

Men have sold their souls for less. Props hadn't seen five dollars for months.

One hour later Props and Plasters, seated as close together in the buggy as was humanly possible, were seen driving toward Carson City, the capitol. They married. We never saw Props again. And the leading man himself couldn't have been a severer loss to the company, for Props had been the support of our back stage morale. After this every man of us had to help shift the scenery, work the curtain and attend to the lamps, and every moment we were not actually on the stage, we were toiling like laborers. But we forgave Props. Many another has turned his back on the home trail at sight of gold.

The same week we arrived in Virginia City, we left it. But we left friends behind us, and have, wherever we have traveled. This time we took the train. Our traveling by stage coach was over for a time. We rode through arid, sunbaked mountains.

July! And over the waste Nevada land the cattle were dying. Thousands of the herds we passed belonged to those great cattle czars of California, Miller and Lux. At this time, it was said, Miller and Lux could ride through California, Nevada, Arizona, Washington and Oregon, and sleep every night on their own land. This starvation among the herds made Nevada pitiful to us, for in our section of California a cow was a family friend who lived in sleek happiness in an alfalfa field. The calves with their innocent, sad faces were like suffering children. For the first time, I wanted to return to California.

"We'll work toward Reno," said Pop.

CHAPTER NINE

NOW ALL ROADS LEAD TO RENO

But when we stormed Nevada, Reno was as innocent as one of the calves we passed in our travels. It was little enough to remember. In '91 divorce in a family was almost as bad as a hanging. A divorcee was somebody for ladies to talk about in low voices while sewing on the front porch, afternoons. To know a person who had a divorced aunt was something to brag about, like having once seen Jessie James, or the Siamese Twins.

We worked our way through a monotony of small towns toward Reno. Today, these towns that slept beside the railroad have revived. But they were dead villages then. It is strange that in such a noted cattle state, we tasted condensed milk for the first time! It was given us everywhere, in country hotels where the cows stared in the windows at us as we ate. But as on most cattle ranches you will find no cowboy who would risk the disgrace of milking, so it was in Nevada.

We followed a zigzag route. Wherever Pop scented a few possible dollars, there did he lead us. There did we rent our hall or Opera House, and night after night we played the two plays left of our repertoire. The other dramas had been discarded as our actors left us. All we had left to play were "Lynwood," and "The Black Flag." Poor as I am at memorizing parts, I could give every line in these two classics, backward. Their authors would never have recognized them. Every man selected his own lines and crammed three or four parts into one. We were presenting plays written for three times as many actors, with our company of ten!

We caught late trains out of the small towns, after the show. Sometimes the train didn't leave until three or four in the morning. Then we sat up waiting on the miserable wooden benches that grace country stations, or if there was no station, we sat on our scanty

89

luggage. Bessie would always be asleep, and George Hernandez or I would carry her gently aboard and tuck her under my coat on an empty seat. These jumps were hard on all of us, but we made them easiest for Bessie. She slept through all the tragic periods of our trip with the merciful innocence of four years.

The rest of us made the best of the hard upholstery and slept in the positions of a group of statuary gone insane. Berths! — say, not one of us had a berth on the entire trip!

But it was fun. I was doing what I had longed to do all through boyhood, newspaper galley and photographic gallery years. Even though there were no more money orders to send home, though Pop Russell recognized no salary days and my one checked, glaring suit was growing shabby, I was happy. The letters we received from San Jose were enraged demands that we return to family life and decency — the aunts regarded us as traveling gypsies, my father's disappointment in me amounted to pain. Still, we were triumphant.

We were actors!

And Bessie, aged four, was our boon companion in guilt. Our families might regard us as three young runaway scalawags, but that only added to the thrill of it all. Merrily, we came to Reno.

We put on "Lynwood" the first night in Reno and "The Black Flag" the next night, and the next day . . . Hattie Ross and Albert Hosmer deserted.

Hattie and Albert were leading lady and man and their leaving was the knockout blow. Not that I blamed them for quitting. Being a star means little when there is no salary to match the honor. Hattie and Albert were tired of the late riding, the dubious hotels and the poverty of our life. They were through with Pop Russell.

"We'll get along without them," said Pop.

You have to admire that man!

Another manager would have thrown up everything and left us to shift for ourselves. Not Pop Russell. There were eight of us left, including Pop and little Bessie. So it was at Reno we reorganized and set our faces on the long gypsy trail. Think of it, a company of eight starting through the great northwestern areas where towns are small and few.

Will Russell's Repertoire Company bravely left Reno on a dust-blown day that was riddled with heat. We did not know what waited for us on the out trail. But one thing we knew, we were real barnstormers now.

90

Jennie and I, the greenest actors present, were elected to take the parts of the missing leads! Jennie the leading lady! But there it was in black and white on the program — "Miss Jennie Bacon," and I played leads sometimes, when the "heavy" man didn't have them, and I had another part as well. Between times I shifted scenery. Although there is much to repent in those poverty smitten days, it is all worth while to have played leads.

We followed the Pacific line to Elko and that was our last railroad town in Nevada. Elko was more sophisticated than the smaller places; she sniffed at our desperate courage and our company of eight. The eight of us climbed aboard a lumbering old stage next morning and departed for Tuscarora.

Tuscarora had been a prosperous mining town even as late as the '70s. But now, by some freak of economics, her main prosperity lay in the saloons and gambling halls. It was still "live". The town lined the sidewalks to watch the arrival of the traveling actors, word of whose coming had stirred the settlement for days. That night the hall Pop hired was packed to that last echo.

The miners, who had come down from far crannies in the Rockies, cheered us in a thundering fashion. George Hernandez's comical prologue sent tears of amusement trickling down through coarse beards. We'd shaved down our productions to such a fine point, there seemed no part for little Bessie. So we brought her in on one scene completely inapropos, and she gave them a couple of recitations in her solemn baby fashion. The child ran out of encores and stood helplessly staring at the cheering crowd.

"— give the White House poem," mother whispered between bows.

We had taught her the silly doggerel to amuse ourselves on the tiring trips. One was about the book by Rose Cleveland, sister of the President and then mistress of the White House. The book had been given great publicity.

Bessie went right down before the footlights and related to them the absurdity:

> "The President sat in his easy chair,
> Reading a book of his sister's,
> He hadn't been shaved for two or three days
> And the wind blew through his whiskers."

Only, she couldn't pronounce the "whiskers," and said "whoofers."

91

The audience whooped and stamped and Bessie went solemnly on with her next favorite, one I had made up for her amusement:

"Way up in the sky,
The moon we often see,
It may be covered with insects
But there are no flies on me."

The expressions, "There are no flies on me," and "The wind blew through his whiskers," were then the acme of slang.

The idiotic doggerel was the hit of the show and Bessie took more curtain calls than the rest of us put together.

Early next morning we caught the stage out of Tuscarora. We left early to avoid the heat. There were only the eight members of our glorious company as passengers and a fat Chinaman who owned a big lottery hall in the camp. We welcomed him into our circle and found he spoke fair pidgeon English. He was delighted with the little girl "act-less," and astounded by Mrs. Bacon's feet, "allee same Chinese lady!"

As we jolted in the direction of the Utah line and the morning sun warmed the stage and its occupants, he grew drowsy. On the contrary, we were all feeling very gay, with that false nervous exhileration often produced by lack of sufficient sleep. So we sang loudly in chorus in his ears, to the tune of a popular song:

"Tuscarora! Tuscarora!
Umphty dadd, dada! Boom!"

He would jerk awake smiling, and say, "Heap much big fun."

Afternoon and sunlight ended our high spirits. Now it was our turn to become sleepy. Bessie slept in my arms as the long, bouncing ride wore on and the heat grew more unbearable. One by one we settled down like lead on the high seats and dozed. Then our Chinese traveler turned the tables properly! All the rest of the way, in his high Oriental voice, he sang joyously:

"Tusky-kee-lora! Tusky-kee-lora!
Heap wake upee! Sabee? Boom!"

And so, damp and jostled in the heat, a weary company kept awake by piping Oriental strains, we "made" our third state, crossing the Utah line.

It was on a Sunday we came into Ogden. That night was the first we spent in the state of Utah and Bessie made it memorable for us. All night she scratched her small body and sobbed with weariness.

"It's the hives," declared Jennie anxiously, examining the white welts on the tender flesh. "Don't cry, dearest, it will all be well in the morning . . ." But in the morning we found the reason for the welts. They were legion, they infested our cheap room. Bedbugs.

We had never seen one before. In California, seems to me, the pests are rare. We looked at each other helplessly. So this was the gilded life of the stage! Bare living expenses and night journeys aching with sleeplessness, bad food and disorganized systems and now, these!

However, we continued in that room while playing Ogden.

We wanted to play Salt Lake, but that was far too grand an ambition for the Russell band. Instead, we played the small towns of Utah, or, as they were still called in the '90s, "the Settlements."

These were the spots settled and inhabited by Mormons. They were like great family groups, and one store served the entire town and was known as the "Co-op." That was colloquial for "co-operative."

There were no hotels. Strangers like ourselves who entered the Settlements were lodged in the "Big House" of the local Elder. Life in the Settlements was severe. The Mormons were a stern and thrifty people, still, they proved good patrons of all we had to offer. They were a people apart. Under their kindness to strangers lurked a resentment against other states and people, for this was in a time when many Mormons were in prison for the practice of polygamy.

The Government was stamping out the belief in many wives ordained by Brigham Young. The Mormons were undergoing the fire of what they felt to be religious persecution. So they spent their hardworking lives grouped together in the Settlements, as if for protection.

I wonder what the Mormon wives thought of Jennie and Helen Johnson! Our actor women must have seemed like birds of passage to the women who were trained to know only four walls, family and religion — "Kirche, Kuche and Kinder."

"Do you suppose there is any face powder for sale at the Co-op?" Jennie asked one Elder's wife, our landlady.

"You mean that stuff you put on your face?" replied the landlady staring. "I don't think there's any in the Settlement. A play-actor left some in her room once — I didn't like to waste it so I put it in the starch."

For weeks, we wandered around Utah, usually playing two nights in a Settlement.

Provo may not create much of an impression on the map, but it was a metropolis compared with the places we had been playing. Hand me the old scrap book, Jennie — ah, here are memories from Utah! Here is the old program from the night we played "The Black Flag" in the Provo Opera House. Have you forgotten how magnificent we thought that theatre, after the country halls we had known? There were coal-oil lamps for footlights, and they raised or lowered to brighten or dim our stage, just as we pleased. That was a final note of elegance. We had never seen anything like that. It was a triumph to play Provo, as this yellowed program recalls:

PROVO OPERA HOUSE

Thursday Evening, Nov. 6th, 1890

RUSSELL'S
DRAMATIC COMPANY

In Mr. Elward Thorne's Great Comedy

Drama in Five Acts

Entitled The

BLACK FLAG

OR

BROTHER against BROTHER

CAST OF CHARACTERS

Henry Glyndon of the life saving crew .... Mr. Oscar Don

Owen Glyndon, with an iron will
Sam Seaton, a prison guide .... W. M. Russell

Lazarus, a London sharper .... George Hernandez

Jack Glyndon, known as Flash Jack .... J. McGlynn

Ned, a cabin boy .... Frank Bacon

Capt. Handysides, a brutal skipper
Scarun, a masher.. A. Rosmore

Prison Inspector
Prison Warden .... W. M. Seymour

Naomi Blanford, an heiress .... Jennie Bacon

Mrs. Ruth Glyndon, the mother
Topay Carroll, of the Red Lyon Inn .... Helen Johnson

Fifty Cents — Adults   Twenty-five Cents — Children

It was after playing out of Provo that Pop acquired a new leading lady.

Miss Pearl Ethier was a Junoesque young woman who had been working around Utah in repertoire. She was given roles that would now be termed "vamp," although the word had not been coined. She was a sister of Alphonse Ethier, now well-known on the stage.

Pearl's arrival enabled Jennie to return to her former role of soubrette and that strengthened our cast. We were having no gentle task spreading our small group over two complete and famous plays. We had to double and twist the parts, and, honestly, our productions weren't so bad! Everyone of us was working like three. Giving a leading lady to Pop's company was handing a wheelchair to an invalid. With this new star to guide us we trekked on across Utah.

And still we were always penniless and often on the verge of entire financial collapse, and the days were growing colder and the mountains steeper, and still I trusted Pop Russell as I never shall trust another manager.

Well, we were all doing our best. I'm the last person to blame anyone. After all, it was harder on Pop than on any of the rest of us, but if the worry hit him harder, he showed it less.

At Spanish Forks, one of the larger Mormon Settlements, I met with a man after my own heart. He was a traveling photographer. There were many men like him in those days, men who wandered the States over to photograph these people who lived "off the beaten line."

"I was a photographer myself once," I informed him — after the manner of Lightnin' Bill Jones, who has been all things unto all people.

Meeting as fellow wanderers far up in the Rockies of Utah, he offered me professional courtesy. He had me invite every single member of the company to sit for pictures. Bessie's turned out charmingly and he let us have several hundred photographs of the child at $10 a hundred. That was mighty kind of him.

After that, wherever we played, Bess sold these pictures of herself to the audience between acts. What is more, she actually sold them at twenty-five cents each. And the profits that infant made selling her pictures furnished the only spending money the Bacon family saw on this historic trip!

Every new town we played we entered penniless. We never knew what few dollars Pop held in his pockets, but we knew they were few. Upon the success of our night's performance depended the paying of our hotel and board bill. Often enough if a town failed to show money, we had to ask the bill be sent on to our eternal new hope, "the next town." And all the time, hopelessly drifting, we were passing farther away from California.

And winter was creeping on us. It met the Russell Company at the boundary line of our fourth state and ushered us with a white cheerlessness into Colorado.

I had never seen snow before! We who hailed from the Santa Clara Valley knew winter as a thrilling benediction of sun and rain, of golden days and gray, that purpled the valley with the prune harvest and left never a dearth of roses. We watched the snow whitening the Rockies with a sense of dread. It was a threat of what winter might mean to us.

I was glad when Pop turned the trail southward. Working down through the mountains and playing the smallest Colorado towns, we came to Salida.

Salida was like a homecoming. Helen Johnson had friends there from her home town and during her stay there she visited them. And if they didn't invite all the Russell company up there for dinner, the whole nine of us!

You have to be a traveling actor to appreciate an invitation like that. Think of a real kitchen stove with good things bubbling and steaming on the top of it! A pantry with a ginger snap jar and a barrel reeking with home-made salt cucumber pickles! And a table to stretch your legs under happily at the meal's end! No wonder Helen wept at the thought of leaving Salida. We all wanted to share her tears.

One member of this kind family was deeply impressed by having a real theatrical company strike his home. He had a little money and he had an idea he'd like to be a manager, just like Pop Russell. Pop never showed the marks of hardship and worry — in presenting a prosperous front he could always fool the public. The Salida man didn't know what trouble meant.

"Sure, go ahead and found a company," our leading man urged him. "I'll go with you — so will Helen."

And instantly trouble fell on our shoulders like a vulture, at Salida. Helen was all for the new company, and naturally, since she was to be its leading lady. The Salida man planned to start a little company with these two as the nucleus, and start playing out of Denver. He came to me about it.

"I'll open with Hearne's play, 'Hearts of Oak', he stated. "There's a clever child's part in the play and I'll let Bessie have it, if you and your wife will leave Russell. Remember, I have real money to offer you!"

It was keen temptation. Jennie was pathetically thrilled at the thought of a real salary. She was tired of the letters from home that referred to our poverty-struck wanderings as madness. Our little group fell into civil war. Hernandez was doubtful. Jennie was for going with Helen. So were most of the nine. But one or two promised to stick with Pop Russell.

"If Pop wants us to stay with him, let him give us some money," said Jennie, furiously. "He hasn't given us a cent since we started. Make him prove he wants us — go and ask him for some money now, Frank."

I was never any hand at business. I'd never been able to wring a cent from Pop, although the other men of the company could strike him for fifty cents or a dollar and get it — sometimes. But he had a way of sending me away empty handed and perfectly satisfied. This time I swore either to get some back salary from Pop or quit him flat with Jennie and the little one. Why, he hadn't given me a postage stamp since I left San Jose to follow him . . . ! It made me boil to think of it.

I went straight up the narrow staircase of the cheap little Salida hotel. Hotel rooms were one dollar a day but we always shared rooms to cut down expenses. I opened the door to Pop's room with great determination, afraid if I stopped to knock my courage would die.

There was my iron-fronted manager, down on his knees in his nightshirt, saying his rosary.

I crept out of the room. The debonair Pop had won again, but never in a way he dreamed.

"Did you tell him?" demanded Jennie.

"I told him — we'd stick," I said huskily.

At least, as I explained to Jennie, Pop was not a drinking man. And although the leading man was a fine fellow and a good actor, there were times when he fell by the wayside. The worst curse a stock company can have is a drinking leading man. For that reason I distrusted the new company as a venture and stuck by Pop.

"Better the evils we know to those we know not of," as I remarked to Jennie.

But Helen Johnson and the leading man and one other made their vow to desert us at the Colorado-New Mexican line. From there

97

they would go to Denver and form the new company. And we who were left would go — whither!

Until then the two forces stuck together and played the small mountain towns nearing the line. Colorado memories are mostly of this conflict between the members.

The towns we played were far up in the Rockies, where the air was clear and brittle as glass, and friendly men of the villages brought wee burros to the hotel for little Bessie to ride.

The poor child lacked the clothing needed in this cold altitude. She was still in the light dresses and underthings we had taken with us from California in the heart of a wonderful spring. And now in the high Colorado winter Bessie went through a series of small colds and finally into the serious horror of whooping cough.

Between the lines on the stage she would have to lisp, "Just a minute, folks!" She would stumble off stage, and the audience, hearing the little thing choking in the wings, pitied her. Jennie was hysterical. But it was Helen Johnson, who had a will of her own, as joining the new company would prove to us, who rescued the child.

"You'll have to get her some flannel underwear," she raged at Jennie.

"Don't I know it?" returned Jennie, at her wits end. "But what am I going to buy red flannel with . . . Frank has been to Pop a hundred times for money."

"Then I'll go to Pop," said Helen with red fury in her eye.

I don't know what she said to Pop. But he came through with a dollar and a half — a fortune to the company. It was probably every cent he had. Then the red flannel was bought and the two women cut it out and sewed it by hand into miniature undies. The whooping cough died in a smother of red flannel. Bessie was well again by the night our complete cast played together for the last time.

Our last Colorado night was played in Trinidad, close to the Mexican line.

"The Renowned Russell Dramatic Company," was how we advertised ourselves that night, played in full force at the Jaffa Opera House. It was farewell.

For then — we all crossed the line together and were in our fifth state, New Mexico. Directly across the line was the small town of Raton, and there it was the old made way for the new and the rebel group, who were to form another company at Denver, deserted us forever.

98

We stood that freezing day on the rickety Raton platform, the sorriest little group of actors under the sun. Bravely we waved to the departing three, who were fleeing to the safety of a big town and a steady salary. Like soldiers, we stood under desolate skies, waving farewell.

There were five of us left. What could five accomplish in the northern wastes of lonely New Mexico?

Jennie sat down with a thud on our miserable little tin trunk. She was the only woman left with us now. And how Jennie had wanted to see Denver!

CHAPTER TEN

WE ARE STRANDED

We were five — stranded in the upper wastes of New Mexico!

Also, there was Bessie, who was studying me now with eyes of clouded brown under a tumble of golden curls. Trouble had overtaken our poor child at four years. She knew something was wrong with the five adults who composed her world.

There was Jennie, seated on her battered tin trunk in an attitude of complete despair. Jennie might have posed then for a masterpiece entitled "Stranded."

There was John McGlynn, tall, phlegmatic and gloomy as a Shakespearian. Heaven knows how Pop had persuaded McGlynn to throw down the pick and try the stage. The last time I saw McGlynn, he had returned to his original profession, mining, in Butte, Montana.

And there was George Hernandez, as sad-faced a comic as was ever left behind by a deserting company. He was little and cheerfully plump — we played together in a motion picture not so long ago, "Rosemary," with Marguerite Snow! But in 1890, who had heard of pictures that moved!

"I wish I'd never left Butte," said McGlynn, dolefully.

Jennie was silent. She hadn't enough courage left to long for San Jose.

How could five hope to carry on "The Black Flag," or any sort of a flag? How were we ever to see California again?

I was reckoning without the iron nerve of Pop Russell.

"I have arranged all details!" said Pop, speaking in Jovian fashion from the cloud of gloom. "We play Springer!"

We stared at him — we lacked the energy that went into our usual quarrels with him. Springer, to be sure, was only a few miles away, and a mere dot beside the railroad line. But, we were five...

100

"Trust me!" said Pop, magnificently.

How could we doubt that seasoned veteran! The wretched five boarded the next train and bumped gloomily down to Springer.

Springer was less than a village — a mere whistling post in the desert. There Pop unveiled his beautiful plan.

"I have wired to Denver for a new leading man and woman," he announced — "we will lay off here to rehearse."

Now this was cheering. With a new leading man and woman, the William Russell Stock Company could travel onward. This revived our fainting hope and carried us to the one small family hotel and through a weighty but cheap family dinner. New actors arriving from Denver. We were saved once more.

I met every train that day, and watched them shoot past Springer and away across the desert with only an insulting whistle for me. They did not slow down for my pathetic form beside the little station.

We slept that night upon beds that were not paid and might never be paid for. The next morning I was again at the little station, whiling the cold hours away, waiting. And there were no actors from Denver.

"I can't understand their delaying matters," said Pop indignantly.

Now, I realize, Pop sent no telegram to Denver, expected no actors. The wire, the actors, the hope — all were part of his undying bluff. But we didn't know this, only that we were truly deserted now in inhospitable Springer, New Mexico.

And now we found ourselves arriving at the long inn table with a delicacy of appetite that must have astonished the Springer host. For how we were ever to escape from the village, no one knew but Pop. Whatever he felt, he did not confide in me, nor in the mournful comedian, Hernandez, nor the actor-miner, McGlynn. We were shut out from the mastermind that was guiding us into starvation. Pop, indomitable as a granite bulldog, had thought up a masterly plan by noon.

"Tonight," he announced to his four satellites, "we play 'The Black Flag!' "

We stared at him, our throats rattling with astonishment. Then four adults found tongue and drowned his voice. Play "The Black Flag?" When only five of us were left to the many characters, and Jennie alone was left for the women parts? Play "The Black Flag", a drama requiring many people?

101

"I've thought it all out," barked Pop, raising his voice over our chorus. "Frank takes the lead. I'll do the father. George and McGlynn are up in the other parts — they can mix them up and play all of 'em. Mrs. Bacon can blend all the women roles in one."

"And Bessie will play the boy!"

Right there the chorus drowned him again. Wonder what that Springer innkeeper thought of the arguments the actor folk were having that morning!

"Your whole scheme is crazy enough without having Bessie play the boy," said Jennie, indignantly. "Ned, the Waif, is a hard part — I know! And Bessie doesn't know a line of it! And the poor baby can't learn it in one afternoon!"

Jennie knew, for when I was assigned to other parts, she had been playing Ned, the Waif, all along the road.

"Bessie DOES know the part!" shouted Pop, furiously. "She rehearsed the entire role for me this morning!"

And she did know it. In amazement we heard our child through the entire difficult role of the Waif. She had learned it by heart while watching her mother's acting from the wings.

Then for three hours there was hot excitement, while we toiled to redeem the Russell Stock Company. Pop rented the little entertainment hall and swept it out himself, and McGlynn and George and I set up the benches and repaired those that were broken, and strewed our few cherished lithographs through the three small stores on main street and in the Post Office.

"Don't forget to go around and pick these cards up after the show," warned Pop. "We can't waste one of them — now."

As if we ever had wasted a card! Invariably, we redeemed our printed treasures from the grocery windows and elsewhere, for they were far too precious to waste. How would we ever afford more?

Our rehearsal was staged in a general hysteria of nervous laughter. This was such a funny, scrambled "Black Flag." No part was as it should be, and everyone selected their own parts and lines and quarrelled over them. Everyone of us was playing part after part, and in no order.

This was not so funny then as it would be now, for doubling was the given rule in stock companies. There is an old story of the actor who played three characters, and was fired.

"You are simply not the type," said the manager in explaining.

"For which part?" demanded the insulted actor.

102

But Bessie's acting sobered and inspired us. Here was no child prattling parrot-lines. Bess was an actress.

"We can't lose — with her," muttered Pop, with as much feeling as I ever saw him express.

"Oh, dear me — the poor child hasn't a costume," burst out Jennie, and fell into a frantic ransacking of her little tin trunk. It held nothing for Bessie. And Jennie's waif costume was miles too large for the child. Some ten minutes before our performance that evening, Jennie created a waif costume by tearing the waist from an old blue gingham frock and "tacking" it onto a tiny pair of gray flannel panties Bess wore when playing out of doors.

And that night "The Black Flag" waved over Springer on the desert.

I believe even Pop Russell felt a touch of stagefright before the curtain rose. This was a desperate chance we were playing. Springer Hall was like a barn loft, and every beam was a miniature stage setting curtained with cobwebs. Our "reserved section" consisted of twenty unpainted kitchen chairs. The rest of the floor was set with wooden benches. For the privilege of sitting in dignity upon these chairs the people of Springer paid fifty cents. The other seats were twenty-five cents.

We hired one of the villagers to work the curtain. The curtain, by the way, was a terrifying device, for it was the old type that rolled up on a windlass, exactly like the one that rose upon "Fashion," in New York in 1845. The heavy wooden roller, thundering down over our heads while we were gracefully bowing to the applause, threatened all our lives and hit the floor with a crash that shook the loft. But the roll curtain was a common curse in country places then. What was that old quip . . . the unlucky actors who played a village although they were starving, "and the curtain came down with a roll!"

Until the last minute, Jennie sat in the narrow wings fussing with little Bessie's curls, and almost crying over her own lines, for poor Jennie was playing every woman's part in the show!

Pop stayed out in front selling tickets until 8:15. He reluctantly tore himself away just before the curtain lifted, leaving that important post to the man who managed the hall. Pop came dashing back stage with just enough time to make-up for Owen Glynden, my father in "The Black Flag." Make-up wasted little of Pop's important time, for while he played Jim Seaton, "the prison guide," in his regular and only suit, he played the father role in

103

the same, adding only a row of whiskers that were always coming loose. Doubling in brass was the smallest of Pop's many troubles.

Eight thirty — time for the play!

George Hernandez slipped out before the curtain in his role of Lazarus, the Jew, and played an overture. We felt that terrible silence "out front" as southerners feel the sudden shock of northern climate. George came off wiping the vaseline and powder from his hot forehead. We knew by his despairing eye — Springer was a lime!

The hired villager began bending slowly over the cranking and as slowly rose that crudely painted curtain. Wretched of soul, we five adults found our places in the play and on the stage, saving ourselves by quickness of mind only when cues were slipped or forgotten, trying miserably to wring one sound of appreciation from that dim group beyond the oil lamp row.

Through our own words we listened tensely for the clatter of departing feet as our audience marched forth to demand "money back." But there was only the hard, unbreakable silence. And I calculated, while in the midst of my role as Harry Glyndon, that at least fifty dollars in cash was sitting out on the uncomfortable benches! And, oh, how large that seemed to the Russell five, and how we needed it! If that audience deserted — would we leave Springer alive?

Then Bessie came running on the stage toward me, a frightened little creature in the ragged waif costume. Her beautiful little face was piteous with fright.

She was crying:

"Hide me! Hide me!"

It was all so violently real, that I remember how fiercely I clutched her to me, fooled for the moment by my child's acting. And that dim Springer mass on the benches was suddenly alive, stirred to the quick by the child.

At four years, Bess was a triumphant soubrette!

At the third act curtain, Little Ned dies. Every woman in the hall was sobbing as the child received the bullet intended for me, and as I flung myself over the tiny frame stretched on the floor, my eyes were wet. One swift moment I looked up as the curtain fell and saw my young wife crying in the wings.

When I lifted the child in my arms at the last moment of the act, Bess put up a tiny hand to brush back her hair, showing a "wound" she had lined on her forehead with carmine.

104

"How did you happen to think of that, darling?" we asked her afterward.

"Hattie always painted a wound for Madame Vine," she explained, referring back to our former leading lady's work in East Lynne. "So I thought I needed one for Ned."

The people refused to leave after our last curtain, but mobbed the stage crying for "Little Bessie." She went out before them like a small princess born to the purple of publicity. Men passed her from one to another. Women caught her up and kissed her, told her of little girls at home, "just like you, precious." I brought out her photographs and Bess sold them. This was her reception.

Back stage, Pop Russell was scrambling through the night's income. We had played to fifty dollars in that small desert village — more money than we had seen since leaving California!

"Bess is star from now on," said Pop, feelingly pocketing the entire fortune after paying the hall manager and the hotel man . . . you don't suppose the rest of us saw a cent of it, do you?

No mention again of the two mysterious stars from Denver! Pop Russell was never a man to regret nor apologize. Nor were we to question him. Lost in the arid territory of upper New Mexico, our goal was home, "across the desert wastes, beneath the blinding sun." And Bess, our baby, was an infant Moses who would lead us through the wilderness. What would have happened to us without that child to lead us? I'd probably be taking tintypes in Springer and Pop would be another Bill Jones grown ancient and still with the village. I have an idea we would never have escaped from there, without Bessie.

The morning after this financial and artistic triumph, the encouraged five met over a hearty breakfast table and dared eat again! Over the home-cured ham we held council. We had a strange feeling of being a troupe newly organized, with prosperity ahead. And yet, what had we to look toward?

"You will have to advance the show, Frank," said Pop, turning to me so suddenly I nearly dropped the hashed potatoes.

A troupe of five requiring an advance agent! To me, that was so much conspicuous waste.

"And anyway, I'm the leading man," I objected hotly among other arguments. "How can I play in one town and paste up bills in another — at the same time . . ."

"I am prepared to play your role," interrupted Pop, generously.

I yearned to wreathe his head with the heavy white iron-wear platter. Why, the man was already playing two roles, the father of the hero and the Seaton character. Now he wanted the hero role as well. Pop was willing to play his own son and his own father and a guide thrown in, all at once.

"Why don't you take over all of Jennie's roles, too?" I suggested, elegantly. "She's only taking the parts of about eight women. And play little Bessie's part, too! It's a shame to have five actors cluttering up the stage when you could play the whole show by yourself."

"That isn't worthy of your usual disposition, Frank," he returned forgivingly.

With magnificent dignity, Pop explained. And as usual, even I had to admit he was right. Trust his canny old brain when it came to making everything from nothing. Pop may have been a poor theatrical manager, but he was a Houdini in tight corners of barnstorming.

I was to go on ahead to the next town. There I would post our few cherished bills, rent and prepare the hall, and, when the others came, be ready to play the leading role on the first night. Then I would hurry on to the next town, and Pop, by carefully juggling the lines, would be able to double in my part as well as his own! Two nights was plenty for the Russell Company in any town. In most towns, it was more than plenty. I would play opening nights only.

From now on, Bess was the star.

We raked over our scanty possessions for anything to serve as posters. As motley a collection of show printing as ever came together was given me at last. With this bundle of worn paper I was to conquer New Mexico.

I left Springer on the next train.

And this is the queerest part of my life to remember, when, as helpless an advance agent as ever lived, I set out through that lone territory heralding as strange a company as ever walked the boards.

I didn't know a thing about New Mexican towns. I didn't know which would prove the "cakes" and which the "limes," meaning worse than lemons for traveling shows. But I always have liked railroad men and whatever train I boarded, the conductor and brakeman became my friends and advised me concerning the towns. The railroad boys were my guides — they steered the Russell Company away from dangerous towns and into those where we would play to thirty — sometimes forty - dollars a night!

Jerking along in this slow fashion, we played right down the New Mexican railroad line. Our success was changeable, but we managed to keep moving and to eat. And we almost always paid our hotel expenses! But the mere fact that we kept moving was enough, for slowly but certainly we were edging homeward to California. And how I talked to those railroad men about California, and to everyone I met! And for that matter, I still love to talk about California. Only now, it is not poverty and a poor show that keeps me from the west. Now, it is the success of *Lightnin'*.

One of my great responsibilities was our printing collection. You know we had very few posters and could not afford more. After playing a town, it was the duty of George Hernandez and myself to go around collecting our posters. To lose one was a dreadful loss. And we had orders from Pop to likewise collect any strange theatrical paper we might find lying forgotten in store window or hall. We had cheap "Russell Company" slips and pasted these over the printing matter on the other lithographs, thereby taking advantage of the picture. We had one of Lillian Russell — I guess most of the natives thought she was in the Russell Company! And we had one of Sol Smith Russell — to whom, strangely enough, critics were often to compare me in later years.

In one of the smaller New Mexican towns I made a great discovery in the rubbish of the hall I was sweeping out. It was a lithograph of a child actress in a company that had played there months before. By straining your imagination you might fancy the picture looked a little like our Bessie.

Somehow I scraped together ten dollars and sent back to Chicago for a lot of these lithographs. I had a lot of cheap "Little Bessie" strips struck off to paste on the lithographs and we used them all the rest of this tour.

One of the towns we planned to make was San Marcial, a railroad junction off the main line. I was pasting strips upon my sorry collection of posters in the smoking car, when the conductor sat down beside me to gossip. We had grown very friendly, considering the shortness of the run.

"You're not the only show fellow aboard this train," he said, warningly. "There are two others — and they're planning to make San Marcial."

My blood solidified with the shock. Two other showmen — but we had to have that date! It meant life to the remaining actors of the Russell troupe. I couldn't let anyone beat me to San Marcial.

Why, I'd been told San Marcial wasn't big enough to support

107

more than one show a month! And here two shows were arriving at once!

"Never mind, I haven't told them you're aboard," said the conductor, realizing how he had startled me.

"Where is the theatre located in San Marcial?" I demanded. "And who runs it?"

The conductor explained that the local showhouse was run by a woman. He drew a sketchy map of the small town, explaining just where the threatre was located and its distance from the railroad tracks.

"And just because Mrs. Blevin is a woman, I'll bet if you reach her first and tell her about your little girl actress, she'll give you the date," he urged, sympathetically. "Tell you what I'll do, Mr. Bacon, even if it is against railroad orders. . ."

You see how friendship always came to our rescue? That conductor did a wonderful thing, for just before the train pulled into San Marcial, he jerked the emergency and slowed down the train, at a point only two blocks from the Opera House.

I was ready on the platform and when the conductor signalled, I leaped to the ground, lithographs and all. One moment I turned to wave him a grateful good-bye, then ran down the two thinly-populated blocks to the little theatre.

Mrs. Blevin lived in a cottage adjoining the Opera House. I almost tumbled inside when she opened the door and blurted out my entire announcement in about two seconds.

" . . . and I'm advance agent for Russell's Comedians, featuring Little Bessie, the child actress," I panted, offering her one of our announcements.

At the bottom of the announcement, as on all our bills and programs, were the words:

> Note — Little Bessie is four and one-half years
> old and plays a leading part in the drama. The
> management claims she is the greatest child
> actress living.

Closely watching Mrs. Blevin, I saw her glance soften as she read these lines and glanced at the child's picture I carried. She was hesitating, when the door of her house banged open. Two men came unceremoniously into her room.

The brand of the theatrical advance man was writ upon their brows. I knew them — they were the two I had left on the train. One

108

was big and good-looking in a swaggering fashion, the other a small man with rapid eyes and nervous hands. They were self-assured and poised — typical showmen.

The big fellow elbowed me aside to hand Mrs. Blevin a roll of beautiful show paper. It made our miserable printed specimens — most of them not our own — appear weak.

"We're representing Turner's English Girls, biggest attraction out of Chicago," he informed her snappily. "Galaxy of pretty girls! Wonderful comedians! New songs from the Big Town! We have a show that brings in. . . ."

"I was talking to this gentleman," said Mrs. Blevin, hesitating.

The big fellow whirled on me like a shot, but he smiled easily.

"What show you got?" he demanded, in the language of the trade I hardly knew.

"Russell's Comedians," I said.

The two men looked at each other. Then their laughter began. They tried to apologize for laughing at Russell's Comedians! But I, as an actor, felt the hollowness of their loud laughter, and guessed that these men were desperate.

"Say, Russell's Company are just a bunch of fly-by-nighters," the big fellow explained, turning to Mrs. Blevin as if he were helpless with mirth. "They are all that's left of a stranded company, and a joke clear down the line."

"Yes, and they have a kid that can't talk plain yet, trying to star her," piped up the little fellow.

I said nothing. I was unhappily thinking of the little group back in the last town depending upon me. I was wondering how we could exist without San Marcial. Then I learned Mrs. Blevin was a real manager. Her voice snapped into the jeering comments of the other two.

"That kid that can't talk plain — she's been the talk of the road for weeks!" she said, suddenly. "Every railroad agent in the towns Mr. Bacon's show has played wires on wonderful reports of Little Bessie. She's the attraction I want for my house."

She looked at the silenced two.

"This town is too small to support more than one show a month, gentlemen, I'm sorry, but we can't do business. Good-bye."

If that once popular song had been written in '90, I would certainly have accompanied those two showmen's slow march to the door by humming, "Lordy, be good to that railroad man!"

The men of the rails had saved us again. But my elation, and

109

pride, and unspeakable relief was troubled by the bitter disappointment of the other two. Didn't I know all it meant to them? Couldn't I have said, if it hadn't been for the friendly conductor, and the kindly operators who had wired on, "there, but for the grace of God, go I?"

I pitied them as only a barnstormer can pity another. I hurried through the business part of the affair with Mrs. Blevin, for I wanted to get outside and start work. I left, promising to return in half an hour, and with a feeling that those men would be waiting outside for me. I should certainly have waited, if my luck had been theirs.

Sure enough, there they were, lurking outside the Opera House.

"See here, we've got to talk things over," began the little fellow, who I found supplied the brains for the pair.

They blustered at first, threatening all manner of things to make me release my date. At last their pride broke — even as mine would have done.

"Ain't you got a heart?" demanded the little fellow piteously. "Sixteen people we got — beautiful girls stranded out of Chicago — and not a booking in sight! Not a date! And chorus girls must eat — oh, and how they must eat!"

"How'd it happen?" I demanded, made wretched with sympathy.

"We were stranded — left out here by the Chicago Company," explained the biggest man, and picturesquely he cursed the heartless crew who had left a company on the New Mexican plains without money nor transportation.

I thought to myself, "Boys, you're no worse off than we are!"

Of course I didn't admit that to them. I knew they wouldn't give in without a fight, for who would, and bluff is the agent's only weapon. It was the little one who at last declared open war.

"Give us your date," he threatened, "or we play against you here the same night."

"That's perfectly all right with me," I returned gracefully.

But as I walked back to the Opera House to make the final arrangements with Mrs. Blevin, I knew what it meant to be scared.

CHAPTER ELEVEN

EVEN A HAT MAY SUFFER

Pop and the others would arrive early that evening, and we would play "The Black Flag" in San Marcial. There was little for me to do, for Mrs. Blevin kept her small Opera House in perfect working order. I walked down Main Street with my wretched posters, and met my two enemy agents.

And they also were putting up posters!

They had scoured the town for a hall. As the Opera House was the only hall, and I had it, they rented a store that happened to be empty. The town being far too small under the circumstances, we met frequently that afternoon and with much scowling. We said nothing, for there was nothing to be said. San Marcial could not support the Russell Company and Turner's Beauties, together. This was not competition. It was murder.

Late that afternoon, in walking to the station to meet my little group, I had the pleasure of comparing my poster display with the Turner. Mine were meagre announcements of a play that featured a child. Looking from them to the violent pink Turner sheets, I felt faint. The Turner sheets were gay with pictures of women, who, in spite of the sad complaint of the agents, fitted plumply enough into their strawberry-colored tights.

At the station my two enemies were waiting. We didn't speak. Listlessly I heard the train's whistle moan over the desert and toward San Marcial. The Turner company had numbers, variety, and the posters. If we failed that evening, we could not pay our hotel bill and worse still, we would not have enough money to get out of San Marcial.

Evening came, and with a beating heart, I stood behind the Opera House curtain watching, through the peep hole in the canvas, the people coming in. It seemed they never would stop coming. Our little hall was packed.

Even little Bessie felt the portent of that hour and played as never before. She had saved us once again. She had turned the faces of San Marcial our way.

And down the street in that echoing grocery store, the Turner chorus girls were dancing to an audience representing only fifteen dollars.

I did not see that forlorn troupe next morning, for our company left on the earliest train for the next flag stop. After that, another flag stop, and still another. We skimmed over the villages and took what small money we could and didn't see the Turner crowd for the rest of the week. Then I crossed their trail on my way to Silver City.

Silver City, the trainmen had told me, was a sleepy little place, suffering a business slump after the silver rush that introduced New Mexico to fame. But I knew there was money in that quiet town. And while I was traveling to Silver City, I met my two Turner agents in the smoker.

They huddled together on the seat and pretended not to see me. The social snub didn't wound my feelings. Perhaps I should have felt more worried than I did, for men with sixteen starving beauties on their hands are dangerous rivals.

The train kindly stopped for me at the Silver City station and I clambered off with much dignity, clutching my inevitable paper roll. No one else got off at the lonely station. I breathed deeply with relief — anyway, why should anyone but our desperate troupe want to play Silver City! — and ambled over to the Opera House.

"I'm on ahead of the Russell Company — featuring Little Bessie," I babbled pleasantly to the house manager, but he had also heard of little Bessie and began writing out my contract without a word.

"Give you a date one week from today," he said looking up.

"Fair enough," said I, trying not to look too tickled. Then one of my rare business hunches smote me between the eyes. "By the way, it won't hurt anyone if you write in a shut-out clause excluding any show playing here before ours."

"Fair enough," he agreed in his turn.

I watched him write that clause with much satisfaction. I knew there was none too much money in Silver City. I did not care to repeat the bitter experience of San Marcial.

112

The manager was just blotting that clause when the door opened. There stood the enemies I thought I had left on the train. But their arrogance had bitten the dust. The little man was clinging to the arm of his big partner and grimacing with pain. In spite of that he was all business. It was he who explained their bitter adventure.

It seems when they saw me in the smoker they determined to imitate my lightning advent into San Marcial, and beat me into Silver City. They jumped from the platform as I had done. But there was no friendly conductor to slow down the train for them. The little one landed badly and his ankle was sprained and swelling rapidly. His determination to save his company, in spite of his agony, touched me.

"These men are friends of mine," I explained to the manager.

"Not one good house did we get yet," said the smaller man, pitifully, and he grimaced with pain like a monkey.

I thought matters over.

"Tell you what I'll do," I told them slowly. "The manager here just wrote a clause into my contract that keeps out any other show until mine plays. That's a week off. Now he and I will canvass the town with the box sheet and get all the reservations we can. Then, after our success is insured, you fellows can put on a show right away and clean up what money is left. I'll break my clause for you."

They nearly collapsed on my neck with happiness. The little fellow, with business lifted from his mind, went to find a doctor and attention for his ankle. The manager and I set forth to patrol Silver City selling seats.

And everywhere we went:

"Oh, is Little Bessie coming at last? I've been wanting to see that child."

The news of our little girl's performance had gone far ahead of the Russell Company, far down the railroad, and off the line. It made my heart swell to hear them praise her.

At last Pop arrived in the little town, and Jennie and the little one and the two others. I met them with the splendid news — a sold out house was assured us.

Then there was nothing to do but wait for the rest of the week to pass until show night. There was little to do in Silver City but watch the two Turner men billing the little town with their pink lithographs, and attend their performance. They did well, astonishingly well, considering the smallness of the town. And the entire company behaved in a distressingly grateful way for these crumbs that had fallen from our table.

I felt the conceited happiness of most philanthropists and, there being no other amusement, saw the Turner company off early the following morning. The girls looked radiantly happy as they hung out of the windows and waved back at me, standing at the Silver City station. Poor dears, I suppose dreams of State Street were beginning for them once more. The little agent, waving from the rear car, was also radiant with smiles.

With this small excitement over, I drifted back to the Opera House to gossip with the manager. Anything to kill time in Silver City. Jennie was fussing around our hotel room with Bessie as contentedly as if the place had been our lifelong home, and McGlynn and Hernandez were ambling down Main Street hunting any excitement that cost nothing.

But Pop was in the little office of the Opera House, solemnly laying down to the manager the varied merits of the political situation. He could talk for hours upon the stirring topic of Free Silver. He knew the United States was facing panic, which was true. And he was tremendously excited over the strange great organization of farmers that had just formed the Populist Party the year of 1890, and the new way of ballot voting, and the threatened trouble with Chile, and the argument between Great Britain and ourselves concerning the seal fisheries in the Bering Sea. Also, he firmly believed with Grover Cleveland, the former President, that we should annex that little-known island, Hawaii.

To all of which the small town manager listened with a depressed air, and brightened when I came in.

"I was just trying to tell Mr. Russell here — but he didn't seem interested," he said, apologetically, "about a date you fellows might fill in this spare time with — over to Fort Bayard."

"Where's that?" said I, instantly.

"Ten miles over from here," said he, meaning over the desert. "There's a lot of soldiers at the Fort and they always turn out for a show. You can get over there in an hour with a good hoss."

"Anything for an extra engagement," I replied cheerfully, and Pop gave me his blessing and returned to Free Silver.

In the town livery stable, after hiring a horse and buggy, I glanced ruefully at my clothes. This was my only suit. I had become its proud possessor while running the Mayfield paper, as the result of a contract I obtained for a set of band uniforms. The Mayfield

114

amateurs, including myself, had put on a little show to raise funds toward buying uniforms for the Mayfield band. The contract for making the uniforms I had secured for one of my San Jose advertisers, who was also an old freind. This suit represented his grateful appreciation.

Proudly, I had worn this suit out of California. It seemed the very thing for an actor. It was an extremely loud check in tan and brown, made in the Prince Albert style and with a double-breasted coat. The snows of the Utah territory, the suns of New Mexico, were leaving their marks upon my suit. Still, it was a matter to be proud of. And then, my hat! It also showed signs of hardship, but it had remained my joy, the outward symbol of theatrical being!

It was a serviceable, shiny silk plug.

The livery stable man was surveying these outfittings of mine with a reflection of my doubt.

"The sun'll eat the lining outta that suit," he commented, sympathetically. "Want me to lend ye a duster?"

Gratefully, I slipped the long thin lined coat over my suit. Also he offered me a rather adolescent-looking old cap, and I hung my "Five gallon Kelly" on a nail. I couldn't trust that glossy treasure to the harsh alkali dust of the New Mexican desert.

That was the dreariest two hours I ever spent. It was the kind of day that coats your tongue with a hot fuzz and makes you feel as if you had swallowed cactus fruit. Several sandstorms passed over me and left me with gritty reddened eyes and a loosened vocabulary. Often that unfortunate horse stopped to turn his head and exchange a look of mutual sympathy. I knew just how he felt.

At the miltary post in the desert, the Commandant saw me arrive with no enthusiasm whatever.

"This is the wrong time of the month for a show," he objected. "The men haven't their money. . . "

I couldn't waste the money I had spent for the horse and buggy ride. I protested, almost pleaded with him. At last he sent for one of the young Lieutenants.

The Lieutenant was affable and obliging. His fellow officers called him "Jack."

"Pay day is two days off, and most of the boys are broke, Mr. Bacon," he explained. "But if you are willing to play on credit I can promise you a full house."

"We have done worse," I remarked exultantly.

He took me to the Sergeant of each company. They promised to charge every soldier for the price of a ticket and hold it out of his pay at the end of the month. On pay day, the Sergeants would settle with the manager of the little show house at Fort Bayard, who in turn would forward the money on to me . . . wherever the Russell Company might then be wandering. I was delighted, for although it meant waiting for our receipts, it also meant an extra engagement. I thanked the handsome young Lieutenant and the drive back was not half as long.

Back in Silver City, woe followed exaltation. I yielded up the horse and buggy to the stableman and went in to the small hole of an office for my hat. It was still on the nail where I had reverently hung it, but alas, it had suffered defilement. Its naked pasteboard stared me in the face. Every bit of its glossy silk had been stripped from the frame. Some desert cowboy had seen it hanging there and neatly scalped it as a warning to any future dude actors who might unfortunately wander into Silver City. I can forgive that cowboy now — he knew not the meaning of the wrong he did me.

The livery man noted my grief.

"Never mind, ye can have the cap," said he.

And what was I then but an eagle made featherless — an actor wearing a wilted, juvenile cap! I wore that liveryman's cap from Silver City to the grateful day that found me, weary after many other tribulations, back in San Jose, California.

The next day — and I with my cap — the indomitable five of the Russell Company drove over to the Fort in a large surrey, a vehicle described by Webster's as a "pleasure carriage." We disproved that definition after the first dusty hour. But that night we played at Fort Bayard. After settling Jennie and Bessie in rooms at the Chaplin's residence, I enquired for the Lieutenant who had so ably assisted me on my former trip — after some search and many explanations, I learned his name was Jack Pershing.

Soldiers made up the audience — the largest we had smiled upon in many a moon. They had only praise for "The Black Flag" and their cheers shook the little hall. At every act's end they yelled and stamped, and at the end of the third, a great cry arose for "The ladies!"

Jennie came before the curtain leading our child — and how those uniformed boys applauded! Our friend, young Pershing, came up to the footlights and presented them with two large bouquets of artificial flowers — the only flowers that grew in that climate!

116

"What a nice young man that Lieutenant seems to be," said Jennie sleepily, as we drove back to Silver City after the show. "And so handsome!"

"The sort of man you'd like to meet again," I agreed, trying not to fall asleep and drop the reins.

And we were to meet him again, after thirty years.

It was after our long march down the street of miracles had ended, and *Lightnin'* had struck Broadway. I had played my role four hundred times, watched record after record break; seen, with astonished eyes, the thermometer of success steadily climbing. Little Bessie was grown and married; Lloyd, our baby, was playing in the motion pictures in Hollywood — we were grandparents now, Jennie and I. Came the day of September 9, 1919, when the war was ended, and the troups were coming home and with them their commander.

General John J. Pershing was home from overseas; the streets of New York were riotous with flags. Women wept in the streets, crowds swarmed about the national hero and paraded in shouting lines.

That night, after the parading and feasting was over, I felt a stirring in the audience of the Gaiety Theatre. I looked across the footlights and saw that always handsome soldier entering a box with all his staff. And this was his first night home from overseas, after the bitterness of war.

So we met again over the footlights after thirty years.

When I came out to make the curtain speech I was to make twelve hundred and ninety-one times in New York, I thanked Pershing for being there and mentioned our meeting once "in the long ago." He stood at attention as I said "I was a General — once." When I mentioned the past, he stared from the box in a puzzled way, and then smiled. But I knew he had forgotten.

Later we met at the Lamb's Club dinner in his honor, and I sat opposite him at the table.

"We were five actors, stranded in New Mexico, and you let me have a night on credit at Fort Bayard," I reminded him. "You were Lieutenant then. Don't you remember giving my wife and little girl the artificial flowers?"

Pershing had not forgotten. We laughed together, and he was a man who did not laugh easily.

"And now they tell me *'Lightnin'* is playing to millions," he said.

117

"But you'll never know what that show you gave us meant to the Russell Company," I told him, mysteriously. "General, the money you sent on to us almost saved our lives — later on."

Today, sailing briskly through the desert country toward Santa Fe, you are likely enough to complain of the discomforts of the journey, and ring for a porter to bring a tall ginger ale and start putting down your berth.

You cannot imagine New Mexico in the 1890s.

We who were left of the Russell Company trekked it by rail and stage, over waste land choking white with alkali and dotted with sage.

For two years there had been no rainfall, and the cattle were dying. We drove over desert roads when the ever-present odor of death made the journey horrible. Everywhere lay sad piles of rotted hide and bone that had been animal. Still the processes of life and death went on in this desert, calves were born with innocent, despairing faces, and died nudging the wicked cactus for the food their mothers could not give them.

One of the cattle shipping towns, Deming, lies toward the lower part of New Mexico, on the railroad. I came into it, nearing the end of our slow progress through the territory. We had hitched our way along — like a child learning to crawl — from pillar to post down the desert, barely making our traveling funds and no more. A sorry set, but brave, for slowly but certainly we were edging homeward.

At Deming, according to my usual method, I first got acquainted with the station agent. Station agents had been my principal salvation. It was the station agent of every town who informed me who was what, and how the town felt toward visiting talent, and what men I had better see. After this was learned, I always went to the town show house or "Opery" and met the manager, and then — invariably — to the little newspaper office, if any. There is something about a local room as irresistible to an old newspaper man as a swinging door to a chronic alcoholic. And because I had founded two newspapers myself and once owned part of another, I found welcome in those littered, lively and enchanting places.

During my first half hour in Deming I found my way into the small press room of the Deming paper. I'm afraid I was not an interesting character, in appearance at least. My one checked suit was fraying at the seams and I had never recovered all my theatrical dignity after the loss of my silk topper. But I never met a friendlier newspaper office.

118

Ross was its editor, and he was a former governor of the New Mexican territory. He treated me like visiting royalty. Then the others arrived — no more prosperous looking than I. Jennie, with the plumes drooping on her only hat like the tailfeathers of a beaten cockerel, and McGlynn and Hernandez with their trousers pressed by laying them under hotel mattresses, and Pop with his plated watch chain.

"I want your wife and little girl to be our guests in Deming," said Ross, and marched my family off to his own house, where they were mothered by Mrs. Ross during our short visit there. It was pleasant to know they were in such comfortable, kindly quarters, when I left Deming for the next town.

As usual, I didn't know exactly where I was going. Tyron or Lordsburg, any of the smaller places, as the trainmen might advise me. I would buy my ticket for that place, wherever it was.

I was leaving Deming on the evening train. I was practically alone on the station platform, waiting for the whistle. It was cool gray New Mexican twilight, and the stinging desert cold was coming down with the darkness. As I walked up and down the station to keep warm, another man was walking, too, and we eyed one another in passing.

"Isn't that a Native Son button?" he demanded, stopping as we passed for the sixth time. He was staring at my lapel.

"Are you Californian, too?" I exclaimed, feeling that twin souls had met in the wilderness.

He was, and with less reason to be homesick than I. He looked exactly what he was, a prosperous business man.

"My name's Fred Hollub," he said. "I'm managing the Opera House at El Paso!"

"El Paso!" I repeated weakly.

El Paso was big league stuff to such wanderers as ourselves. I felt as if I had fallen in with Dave Belasco. On the train, I found myself telling the El Paso man all our troubles. Of how we had been stranded, of how we were fighting to get home at any cost, and how Little Bessie, our sole attraction, was doing her childish best to lead us home.

"Come to El Paso," he invited, an easy invitation to follow, since Deming is the town where the rails divide and one road leads to Texas. "Joe Jefferson has just cancelled a date with me. I'll let you have it."

The prompt way I answered his invitation must have startled him. One week later my company was in El Paso, Texas, the sixth state since leaving home. I wasn't taking any chances those days.

But between El Paso and Deming, we played the little town of Las Cruces to fill in time. The town was all Mexican, which promised a large and appreciative audience. We played in a long adobe, which was the combination theatre and livery stable, and had a perfectly lovely time cleaning it out before the performance.

We hired four Las Cruces Mexicanos, one to turn the curtain and three others to act as supers in the "revolt." We owned three faded convict suits, our chief pride in the property line, and the Mexican supers put these on. The "revolt" was accomplished by the three of us not on the stage bellowing "OYOYOYOY," in the wings, while Pop pounded on a drum.

The revolution started all right. Then McGlynn, according to the play, fired off a blank cartridge in his prop revolver, the rest of us yelled, "Oyoyo," and then Pop, who was pounding the drum offstage, noticed the curtain tender was not turning the windlass fast enough and hit the man over the head with his drumstick. It all happened at once to our three Mexican "convicts," who evidently thought we had planned a real revolution. They tore off the stage and out the rear door. We saw them no more — not even for the next act. But what was worse, neither were we ever to behold our three convict suits again. And that was a real blow.

El Paso, small and sun-warmed, climbed a stony hot hillside up from the banks of the Rio Grande, which river was a strong disappointment in a romantic way. Jennie had never failed to stir an audience in her elocutionary days with the old poem, "Lasca." Her voice had thrilled at the words:

> "And I wonder now why I do not care
> for the things that are, as the things that were;
> Does the half of my life lie buried there
> In Texas, down by the Rio Grande?"

How we stared disconsolately across a low, wide and yellow river where dark skinned children were bathing, in public and naked as frogs. And across the Rio Grande, was Mexico!

The first thing we did, after talking over business matters with Hollub, was to cross the river. Every American did — and still does. But we didn't find the opposite shore as strange as it would have seemed to an Easterner. Remember, we were Californians, and

I recalled a few words in the Mexican tongue that nearly every born Californian knows, and ordered enchiladas for the company in a squat but picturesque adobe.

For in San Jose, at that time, the old Mexican tamale vender was still hawking his pungent wares through the streets, and in private Latin homes Jennie and I knew where we could buy the tastiest chili con carne and frijoles. In San Jose, the legends of the city were all of the Spanish pioneers who founded the Mission and the town. So Mexico did not seem foreign soil.

Juarez was then a simple Mexican village of adobes clustering around the old Mission. It had not acquired its name of wickedness. American visitors would give it that, long after the Russell Company played El Paso, "down by the Rio Grande."

"I knew Texas was lucky," said Pop, triumphantly, as if he had arranged it all.

We were pleasantly thrilled by playing El Paso. This city was our masterstroke. We made violent efforts to leave our memories behind us in the quiet town. I had very little money, but I lavishly invested all of it in extra printing. I even advertised in the El Paso papers. And in return, of course, the papers were unusually kind.

"Little Bessie Bacon was fine, but her support was very poor," was the review one paper gave us. Think of that! The rest of the company were cut to the heart, yet we couldn't but be proud of the child. Our first night had been triumphant, and when, the second night, we again played "The Black Flag," Little Bessie was called before the curtain like a star. She was the pet of El Paso.

"I'm going to let you have another night," offered Hollub, whereupon the entire Company nearly fainted with happiness, "but put on another play — we've had "The Black Flag twice."

Well, we had to do it, so we put on what was known by the name of "Lynwood." It may have born some faint resemblance to that great old masterpiece of the dramatic age. I was playing the lead as usual, but that didn't matter, for Bess was our only attraction. We were puppets that danced to her playing.

When at last our three nights spoil counted, the Russell Dramatic Company had cleared sixty percent of $750, or $450.

Think of it — ninety dollars each! It was a fortune. In our minds we spent it a thousand ways — in our minds only. For think you we saw our ninety dollars? Pop Russell saw it first.

But by putting up a rabid struggle, I won several things from Pop out of this manna, and one was a little boy suit for Bessie. It was to wear as Ned, and she looked so adorable in it we took her straight to the leading photographer in El Paso and had her picture taken.

I also bought a new suit! Perhaps I didn't deserve mine as Bess did hers, but I needed it more. My new suit had even larger checks than the old one, and I looked more like an actor than ever, and also, I wrung thirty dollars more from Pop, and this was rushed on to San Jose. That made me feel the weight of coming prosperity — but the dream was to prove a lie. Pop believed in it, however.

"El Paso has given us the test," he said, grandly. "Now we have shown what we can do, we will go on and play all of Texas and head for New York . . ."

"We go West!" I replied, firm-minded as never in my life before.

Mother Nature had borne too much. Jennie's heart was in San Jose with her baby boy, and no matter what Pop might say, we were going home.

Bessie Bacon, child actress, in costume. Photographed by F. Parker, El Paso, Texas, 1890.

Bessie Bacon in little boy suit purchased in El Paso, Texas during 1890 barnstorming tour.

CHAPTER TWELVE

A BARNSTORMING CHRISTMAS

We were longing for the sunshine and shadows of the Coast Range. We wanted California. If Pop Russell insisted upon the Russell Company playing on through Texas, he would go alone. At that, he was perfectly capable of it!

But Jennie and I, and McGlynn and Hernandez, refused to move eastward from El Paso. And with Pop's reluctant consent, we crossed the westward line into Arizona.

Arizona was our seventh state, although it was not actually admitted into the Union until many years after our playing there. I am glad we knew Utah and Texas and Arizona in their territorial days. I am glad we knew their pioneer hardships, even if it was a make-up box we carried, instead of a ploughshare.

If you believe in the magic of the lucky seven, Arizona should have proved a fortunate country to the wandering actors. Instead, it was our worst.

Under the wintry Arizona sun our El Paso fortune melted away. We entered by lower Cochise County, and played Bisbee, the mining town in the mountains the great strikes were later to make famous. We traveled by stages pulled by six horses, and by night to avoid the heat. The stagedrivers rode armed, for the country was ridden by bandits that pillaged the silver and copper mines. There were Indian troubles and uprisings and the name of the famous chieftain, Geronimo, echoed in the Territory.

It was while I was riding on ahead into Benson I met Dan Mahoney. He was conductor on the train, and when he took my ticket he stared at me before punching it.

"Say, ain't you from San Jose?" he demanded.

And so was he. Dan, bless his heart, got hold of a pass for me, and after that I rode free all along the line.

At Benson, we attended the Mexican circus.

These circuses played, and still play, up out of Old Mexico, and should be famous for their acrobats — also for their freedom of speech. The clowns are so natural in their remarks it is embarrassing to anyone from California, who usually comprehends enough of the language to know when to blush.

Jennie had her doubts about attending the affair in the first place. She had heard the performers danced a can-can and there is nothing in this age could express the moral horror people had for the can-can in those days. Nice people hadn't heard the word. We should never have seen it, perhaps, if we hadn't played Benson.

Benson in those days was as open as a steamed clam. The town was running riot with "bad men" and painted women, and gamblers. In '91 Benson was still totin' its gun when it went forth to such places as this Mexican circus. Even Jennie changed her mind at last, for she was just starting in with a terrific toothache and needed distraction, and she came to the circus with the rest of us.

All of Benson was gathered under the Mexican tent that evening. The painted ladies were there in their brightest colors, eyed askance by the Mexican matrons in respectable black shawls. All the cowboys were there, and the miners from the shafts, and the Indians from the village outside of town, and the Chinese and Negro inhabitants. The West was represented under that shabby tent.

The circus consisted of a man and his wife and their children, and a few horses and dogs. The children were marvelous acrobats, trained to the ropes from their cradles. We enjoyed it, for we had seen so few affairs of any sort since leaving home, and also we appreciated the work of it. But it was the toothache, and the can-can danced by the man and his wife — she wore a flaming ballet skirt — that finished Jennie. We left early.

Jennie's toothache grew agonizing. There was no sleep for either of us that night. There was not a dentist in Benson and the drug stores were simply part of the general stores, and the drugs consisted principally of pain-killer. Poor Jennie played our night in Benson with locked jaws. She could hardly speak with pain.

And when at last we got to Tucson, it took the Tucson dentist and a doctor to extract the tooth!

Tucson was bigger than Phoenix then, mostly adobe, and with part of the old Spanish wall around it still. Tucson is the "only

124

walled city in America," you know. Beautiful San Xavier Mission, the Taj Mahal of America, is at Tucson. It is a show city now, but in our day the Mexicans were our greatest patrons and the principal citizens. They gloated over the golden curls of little Bessie. They would give their last centavo to see the child. But, although they were ardent play-goers, they had very little money. So we found ourselves working northward through Arizona, facing the winter and poverty. Again we knew what it was to be two dollars ahead of the game. Again I felt as if I were turning gray with worry.

We came by stage through the Gila valley, beautiful with a lonely desert grayness, and played Florence, a town of neat adobes on the Gila river. We played in the little Opera House there, run by "Dad" Keating, a popular saloon man, and left the next day for Phoenix, the Capitol, some seventy miles north. Later, the Roosevelt Dam would bring green life to this country. In our day it was a land of the dead. Great cacti shot twisted green shapes into the air. Cholla lathered the scene with gray foliage that looked like coral. The whole country was like a scene under the sea.

Adobe hotels and stage fare took all we could make in Arizona. We worked down to Yuma — the line. We felt as if we were escaping for our lives from Arizona. We took the train at Yuma — there was little there to keep us from crossing the river, and that night we kept awake for the joy of watching the Colorado slide below us like a rattlesnake. We were over it, and the Colorado river was the line — we were back in California!

I think even Pop felt like crying then.

In California! — but we were poor as the day we started, and we were hundreds of miles from San Jose.

Colton was our first stop. It was good to play a California town after our wandering, and we played with thanksgiving in our hearts. The psalm died. For the rainy season was on, and every reasonably large town in Southern California had a well-organized, regular stock company of its own. We played Riverside, and around Ventura. Our brave efforts were scorned. No one cared to see a company of five present "The Black Flag," when there were real shows to be seen. Our ship was close to the rocks again, although so close to home.

And Christmas was coming on.

Christmas is likely to be a blue season for the actor. He nearly always is in a strange city. As I look back upon my Christmas Days, it seems to me they have nearly always meant an extra performance and no extra pay. Christmas Eve is the worst theatrical night of

125

the year, every actor knows. Folks want to be in their homes that night, around lighted trees.

On this Christmas of 1890, we were booked to play San Bernardino.

We came into San Bernardino the day before Christmas. It was pouring rain when we left the train.

"Is this bus free?" I demanded of the dampest driver at the station.

Having been carefully assured that it was, we clambered aboard and drove to one of the smaller hotels. We were wasting no thirty cents on bus fare! We had to pay in advance for our rooms. After that nothing was left but our future.

The manager of the Opera House, where we were playing that night, Christmas Eve, came through the rain to call. I had expected a man, but the manager was a woman, Mrs. Kipplinger.

"Can't you advance us any money?" asked Pop, almost pleadingly, for we hadn't enough money between the five of us for a complete dinner.

"We haven't made a single advance sale," she answered, to our despair. "Wait until after the show. We may do better than we expect. . . ."

But it was Christmas Eve! Who wants to go out on a rainy Christmas Eve, when of all nights home is the sweetest place on earth!

I went upstairs to our room. Bessie was curled up on the bed with one chubby fist buried in her curls. She was taking her delayed afternoon nap and Jennie, unpacking the wretched little trunk, looked up at me with hot eyes.

"Then there's no money?" she demanded quietly, as I said nothing.

"The manager said we'd have to wait until after the show," I told her hopelessly.

Her lips were white and she looked from me to the sleeping child.

"And after the show it will be too late to buy Bessie a Christmas present — every store will be closed!" she said, tensely. "Frank, you know Bessie is planning to hang her stocking up, and that baby isn't going without her Christmas — give me all you have!"

Together, we produced forty-five cents. We hadn't another penny and we knew the show that night was going to fail. Knowing that, Jennie went out in the rain to do her Christmas shopping.

126

She found a little doll with a very sweet expression for twenty-five cents. Five cents she squandered on peanuts, and five more for that cheap striped Christmas candy you buy in groceries. With the remaining ten cents, she bought two packages of cigarettes — yes, they were five cents a pack then — and these were to be divided between Pop and McGlynn and Hernandez and me. She went home and had the dolly dressed grandly in some velvet scraps before it was time to start for the Opera House.

That night little Bessie played the part of "Gay Carlyle," in "Lynwood," and played it beautifully, we thought. But there were few there to appreciate the four year old soubrette. It didn't take us long to count up that night. There was $38.00 in the house. That came to about four dollars apiece, and we had our hotel bill for the morrow to pay, and our meals to buy, and our future train fare to reckon against. And it was Christmas Eve!

"You may do better tomorrow night," said Mrs. Kipplinger, kindly, seeing the grief on Pop's face as he pocketed the money for all of us.

We could not be comforted by promises. We had seen too many fail us. We were hopeless as we splashed back to the dismal hotel, I carrying the drowsy Bessie. The child fell asleep instantly after her tiring work on the stage, and I sadly helped Jennie fill that tiny stocking hanging on the foot of the bed, with the twenty-five cent doll, and the striped sweets and the peanuts. Our hearts were aching, but we did try to laugh.

"I — I'm sick of the stage!" Jennie burst out despairingly, and in this hour only I saw Jennie's courage die.

Christmas morning was brought to our consciousness by a knocking on our door. A husky voice was demanding, "Frank Bacon."

Jennie and I, jerking awake abruptly, exchanged startled looks.

"You answer!" I whispered hastily, for Jennie has always proved much more effective at conversing with sheriffs than I, and of course my first thought was that the show was being closed for debt.

But it wasn't the San Bernardino Sheriff. It was the Wells Fargo delivery man, a very large person carrying a very small package.

"This came in on the early train and I just thought I'd bring it over to you — seeing it's Christmas," he said with a heart-warming smile.

I tore the package open. Ten twenty-dollar gold pieces crashed to the floor. They were wrapped in a statement from Fort Bayard.

That performance young Lieutenant Pershing had arranged for us on the credit system was paid for at last and the money came in time to turn our blackest Christmas to sunshine. Jennie and I kept turning the gold pieces over and over. They meant release. They meant — home. Bessie, awake at last, was rapturously crowing over her twenty-five cent doll. Christmas was complete.

The old tattered scrapbook stares at me again:

CHRISTMAS EVENT

RUSSELL'S COMPANY

Friday and Saturday, December 26 and 27, 1890

— TWO BEAUTIFUL PLAYS —

"LYNWOOD"   **"THE BLACK FLAG"**

But we gave our best, and Lower California found us wanting. We found ourselves without audience and without hope. There was too much competition. And all we had was this money from Fort Bayard.

Jennie and I looked at one another, and at the money. We spoke in one voice:

"Let's go home!"

We came into San Jose shortly behind the New Year of 1891.

The Russell Dramatic Company lay behind us like a dream. No more would the indomitable five face together the acrid sunlight of Nevada, the snows of Utah and the loneliness of Arizona. And yet, we parted from Pop, and the gloomy McGlynn and the comic Hernandez, as if from brothers. Had we not faced the end together many times, only to find it one more chapter in the glad novel of life? We had known the piteousness and the humor of poverty. We had practised all its droll little camouflages of the poor. Whenever our paths might cross in the theatrical wastes, we would mean much to one another.

And we were to meet again. Pop would take us into his arms again in Seattle, and Hernandez and I would play together in the Hollywood films, and McGlynn, we would meet in his mining togs, when he returned to his original calling. Pop, courageous veteran that he was, died many years later playing his favorite role, "East Lynne," to the very end. He would barnstorm to his last day on earth, but

128

not with us. We were going home, although the parting was a mournful one.

Our homecoming was sadder still.

We arrived at the San Jose depot without an extra cent. But we were home, by the grace of God! We breathed in the air of the old Alameda, and hung out of the "dinky" street car windows to see the palm tips over the high stone fence surrounding the convent of Notre Dame. Around the corner, hidden by the pepper trees, was the little home where Jennie had been reared. Now our son was there! We ran up the little porch steps with the lightest hearts in the world.

Inside that home was the misery of disgrace. We were received, Jennie and little Bessie and I, like naughty runaway children. Jennie wept, gathering her little son into her hungry arms. Lloyd stared at her suspiciously, turned his stormy infant gaze away, looked again and puckered up his rose wet mouth. How he howled!

"He doesn't know us! Our baby doesn't know us!" wailed Jennie, and that was the blackest moment of all.

The aunts were passing Bessie around like a charm, hugging her within an inch of her life. Poor child, she wasn't five, and not to be blamed if her wild young parents chose to drag her over seven states with a barnstorming troupe! Bessie was out of this. It was Jennie and I who had to face the stern Methodist music.

You see, we had come home because the chance offered, but with not an idea of staying home. We didn't dream but that our careers would go on and on. The Russell Company had been "experience." But Father nipped our young dreams in the bud. He was the sternest of all.

Father had also had his dreams, perhaps, but he had done his very best in the world. He was determined to save me from what he felt was failure. And he talked to me, in the little side bedroom with the dimity curtains, as if I were his little Frank again, and not a grown man with a family.

I felt as I had, years before, when he had led me behind the stacked redwood in his lumber yard to meet punishment, far from family ears. I wished Jennie would come in. Somehow people never got quite so angry with me when Jennie was around. She was little, but she could look ferocious. But I knew Aunt Em was giving Jennie her share, for I heard her high voice saying in the kitchen:

"Sending home forty dollars in nine months! — the very idea of such a thing!"

Father was saying practically the same thing.

129

"Son, I'm ashamed of you at last," he was saying, in his slow, careful way. Father was never anything but dignified. "You haven't been able to send home five dollars a month for your son! Gypsying around in all sorts of places and nobody knowing where you are — why, Frank, the whole town's talking about you!"

It came upon Jennie and me like a thunderbolt, that our careers were to begin and end at home. The assembled Jeffreys and Bacons decreed that. Like remorseful children, we sat in penitence before this family legislature, and promised never to think of the stage again. Never! Or, as it happened — hardly ever.

Ed, my big brother, who was the steady, dependable member of the family everyone admired, was not in at the family reception. Ed had bought out a little photograph gallery in Salinas and was doing well.

"You ought to go down there and help him in the gallery," said Father. "At least you'll be able to send home some money once in a while."

I wasn't so sure of that. I knew what gallery work had ever meant to me. But I was voted down, and off I went to Salinas. I went alone. The aunts not only kept Bessie, but Jennie. I guess the family felt I was safe if the wife and child were not along. I wasn't likely to get very far from the beaten path myself. I am only stating what the family thought, remember. I was to disprove their pleasant theory.

Ed welcomed me to the little studio on Main street with much satisfaction. It is now the Vassar Studio. He didn't mention my barnstorming career — very much. Oh, well, you know how brothers are, that way! Ed was only human. And he was doing well with the studio. He had a nice home of his own, on the outskirts of Salinas, think of that! The family had mentioned it to me, frequently, before I made my sad little trip down there.

"Ed has a nice home of his own — but then Ed knows how to stay in one place," the family had informed me kindly, while Jennie, with the make-up box hidden away and her reconciled and adoring son in her arms, had watched me go in complete despair.

I felt as if I had been set back one hundred years, as the theosophists believe happens to evil doers. Here I was, back in a small California town, in a studio I hated, on another main street. That night, after Ed went home to his family in the nice house on the outskirts, I was alone with myself in the echoing gallery. Behind the main room were two tiny rooms, and that was where I was to batch

130

Jennie Bacon, photographed in Salinas, c. 1891.

Frank Bacon, photographed in Salinas, c. 1891.

and cook my meagre dinners. There was not another soul in the building at night. The dentist below stairs and the storekeeper and the attorney whose office was next to mine, went home for the night. Then the hallways creaked and the wind came sighing from the drying bed of the Salinas river, and in the studio the tall tripod and camera stood shrouded in the black cloth like a monstrous-headed ghost. I was lonely. There was only one talent I was left free to exercise and that was — making friends.

I made them, slowly but surely. Before long, for fame and infamy ride fast in small towns, people said of me as I walked down Main street, "There goes Frank Bacon . . . he used to be an actor."

I couldn't forget my nine months of barnstorming. I recalled, longingly, while I posed giggling Salinas brides and cowboys from the big Miller and Lux rancho that surrounded the town, that once I had starred in "The Black Flag." I posed the brides with their veils, and the cattlemen with Stetson hats that cost a month's salary — I clamped their necks viciously with the adjusting iron and ordered them to smile, but my thoughts were with Pop Russell. Still, I worked steadily in the gallery.

And since I was in the work, I wanted to feel that a small part of it was mine. Horace Keesling, my brother-in-law, was again kind enough to sign another note for me. It was for one hundred and fifty dollars. Now a part of the gallery was mine, but it left me in a strange mood. For I had once sworn never to develop another plate. And here I was once more, alone in a small gallery, without Jennie, cooking my own meals and in debt! Just as in the Napa studio before Bessie was born! Fate turning the pages back, as if the barnstorming had never been, and I never had met with Pop Russell.

Salinas is not, and was not then, a lively town. The usual Bill Joneses of life sat in the sunlight on the porch of the old Abbott House. The Salinas river passed the town silently, a true California River, "one mile wide and an inch deep." There were many descendants of great Spanish-Californian families living there, the Mission Soledad was in ruins not far away, and the crumbled adobe walls of the first college built in California. There was a sleepiness in Salinas, as in many California towns. But there were live souls living there!

Within three weeks, I knew every person in town who had ever read a play. I couldn't help it. And before long, a little group was

131

forming. We talked acting. We read plays. And then the words leapt from the sky:

"Let's get up a show!"

I'll never know who said it first. I'll swear I wasn't entirely responsible, although the group did look up to me as a "professional," with the profound experience of seven states to my credit. Poor Ed heard the news with the sensation of a man whose drunkard brother has just returned to drink. He recalled father's words to me:

"No Bacon went to jail yet for being a play actor — till you came along."

But I didn't consider an amateur performance in Salinas would break my pledge never to return to the stage. For I had promised, faithfully. But, I guess it isn't safe for a chronic drunkard to order even a vanilla soda. It's likely to renew old desires.

There were a great many of us in on the plot. There was Henry Andresan, who later became Superior Judge, and there was a rather bashful fellow with leanings toward Shakespeare. There was Peter Krough, Dr. Edwards, Roy Alexander, Sidney McCollum, Jimmy Hughes and Karl McCandless and a lot of others. We decided to put on "The Black Flag" in Central Hall.

"Come to Salinas at once and bring the manuscript . . ." I wrote Jennie, happily, and she arrived on the earliest train.

She brought Lloyd, curly headed and brimming with mischief, and Bessie, who was lovelier than any picture I have taken in my entire photographic career. And Jennie also brought our famous little tin trunk containing the few costumes we had saved from the barnstorming, but she did not bring the manuscript of "The Black Flag." Pop Russell had taken that.

"Never mind, Frank, I know every word in the old thing by heart," Jennie assured me, and set about in the little room behind the gallery writing out the entire play from memory.

And we gave the show. We rehearsed in private homes, or in old Central Hall where the great affair was to take place. It was also known as the Opera House and was upstairs over a livery stable on Main Street. Today it is a motion picture house, the Crystal.

We had three sets, a woodland scene, a kitchen and a parlor. We had to fit the "Black Flag" into these sets, and we did. That was easy compared with some of the stunts we had accomplished with Pop Russell.

Little Bessie, as always, was the star. Children forget, and we had to coach her again in the simple lines. Bessie, who had lapsed easily into San Jose and a pinafore, never recalled the fact that she had once been a soubrette. In this happy forgetfulness she was luckier than her father.

Central Hall was crowded to its topmost bench that night. Seats sold at fifty cents each, and I made $150.00.

"Jennie, this means I'm out of debt," I whispered to my wife before the show started.

There are five acts in "The Black Flag." At the end of the fourth act, Little Bessie was called before the curtain. Andresan was there in his make-up, with two little gold bracelets in his hands. He made a speech:

"Little Bessie, I am called upon by the Band boys to present to you, for them, these two gold bracelets. They are interested in you because they believe you to be a good little girl, and the prettiest and cleverest little actress that has ever appeared on the stage. And it is the wish, expressed by every member of the Salinas Band, that your future life will be banded by a golden circle, as will your tender small wrists when clamped by these."

Bessie heard his words with the deep seriousness of the very young, and slipped the bracelets over her little hands with the deepest, loveliest interest. From behind the wings I was watching with Jennie. Something was stirring in my soul again. A horizon of belief lay before me. I knew that one of us, at least, would win!

I dreaded next morning and the squalor of the gallery again.

CHAPTER THIRTEEN

A FLASH BACK TO FOOTLIGHTS

The Salinas studio was not a lonely place during the time we were putting on the amateur "Black Flag." No, for Jennie was there, and the two children, crowded together and happy as larks in the little rooms. If I happened to be out, and a customer came, Jennie never admitted the photographer was not in, for as usual, money was scarce, and we always had a place for the "deposit" demanded before a sitting.

"Sit right down and I'll take you," she offered, readily.

She knew as much about photography as baby Lloyd. But she would adjust the iron clamp to the subject's ears, and make him smile beautifully and hold that position minutes longer than it takes now, and dash behind the camera and throw the black cloth over her head.

"There. Return Saturday for your proofs," she would say, coming out from under the cloth.

And when the customer returned for the proofs, of course I had to tell them they turned out badly and they must pose again! Anything to hold the fort — and the deposit!

The $150 I made from the "Black Flag" just paid my brother-in-law's note. Now I was out of debt. I felt free. Now I might return to my chosen trail — but no! There was my pledge to Father. I had to remain in the gallery.

I forgot my restlessness as long as Jennie was with me. Henry Andresan and the other boys would come over evenings, and we would have a game of whist. Jennie didn't play, and one of the boys taught her solitaire. After that she played solitaire by herself evenings, while we played at another table. Jennie wasn't altogether sure she was doing right in learning the game. Remember, she had

134

been raised a Methodist. But so had I, and I hold that to blame for never having become a good hand at poker.

But Jennie couldn't remain with me in Salinas. Things weren't going smoothly enough for that, and she had to return with the children to San Jose, returning now and then to Salinas for another show.

We worked for many months among the amateurs of Salinas. We put on all the old Russell repertoire, "East Lynne" and other classics of yesterday. We discovered talent in the little town by the salt river. But between shows, and with Jennie in San Jose, I found time weighting down my hands and I wrote a play.

I wrote that play with the hopelessness of a man in prison. There had to be some way out of the grind! I couldn't stick much longer to photography, in spite of the family and need of money. There must be some key to the door. Writing might be the way.

It was a rambling sort of play. I tried to put into it the spirit of all the Bill Joneses I had known, beginning with Uncle Morris of Marysville. The lead character was an old fellow spiced with a large sense of nonsense. He was a tramp printer and veteran of the Grand Army of the Republic. He had been parted from his much enduring wife. He drank. He told tall yarns concerning his own importance.

This was the play, *Lightnin'*, its seed and beginning.

Henry Andresan takes a wicked joy in telling how he visited me in the gallery one day. And how I locked the door and made him listen while I read him my play. He said it was awful. It probably was.

After I had toiled over it for months, I tucked it down in the old make-up trunk with the rest of my relics of dreams. And there it lay, for many years.

During this year of Salinas, Ed was branching out rapidly. He bought another gallery in Monterey on the coast, and now he went on a visit to Hollister, a pretty town beyond Salinas toward the east, and returned with the news that he had found a bargain of a small gallery there, and was going to let me take charge of it. Ed was going ahead. No wonder the family pointed him out in comparison to me, to my humiliation.

Also, Ed added that he was pleased with my year's industry in the Salinas gallery! I shall always be grateful for that.

I was glad to go over to Hollister. It wasn't far away, but a year's end marked my usual cycle in a town and I felt I needed a change. But I left many friends in Salinas — just the other night an old neighbor called to me across the footlights in *Lightnin'*.

Honestly, I moved over to Hollister with the virtuous belief that I would make a "go" of the gallery for Ed. I knew that back home in San Jose, Father was watching my sobered progress with much pride, pleased with the son who had kept a promise. I knew that the future of Jennie and the children, also in San Jose, depended on my work in this new town.

My first day in Hollister I met James Piratsky.

For many years now, Piratsky has been owner of the Watsonville *Pajaronian*, a small-town newspaper with a big personality. But then he was the energetic young editor of Hollister, and likewise managed the Hollister Theatre. Later, when Jennie visited Hollister, she discovered she had met Piratsky at an entertainment in San Francisco some years before, where one of the striking amateur performers was Frank Murasky, now a distinguished San Francisco judge.

Piratsky became my friend. I notice it is always a friend who brings about one's downfall.

For I cannot remember what the inside of that Hollister gallery was like. It seemed to me I merely walked into it and out again, and that it was all Piratsky's fault. Without Piratsky, I would probably still be in the Hollister gallery.

But James M. Ward was playing in Piratsky's Hollister show house just then. Ward, known as "The Irish Comedian," and his wife, Carrie Clark Ward — she is well known in motion pictures now — were to be listed among the noblest of Coast Defenders. With a small company, they were touring the coast in various repertoires, "Through by Daylight," "After Dark," "Ranch Ten," and also a few of the well known Irish comedies, "Shaughran," "Colleen Bawn," and "Shamus O'Brien."

Ward came into Hollister with his company just as I arrived. He had been doing very badly in other towns. Two nights after my arrival I treated myself to the pleasure of attending his opening night. A man must have some amusement in a strange town. I noted with great pleasure, having once been an actor myself, that the house was packed.

The next day there was something to gossip about in Hollister. Ward had been doing so very badly, that he could not pay his salaries. Two of his actors quit that morning. Was the Ward Company to break up in this quiet town among the wheat fields?

They were playing that night. Where could they find an actor!

"There's a young fellow just came to town — a photographer," Piratsky, who as manager of the theatre was naturally anxious, informed Ward. "He has played around the States, he tells me."

Then Piratsky told me what he had told Ward, and quite casually I locked up the gallery and went down to the theatre to investigate the rumor.

That gallery door was not to open again by my hand.

My hands were drawn from the acid tank forever. My promise to Father was broken. For it was less than a week after my coming to Hollister, determined to make Ed's gallery the finest on the coast, that I was again an actor, with James M. Ward.

I wonder what Ed thought in Salinas, when he learned I had fallen again from family grace and was on the stage. Not that the fall was very far, for the Hollister theatre was small and Ward's company not noted for its successes. But my broken pledge to Father troubled me nevertheless — troubles me still. I wonder! Without that broken promise, there would never have been Broadway!

For one solid week I played in that little Hollister theatre. Ward was not deeply impressed with my talent, but anyone would do. He was close to the rocks.

And another night we needed a little boy to take the part of a child that is kidnapped in the play. In the very last hour we found one. Inside the theatre, and face to face with the painted actors, he went into hysterics. We had to send him home. But there was eighty-seven dollars out front! We couldn't send that wealth away.

"Go out and get a child!" Ward shouted to Joe Muller, who was the property man and destined to play a large role in my future life. "Get any sort of kid, as long as he's under eighty — if you have to kidnap him. Don't come back here without one!"

Joe rushed out, and being a resourceful property man, was back just before the curtain went up. He was panting. He was dragging behind him, like a cross puppy, a grouchy little chap in ragged overalls.

"I found him in front of the French Laundry," panted Joe.

Ward shoved the child to the wings. "Don't say a word to him!" he raged, as we fought to teach the new find his one and only line in the play — then to the boy — "and here's your cue — go on! — for the Lord's sake — Go on!"

The boy walked on and stood glaring across the footlights at the audience. The villain approached him with an ingratiating smile. He was laying his wiles for the kidnapping scene.

"And whose little boy are you?" he sweetly questioned the infant Goliath.

"I'm the laundry boy!" yelled the youngster. That finished the scene.

It was a desperate week, with everything wrong from the very start. I sent to San Jose, and Jennie brought little Bessie down for one night to play in "Ten Nights in a Barroom." Even that failed to interest Hollister.

At the week's end, word came from Ward's advance man. He was discouraged by the poor showing. He was quitting the company.

Now there was no one on ahead and no one to send. I don't know why Ward thought of me.

"Didn't you say you acted as advance man with Russell?" he demanded.

Reluctantly, I admitted that I had. I know I had too many professions, as newspaper man, advance theatrical agent, photographer and actor, to impress Ward. But I lost. Ward took me bodily.

"Just trust to luck from the boards," he said, and made me advance man. Little as he could spare the worst of his company, he had to have someone ahead of the show.

"Then, I'll go over to Salinas and make arrangements there for the Central Theatre," I said hopefully.

"That you will not," said Ward, flatly.

"Why not?" I returned.

"Because 'tis Holy Week," said Ward. "And because we played Salinas but a few months ago. And because it's too small a town to stand us twice in the same year."

"In that case," I said, stubborn as an Arizona burro, "Let's put the Company on the commonwealth."

Ward looked at me with the first respect he had shown. He hadn't suspected I knew this last device of theatrical poverty. On the commonwealth is where no salaries are paid, but the actors divide the profits of each show in proportion to their salaries. And because he knew matters could not be much worse for him, Ward agreed.

And back I was in Salinas, within two weeks of my leaving there. Back, to Ed's dismay, with the Hollister gallery a matter of the past and the job of advance agent for a desperate company.

You see, I had lived nearly a year in the little town, and I trusted it.

I made a personal canvass of Salinas, and made every friend I had promise to see our show. We were putting on "East Lynne," and Jennie again made a flying trip down from San Jose, for little Bessie was to play. And Bessie had more friends in Salinas than I. Between the two of us, I think, we won a promise of a packed hall.

When Ward came over with his people, he didn't think much of my preparations, nor of Central Hall. But I fooled the company. Our first night we played to a crowded house.

"Fool's luck," said the scoffers — there are a few in every company.

They did not know the value of friendship. But the next night Jimmie Ward came and stood beside me in the wings and watched the seats filling again. We were making money in Salinas. And on the commonwealth, the actors drew money that doubled their usual salaries. From that night on they were for me to a man.

Little Bessie was given a reception when her mother brought her down from San Jose. Everyone in Salinas knew the child. "East Lynne," was our best night finanically, for that night Bessie played. She did not know the part, however, but that did not bother us. Bessie died on a couch in the play, and no one in the audience dreamed that, lying on the floor in back of the couch, and completely hidden from them, lay Jennie. In whispers, Jennie "fed" each arduous line to the child.

"Boy," declared Ward, after this fortunate Salinas week, "You are welcome to head us south."

Jennie returned to the little house in San Jose, and the protection of the aunts. I said good-bye to her, and to Bessie, a little bitterly. It was hard to be forever bidding them good-bye. But now there was hope for me, for I was branching out in the line desired! With this thought in mind, I paid one last visit to the Salinas Gallery. This time, I knew I was through with tripod and tank. For once, I was right.

I led Ward's company out of Salinas. We were to play south, toward Los Angeles. I did not go to San Jose first to apologize to Father for breaking my word. I did not have the time. Besides, I was not so certain I was sorry for having broken it. But I sent home a few dollars instead — coin from Salinas. And I started out from Salinas again, alone.

Fresh from the gypsy trail with Russell's Comedians, I knew every neck and corner of the coast. In nearly every town I had friends. I knew what to expect in the way of houses. By short train journeys, or by stage where, at Santa Margarita, the railroad was not completed, I moved slowly to Los Angeles, booking the company all the way. I booked them through Santa Maria and Lompoc, into Santa Barbara. Then I doubled back on my tracks and met the company at San Luis Obispo. I would keep pace with their slow march to Los Angeles — lead them into the towns I had booked for them.

The Southern Pacific went only to Santa Margarita — from then on was a gap of fifty miles to be covered by stage. California was greatly excited over this gap. Say an actor was missing at curtain time and there was inquiry.

"Oh, he's closing the gap."

It had become California slang.

Ward and the actors left Santa Marguerita on the stage, behind sturdy horses. Joe Muller and I were to go with the baggage. The wagon we had rented, piled with our drops and trunks, was like a small distorted mountain under canvas. We started early, but not early enough.

We were to meet the company at Golita, a small village I knew that huddled down beside the Pacific. There, we would picnic together, Ward, the actors, the property man and I. Then we would mush on, and we would have to hurry to reach Santa Barbara by night. Fifty miles was not to be sneezed at, in '92.

There was no Lincoln Highway. In places we found the road a wicked one, particularly as viewed from a high and weightily piled farm wagon. The farmer himself had consented to drive us down, for neither Joe nor I were up to handling a four horse team. He rode, swaying on the stilted seat like a canary on its perch; we clung to the roped peak of our mound of property.

The ride along the coast was a lonely one in those days, over cliffs where thousands of automobiles whiz today. And the road was not level then, but patiently dipped into every little gully and mounted every rise of land, as if determined not to miss an inch of the scenery. Toiling up one of the steepest "hard-scrabble" hillsides, we ran into a party of cowpunchers, — "vaqueros," as we call them out West, and pronounce the "V" like a "b."

They were evidently celebrating the monthly payday, and were immensely drunk. As they rode past us with thundering heels and spurting dust, they whipped out their revolvers and fired. They

140

whooped like warring Apaches. There were no reasons for this except high spirits and hard liquor. I suppose a farm wagon piled with theatrical scenery was a queer sight to them.

The horses had seemed half dead until that moment, when each took his bit between his teeth and bolted. Over the hillcrest they raced, and down the steep side, tearing along like wild stallions. The great, awkwardly piled wagon swayed drunkenly, while Joe and I clung to our seats on the top of the pile, screaming to the driver to slow his horses down. At any moment we would be slung into space. But the driver flung on the long iron brake, sawed with the four reins and impotently yelled, "Whoa! Whoa! Whoa!"' The lumbering mass tore on, and all he could do was try to keep the wheels in the rutted road.

The trunks were tied to the scenery with baling wire — the wires snapped. At our backs we felt the great mass move dangerously as an earthquake, and I guess that was when Joe and I jumped. Then the wagon dropped into a chuckhole and bounced out, and the trunks and scenery rose from the lurching wagon to shoot forward in a heap over the wagon bed, over the road edge, and down a gully.

After another wild half mile, the tired horses stopped suddenly. Their owner drove them back to the wreckage.

Trunk by trunk and wing by wing we got that load back upon the wagon. We unhitched two of the horses, fastened ropes to their collars and had them drag the luggage up from the gully. It took four sweltering hours! When again we took our places on the load, we felt faint with weariness, and heat, and hunger.

And Golita was still thirty miles away!

Joe cursed the wagon and the horses in the picturesque backstage language of the property man.

At last, after a few more hours, we drove wretchedly into Golita and out, looking for the company and the stage.

"Will you look there!" exclaimed Joe in loud despair, pointing to a litter of paper bags and edible remnants under an oak. It was the spread evidence of a picnic. The troupe had despaired of our coming; they had dined and driven on.

Joe cursed Ward and his actors.

Just beyond Golita was a little ranch where stood a small weather-beaten farmhouse. Timidly, the three of us went to the door and recited our mishaps to the farmer's wife. She was suspicious as only a farmer's wife can be of travelers, but she handed us out a plate of raised bread and a hunk of cold salt pork that had been cooked with mustard greens. We manufactured a pile of crude sandwiches and munched them as we rode on again. They were the best sandwiches I ever ate.

We were hurrying the horses, for evening was joining our little troupe. The sun melted like an hourglass into the Pacific. Darkness hid the dangerous cliffs. But, sometime that night, we had to reach Santa Barbara. And the road was bitter going, for all along it were washouts from the recent rains.

"You feller's better get out and blaze the trail ahead," advised our driver as it grew darker and we rode like blind men on a top-heavy wagon that tilted crazily in the ruts.

Joe cursed the road. I have never heard such fluency of speech.

He and I scrambled over the high wheels and fell to the uneven ground. We walked on ahead in the dark, following the road by instinct. We lit matches and held them over our heads to guide the driver. Oh, for an electric flashlight then, even the toy kind our children have today! But Edison was still in his youth and the electric light, by most methodical citizens, was to be looked upon as a mechanism of the devil and not altogether moral.

The matches flared for a moment in the sharp salt wind, and were out. But not before the driver had seen their flame, and we would hear behind us his furious:

"Gee up there, Barney — come along!"

We had but two small boxes of matches between us. Soon the last match was gone. Then we would call back to the driver and he struggled to keep his horses to the road from the sound.

Far out in the pool of night went the lights of a passing ship. I said, unluckily:

"Gee, I wish I was going out with that ship . . . anywhere from this!"

Then it was Joe whirled on me at last, and as we stumbled down that endless road together, he cursed me thoroughly for booking the Ward show in such fool territory off the beaten road! Between curses, he paused to shout back to our luckless driver.

After many hours we sighted another light. This was no ship, but a farmhouse, and we were getting nearer to it. We went in there and asked to put up for the night. We were exhausted, for our salt pork sandwiches had been eaten that afternoon and now it was midnight.

The farmer who owned that house put our sweating horses in his barn and gave them fodder. Make-shift beds were spread out for us, and three weary travelers huddled down on corn-husk mattresses and slept like dead men. Wearily enough we were out again at four the next morning. For the company must play in Santa Barbara that night, and we had their scenery and costumes.

We didn't get into Santa Barbara until three that afternoon, one whole day behind schedule. Ward we found in a raging fury and the rest of the company badly scared. They thought we had been murdered by bandits. Joe and I were welcomed tearfully by everyone but Ward, who couldn't forgive us for nearly losing him a night's performance.

That crazy trip cemented a friendship between the property man and the advance agent that was to serve Joe and me through to our palmier days. Joe is managing the Palace-Hippodrome in Seattle now, but we were to see many hardships together before we landed in snug harbors. Joe is the possessor of a pungent wit, as well as a large vocabulary, and one of the laughable lines in *Lightnin'* is his. Remember where old Bill says:

"I druv a swarm of bees across the plains in the dead of winter."

It was Joe who added:

"And I never lost a single bee!"

Santa Barbara was soon done to a turn. We hurried down to Los Angeles. My bookings there were quite a victory, and I was very proud of them. For we had an entire month's engagement at Hazzard's Pavilion, where the Philharmonic Auditorium stands today. Naturally, I was to remain with the troupe this month, and Ward, who wept at the thought of having anyone idle on the payroll, offered me another chance at acting. He had been far from impressed by my histrionic ability back in Hollister where I had cut the traces and deserted Ed's photography gallery to join him.

"Guess I'll give you a part in "Through by Daylight!" Ward informed me.

I was determined to show Ward I could act. Grimly, I learned my lines, always a hard task for me, and then forgot I had learned them, and lived them. I really think I showed some talent in that small roll. But Ward, being a wily veteran, didn't tell me if he liked my work or not. That worried me, along with something else.

The troupe was breaking up at the month's end!

We were going to close after a long jump back to Oakland. Ward told us he would carry a stock company, the following season, up to the Clunie Theatre in Sacramento.

It was, to me, like one of the balloon ascensions that were so popular in those days. I had been lifted above the clouds, to be dropped again. There was little chance of my being taken to Sacramento — poor actor, as Ward seemed to think me.

During the last two weeks, we watched one another with troubled eyes. We knew many had been called but few would be chosen. To me, if Ward dropped me from the payroll, it meant once more San Jose, and the bitterness of defeat. It meant being given another chance by the family, and probably a return to the gallery. It meant heartbreak to myself, and to Jennie, who was counting on this last chance.

Scarlet fever saved me.

I didn't have it, but little Bessie and baby Lloyd did, both of them. The little brown home on Santa Teresa street in San Jose was under quarantine, and Jennie and the aunts were nursing day and night. Then the Ward company came to Oakland and closed in the old Oakland theatre. Before we closed, the two children were declared well but that was the very day Jennie was taken down.

She was dangerously ill, worn out with the long nights of watching. They telegraphed me, and I thought she was dying, and with tears in my voice, begged Ward to pay me off and let me go home. Ward was broke. He wasn't able to pay me, or any of his actors. And all he could give me was my fare from Oakland to San Jose — two dollars and a half — and a quarter extra. I would arrive home with twenty-five cents!

"Tell you what I'll do, Bacon," he said, wretched as I was when he saw my despair. "Come to me in Sacramento when your wife gets well, and if she can act, I'll give the pair of you work in the new company I'm starting there in September. Forty a week for the two of you . . ."

That was the golden news I could impart to Jennie, when at last the fever had left her and she could sit up and smile at me. Ward had hired the two of us! September was only a summer away, and then we would start in on our first stock engagement, together! And forty dollars a week between us!

In the meantime I lived ignominiously in the aunts' home, without any money save my twenty-five cents. That was all the money I had all summer. For I could find no work in San Jose. And I was glad to escape with Jennie at the summer's end, and join Ward in Sacramento.

144

It was glorious to play a city we had skirted so cautiously in our barnstorming days. Sacramento is the capitol of California, and an honor to play. Jennie and I found a small furnished rooom at "Seventh" and "I" streets. We were alone and gypsying again, for the children were with the aunts in San Jose. We were happy. We had this room and the use of a kitchen, where we cooked on a coal oil stove, and for all we paid seven dollars a month.

Then there was the joy of arriving at the theatre together, our theatre, the Clunie! Ward was to open with all his old successes and play the repertoire through. He began with "Shamus O'Brien."

I was given the comic soldier part and was greatly pleased. But Jennie came home after the opening rehearsal close to tears. She had been given her first character role! It was like the discovery of the first gray hair.

"Making up like that makes me feel like an old woman!" she said unsteadily over the oil stove.

This was in September, 1892.

As the weeks went by in Sacramento and we played on at the Clunie, I became aware of a wonderful thing. Ward was beginning to notice me. He was giving me better parts. Suddenly it came home to me — Ward liked my acting at last!

CHAPTER FOURTEEN

A COMPANY NAMED FOR ME!

Jimmy Ward was growing old, and how he hated learning a new part! And as the months went by and we continued to play with a fair success in Sacramento, he began giving any new parts of his, to me.

That pleased both of us. Slowly I became known in Sacramento. And I learned to love the applause that greets a known local favorite each evening — music to the stock actor's ears!

It seemed to me I had arrived! What more could I ask for? Jennie and I were making forty a week between us — think of that! Nothing I have made since has looked so large. We did wonders with that salary. No matter what happened, we sent home ten dollars every week to Auntie Em in San Jose. That was for Lloyd and little Bessie, for Bessie was starting to school and needed a surprising amount of things for such a little bit of a girl.

We lived happily. Seven a month was all we continued to pay for our furnished room, "with the use of the kitchen." And best of all, every week we managed to put by something in the Sacramento bank. We had learned one bitter lesson from the book of the theatre. We knew the treacherous ups and downs of the stage. Someday, we would need every cent we could put by.

And yet, the sunlight lay along my horizon for a time. Ward had introduced me to comedy drama, and it was to be mine ever after. I played straight parts as a rule, but in one play they gave me the Jewish peddler character.

I determined to make the best of it and featured "Uncle Ike," who ran the big pawn shop down on "K" street and was quite a Sacramento character. I bought Jennie's first diamond ring from "Uncle Ike" along about this time — paid one hundred dollars for

146

it out of our forty a week! This ring was to start our fortunes again — but I'll tell you about that later.

There was a song George Hernandez had sung in our barn-storming trip with Russell, "I'm Going to Hang Three Balls Above The Door." It had always been a comic hit and was a parody on an Irish ballad. If it had made a hit in all our seven "paloose states," thought I, it might go in Sacramento, and I sang it while taking off the character of Uncle Ike.

Uncle Ike was tickled by the attention. I suppose he appreciated the advertising it gave him, and he sent word he was sending me a present. The present arrived — it was a trunk — an unredeemed pledge — left in Uncle's by some forlorn actor. Jennie and I delved into it like Aladdin into his treasure chest. What wealth it yielded! There were wigs, the very first wigs we had ever owned, and all of them in fair condition. Black wigs, gray and white and curly and kinky and juvenile wigs! There was a wardrobe! Those I gloated over longest and wore the most were on old patchwork vest, a bob-tailed coat and an ancient dress suit.

The dress suit almost reconciled me to the sad loss of my precious silk high hat on the New Mexican desert. It set me apart among actors as an aristocrat. Only one other man in the company boasted his own dress suit. If we needed one for a part we had to send all the way down the river to the costumer in San Francisco, and in the meantime pray that it would fit. But with a dress suit of my own, as we used to say, I felt I could neither borrow nor lend.

I did lend it, however. I guess dress suits and silk hats aren't in my line. The minute I try anything fancy I get into trouble, and it wasn't long before one of the boys in our company was called for an out-of-town part. He had to have a dress suit immediately or lose the part. And as he would be away from Sacramento only a few days, of course I loaned him my cherished costume.

Over a month went by, and still he hadn't sent it back. But I trusted him — besides, I didn't need it. We had been playing a lot of costume bills. But finally Ward got hold of a play that called for a dress suit, and I set forth hastily to recover mine. I knew the private family where my friend had been boarding, and I hurried to them.

"Is Splivins back from his trip?" I demanded of the landlady, being accustomed to the race and knowing I must talk fast. "I'm Frank Bacon of the Clunie — I loaned him my full dress suit a month ago. Do you know where it is? Can you get it for me?"

147

"Don't believe I can," she said thoughtfully, as if solving a problem.

Her slowness provoked me. I spoke sharply.

"And why can't you?" I demanded.

"Because," she replied, and hesitated, "we buried him in it last Monday."

I have said luck shifts on the stage. The star of today is the extra tomorrow. Now something happened that hurt me cruelly at the time. But somewhere or other I've heard a verse that runs something like this:

"To those who held me cheaply,
To those of harshest touch,
Because they hurt me deeply,
Because — they taught me much!"

And so it has always been, for my disappointments and my failures have taught me much. And one of my greatest lessons came this first season in Sacramento.

From my good parts, I was switched to playing a "bit."

It came about in a natural way. Ward decided to put on a play written by a young Sacramento attorney, Judson Brusie. Brusie, being a young fellow with political leanings, called his play "The Assembly Man." Brusie himself would play in the cast, and also his talented sister, which would make a big hit with the Sacramento folk and mean high receipts for the Ward Company.

"I'll put your play over with a cr-rrash," Ward promised Brusie.

Big preparations were made by the management. Among other things, they decided a couple of new faces would add to the strength of the company. Two new actors were sent for, both of them having been successes with a former company.

The first actor to arrive was given the script of the "Assembly Man" and told to choose his own part. He selected the one that had my name written after it, and it was given him. When I learned that my good part had been taken from me and I was to play a "bit", I was startled and badly worried. Jennie and I studied the "bit" lines together, and we both felt badly about the matter. It seemed like a "come-down."

"Jennie," I said, grievingly, "even if it is a bit, I'm going to give it all I have!"

And the part wasn't without its opportunity. It was "Rube" stuff. The character was an old, lazy fellow with endearing ways and Jennie looked up at me suddenly over the script.

"Why, it's like your Uncle Morris!" she exclaimed.

As I read the part, Uncle Morris came between the lines. Certainly, it was mother's brother from Marysville! I remembered how he had been disapproved of — and yet loved! I recalled his droll, whimsical ways. His talent for getting out of any small house chores mother expected of him. His tales of what he had been, and said, and accomplished. His appealing, innocent vanity, and his habit of carrying about any small sticks that looked whittlesome. . . .

"I'm going to play Uncle Morris!" said I.

That was my first old man character. This rube role was the ancestor of "Lightnin' Bill."

I put every bit of Uncle Morris into the thing I could remember, because I didn't want to disappoint those friends "out front" who had clapped at my first appearance for so many moons. And I think it always pays to work our hardest with any little material we have. Because after the performance Judson Brusie came up to me.

"I'm going to write a play for you, Bacon," he declared, enthusiastically. "It's going to be an old man part, droll and Rube-ish and yet appealing."

And what is more, Brusie started to work on that play at once. But before it was written, many things happened to me.

Shortly after, the show broke up for the summer, and Ward was not to return to Sacramento. However, the company would remain there, for Ward was not the owner, you understand, but the star. Jennie and I were to return to the Clunie for the winter season of 1893, and we did, after a short and pleasant vacation with the children and the aunts in San Jose.

This marked the year's end in Sacramento for us, and of course I had to start something else. This season, being without Ward, the Company was to play visiting stars. The first stars to join us as the company's attraction were D. K. Higgins and his wife, Georgie Waldron.

They had come west on a starring engagement at the Old Grand Opera House in San Francisco. From there, they came to us in Sacramento, and opened our season with three plays written by Higgins, for he was an author as well as a star. His plays were "Kidnapped," "Vendetta," and "Burr Oaks."

"Kidnapped" was simply too grand a drama for words. It had wonderful printing, and we played it with a real hack and two live horses, on the stage! Only, sometimes we couldn't get two horses and had one!

149

I knew these plays were good. My business instincts rose — also. I guess it was the fact that my cycle of one year was over. Whether in drama, photography or the newspaper game, at the year's end I had to make some sort of a change.

"Let's you and I start a stock company of our own!" I suggested to Higgins when his engagement was over at the Clunie.

Well, we did it.

I told you of buying Jennie's first diamond ring from Uncle Ike. I took it back to his shop now, and he returned the one hundred dollars I had paid for it. And I borrowed my customary two hundred and fifty dollars from my brother-in-law, Horace Keesling, back in San Jose. With these funds, I joined forces with Higgins.

We founded the Higgins-Waldron company, named in honor of our stars. I was manager and advance man and would share the profits with Higgins. Miss Waldron and Jennie were to get five dollars a week and expenses. We hired six other actors at "fifteen a week and cakes," meaning, they were to get their board as well as the fifteen a week.

There were ten in the company. We went down to Oakland, across the bay from San Francisco, and rented the People's Theatre. I had played there before, at the close of my first unhappy season with Ward.

We would open our season at the People's, and the Theatre would build the sets for our plays. Afterward, we could buy these productions, and that meant a big saving to our small but select company.

I repeat — select! For Higgins was a seasoned player who had made many eastern tours, and he knew how to judge acting material. We were one of the best companies ever on the coast, all young, burning with ambition.

Guess who was general stage manager!

Joe Muller, who had cursed me on that fatal trip down to Santa Barbara, when I had been advance agent for Ward. Joe's fortunes were also "on the rise."

We did not "knock 'em dead" in Oakland, but we did come out of that city with a little extra money. And I had the company booked down the coast to the Burbank Theatre in Los Angeles, and there we played one solid month.

That month was the glory of our lives. Every week Jennie could proudly watch me seal the home letter that contained money for the children. We didn't miss a week. And that month proved we could remain some time in a city and not wear it out.

"Let's not tour any more," suggested Higgins, who hated the rapid road jumps. "Let's go back to Sacramento and stay there."

The Higgins-Waldron Company returned to Sacramento in one long leap. And there we played stock through the entire season of 1894. New blood joined our group as old actors drifted away, but the company we had created lived on.

And George Webster came to us! George Webster, whom I had idolized in my San Jose youth, as a young shepherd of the hills might worship Orion. And here he was, leading man in my own company, and life was like that — quick with changes and miracles! He joined us to star in his two favorites, "Bottom of the Sea," and "Under the Polar Star." He remained to play leads, Higgins and his wife being the recognized stars.

Higgins was always using his brain. He was ambitious as a playwright, even more than as an actor. During this season in the capitol, he wrote another play and we put it on. That play was "Piny Ridge." It was to make his fortune.

You remember Judson Brusie, the attorney at Sacramento, had promised to write me a play. Well, many make promises but a few keep their word, and Brusie was one of the few. He came to the theatre to see me toward the end of the season.

"Well, I've finished your play," he announced.

Brusie had not neglected politics for art. He was now a member of the State Assembly, which gave him, and incidentally the play, great prestige. Besides, I liked the play.

Perhaps it was crude melodrama, but the star figure was a simple, loveable old farmer, rather of the type of the "bit" in Brusie's first play I had scored in before we went on tour. It gave me another chance to imitate Uncle Morris.

Brusie called his play "The Estate of Hannibal Howe." Years later it was to be written over into my "Hills of California," and serve me well for many years. Jennie and I rewrote it.

"The Estate of Hannibal Howe," was to be put on in San Francisco! This was because of the fact that Brusie had many friends, and many of his friends had influence. Someone secured his play an opening in the "big town."

Walter Morosco was operating a stock company just then in the old Grand Opera House at Third and Mission streets in San Francisco. That was a magnificent place in my eyes, with a gorgeous stage where the operas sang when in town. "Hannibal Howe" would be presented on that stage.

151

And I would play in the Grand Opera House, as visiting star!

This was my first appearance in San Francisco, a city held fast by all Coast Defender's dreams. It seemed the Great Chance had been given me. I felt, at last, I had arrived.

And yet, my salary was only forty dollars a week!

First night was gala. The fact that a State Assemblyman had written the play made its production an event. There was Governor James Budd, seated in one box with all his staff! There were the front rows impressively filled with gentlemen of the Legislature and the Assembly. Every county was represented there behind a frost-white shirt front. The moment I set foot before the lights, I knew success was sure. The politician-playwright, Brusie, was called upon. I was cheered as star. It was the warmest, heartiest audience I had ever known.

Jennie and I had maintained a habit, from the very beginning of our lives together, of celebrating all our small triumphs. I celebrated now — took my magnificent salary for the week and blew the whole forty dollars for a front page picture in "Music and Drama."

"Music and Drama" was the only theatrical paper on the Pacific Coast. When my picture came out in it, every friend I had ever met on the road, it seemed, wrote or wired to congratulate me. Publicity does that to a man. For this entire San Francisco week, I tasted the wholesome sweets of success.

But fame must be eternally fed, in the theatrical world. An actor's past is known but to himself. It is not "What have you been?" It is, "What are you today?" I found that out when I returned to the prosaic triumphs of my own company in Sacramento, with the glory forgotten and hard work ahead.

"The Estate of Hannibal Howe," was shelved for a time. Directly after my return to the company, we left Sacramento for the road. We had remained beyond our time in Sacramento.

The road was hard to face after the easy quiet of a long run. Trouble took the trail with the Higgins-Waldron company, and camped with us through the small cities and towns. Our company had grown too large to carry easily on the road. Expenses were heavy. Higgins and I knew, before long, that the breaking-up must come.

We were playing in Santa Rosa, a beautiful small city not far north of San Francisco. It was not a show city, where companies were concerned. One night I turned from the wings where I was watching a frail line of theatre-goers trailing in and I said to Higgins:

"Higgins, we might as well close in Santa Rosa."

152

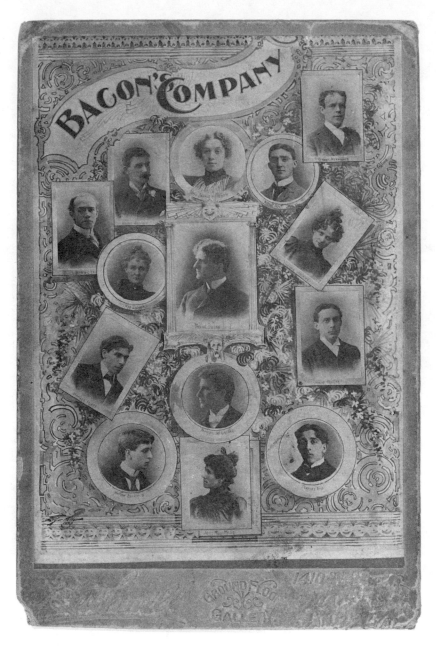

A publicity card for Frank Bacon's Company, c. 1895.

Frank as a young man. Photographed in San Francisco.

Closing the show!

Every actor knows the heartbreak in that line. We who had played two years together, quarreled and made friends and loved and hated, become intimate as people can, who suffer the discomforts of travel together — were to scatter like dust before the wind. "You to the left and I to the right." That hurts! It was like the breaking up of a large family. Our last week in Santa Rosa was sad for the Higgins-Waldron.

We were playing the last matinee of our last stand on Saturday. To lighten our hearts, we played at "hokum," tangled up one another's lines, slipped cues to puzzle the players, played jokes throughout the play. In the midst of this nonsense, which is great fun for the actors but deeply resented as a rule, by the puzzled audience, a telegram came back stage for me.

It was from Pop Russell! What flooding memories swept me as I stared at the yellow slip. Pop and the five members of the Russell Company, snows of Colorado and Arizona sun, dying cattle and yellowing sage, small town people applauding on hard wood benches, and our little Bessie leading the barnstormers home! I laughed till the tears wet my cheeks.

Pop was prospering now. He had the Third Avenue Theatre in Seattle, Washington. He wired:

"Saw your picture Music and Drama . . .
Can you bring company to Seattle at once . . . answer."

"What a shame we can't make it!" I exclaimed, showing the wire to Higgins when he came off stage.

"What's against it?" he answered.

"Because we haven't enough money to hold this show together. Because we're breaking up as it is. Because we couldn't raise enough for our fares . . ."

But Higgins, as I have told you, was a seasoned showman.

"Wire Russell for advance transportation and to lift paper," he ordered.

"Lift paper" being paper we would order from the East, to be sent out C.O.D. to Pop, as local manager. He would "lift" it for us, as we had no money.

I sent the wire, but with little hope. Faithful old Pop wired back instantly, and the telegram was in my hands before our show opened that night:

"How many fares . . . How much paper?"

153

Two days later the Higgins-Waldron company was off for Seattle!

There were fifteen of us who went up the gangplank of the boat at San Francisco, and sailed through the Golden Gate, bound for Washington state. The fact that we were all together, after the gloom of threatened parting, made us gayer than usual, and actors are usually gay. Maybe it wasn't a treat to see Pop Russell again, the old sinner! He was wearing a new watch chain, the plated one had gone with poorer days. Pop was enjoying one of his rare spells of fortune. They never lasted.

We arrived just in time for one of Pop's usual shifts of luck. This was in the summer of 1895.

Afternoons and evenings the Seattle parks were thronged with people, for the parks were beautiful and cool in this summer weather. And every park was running some sort of a show! You can imagine the chance we had, cooped up in the Third Avenue Theatre. People simply would not come in. Before our first Saturday came, we knew we had to leave Seattle.

It was no use trying to stick for Pop's sake. We weren't helping him any. Higgins and Miss Waldron and Jennie and Joe Muller and I talked it over, and decided on Portland.

At the end of our third week, we left. We bundled the company onto the train and fled down the coast to Portland. There we found shelter in Cordray's Theatre. We felt secure. And we were right, for that old house proved a sanctuary to us for nine long months.

For some time I knew Higgins and his wife were getting restless. I expected them to leave any time, and they did, at the end of our fifth Portland month. Ambition carried them, with their play "Piny Ridge," to New York, where the play made them wealthy and famous. That was how, overnight, I found myself in Portland with a company on my hands.

"The Bacon Stock Company!" The Higgins-Waldron company selected its new name from mine. Suddenly I realized to the full the woes of a manager who has a dozen people and their futures resting on his shoulders. San Jose had never seemed so far away. It was up to me to carry this company through.

But I didn't worry about it. Jennie and I were living at the Plaza Hotel, which was then a quiet family place. All the company lived there. We lived quietly and simply, as we always had, and spent very little — we had little to spend — and sent home what little we could. That little grew smaller week by week, as we played on in Portland.

154

We put on new plays and old, and they were always well attended. It was a "supporting" success we were having, not a howling one. The months passed and it seemed the city never would tire of us. We had a faithful audience that returned for every change of program.

A traveling show came to Portland and needed Cordray's Theatre. I let them have it for a short time. Not to lose any money, I took my stage family on a short tour, which would relieve the monotony and mean a certain reaping of shekels. I booked them first for the little port town of Astoria, Oregon. It lies at the mouth of the Columbia River, and then, I imagine, contained some three or four thousand souls.

Astoria's main industry, as our noses informed us when within twenty miles of the place, was fish canning. And we arrived in the very height of the canning season.

"Salmon are as good as cash here," the local manager took pains to inform me when we entered his theatre, "So if any fellow offers you a fish for a ticket, take it. You can sell fish at a dollar each at any of the canneries."

That seemed fair enough, for we knew money was scarce in Astoria. We put out the announcement that fish would be taken at the box office: One salmon for one seat!

We hoped to entice all the cannery workers to our show. We did.

We took turns in the box office with a large crate beside us to hold the salmon, had the orchestra run off a few scales and watched the fish come in. I never saw so many fish at one time and came out after my turn at the crate smelling pleasantly like the school boy Saturdays I had spent with a line and willow pole on the shores of Coyote Creek in San Jose.

All that afternoon we gathered in the glittering salmon. There was certainly more fish than dollars in northern Oregon. But it was when Joe and I carried our full fish crate to the nearest cannery, that we learned something new about human nature.

Most of our fish were worthless! It seems that the Pacific Ocean salmon is worth a dollar, but it has a poverty-struck and non-union relation known as the dog salmon. The "Dog" is worth absolutely nothing. Many of our patrons of the drama had wrung in this tramp variety on the visiting innocents.

155

After our good fish were sold, after we counted up that night, we found we had taken in only twenty-nine dollars for our night's work in Astoria.

But we were not through with the fishing industry. From Astoria we went up the coast a short distance to Aberdeen, Washington, across the line. We found that the Bacon Stock Company was booked to play there in a theatre built over a creek that empties into the Sound.

Then we had an enchanting stay, mixing sport with drama, for in every dressing room, and in the orchestra pit, were knot holes of a huge width. We dropped baited lines through these, and fished blissfully.

We finished during rehearsals, interrupting the work with cries of "Wait a minute — gotta bite!" We fished between the afternoon and evening shows. The actors fished while slapping on make-up, and the musicians fished in the pit between "turns." If the violin stopped suddenly during a musical rendition, you might know the violinist had a nibble.

I stood in the back of the house watching the show one night when a terrific commotion started down front. At first I thought it was a fire or a riot. The audience were standing on their seats, the orchestra was demoralized, and even the actors were poking their heads around the proscenium. I raced down the center aisle and slid under the railing into the orchestra pit.

The drummer was guilty. He had been fishing through a knot hole directly under his music stand and caught a fish too big for the opening. He couldn't get it through. He wouldn't let it go. Just then the comedian came on the stage, and was going to do a funny fall and needed the drum to "bump his drop."

"Drop that line!" I hissed.

The drummer's excited and woebegone face turned up to mine, but he clung to his line. I grabbed the drum stick, I was angry. In a flash he let go the line, and it vanished through the floor. The show went on while a saddened drummer played.

156

CHAPTER FIFTEEN

OUR COURAGEOUS COMEDIAN

We were not out on the road very long. I hurried my company back to Portland, to close the season there. Closing night was a jubilee, for we had given a banner run of sixty performances at Cordray's Theatre! That was a record for those days, and for Portland. I felt as I did, not long ago, when we closed *Lightnin'* in New York, after its world record run of three years and a day!

I had some very special programs printed for the closing performance. Everyone in the company had plenty of curtain calls, for everyone had made friends during the long run, and there were great bunches of flowers handed across the footlights for the leading lady and for Jennie, and a few farewell cheers for me. We were very happy, and a little sad at leaving Portland, even if we were hurrying home.

It was a long time since we had seen San Jose! Nothing had changed in the old town or in the little house on Santa Teresa we called home. Only Bessie had grown taller and important with school affairs and Lloyd was attending kindergarten. Our two families were reconciled at last to the stage—or almost. It was paying as well as photography, admitted father!

Then we played Oakland. And on this jump down from Portland we lost George Webster. He was a real loss. George had played with William Brady before he came to the Bacon Company. Now he heard from Brady, who had the Australian Company of De Maurier's "Trilby" and wanted George. So George sailed away for Australia and we started life anew without him in the old Oakland Theatre, where I had closed, long before, with Ward, and he had been able to give me twenty-five cents against my salary. I had also

157

played the Higgins-Waldron Company at the People's Theatre, and this made my third visit there.

It was a hoodoo house for me.

The People's Theatre was a very old house, down on Thirteenth Street near the depot. People simply would not attend. I don't know why but once a jinx strikes a theatre, it's just as well to turn a few black cats loose in it and nail the doors.

In no week did we make any profit. But in the beginning, at least, I managed to pay every actor's salary. There was little money going home now, and although Oakland is close to San Jose, there were few visits home. The children came up to visit us sometimes — those were great occasions for the four members of the family.

But my company was loyal and stuck through much trouble. That was a good company. Good actors, and good women and men. It wasn't our fault if people refused to be tempted by our offerings. We tried everything, from the comic simplicity of the "Corner Grocery" to the rigorous "Michael Strogoff," with a ballet as added attraction.

"Ballets" in the nineties, were composed of plump young ladies in tights who did fancy marching and formed picturesque groupings after the fashion of "The Black Crook." Even our ballet failed to attract the Oakland public.

And one by one my people fell away for other engagements. I couldn't blame them. An actor must eat, and the Bacon company was dying in its tracks. As they left, I filled the vacancies left with Coast Defenders.

Just as in our barnstorming days, I found my company struggling for life. I had to play all the comedy parts. And I couldn't do that and be manager at the same time, so Joe Muller was promoted. From stage manager, he became company manager and that was a great relief to me. Joe did most of the worrying after that, even if the company was mine.

We went on the commonwealth, as I had put the company with Ward years before. Every night after the show, when the receipts were counted, I divided the money fairly between the actors, the orchestra and the stage hands. Each received a share in proportion to their salary. Only we did not mention salaries. We ate, and no more.

And many a morning Jennie and I waited in the box office for our breakfast until Joe sold a thirty cent seat!

William Sterrett over in San Francisco was our printer, and he thought the Bacon Company had ability, and he believed in me as a man who paid every owed cent when he could. He saved the company these days. Kept on furnishing us with paper and was willing to wait until I could pay. Every once in a while we had a good week and I would be able to pay Sterrett.

And again Jennie and I found the shadow of family disapproval heavy over us and the life we had chosen. For the years were passing and what had we to show for them? And we were not so youthfully careless of disapproval now. We had worked hard but something was wrong.

I tried playing visiting stars — they would furnish their own plays and display paper. But they failed to improve matters out front. The box office reports grew more cheerless. Among the last of my visiting stars was L. R. Stockwell.

"Stocky", as every member of the company was calling him after the first rehearsal, was little and fat and homely and a brilliant comedian. All California knew him, and particularly San Francisco. He had been one of the original lessees of the old Alcazar Theatre. He was the original lawyer Marks in "Uncle Tom's Cabin," on this coast. James Flood, the millionaire, built the original Columbia Theatre for Stocky, at Powell and Eddy Streets. It was first known as the Stockwell Theatre.

But Stocky had played in a run of black luck that comes sooner or later to all who woo the stage. He lost the management of the Stockwell Theatre through financial reverses.

At last he crossed the bay to star for me.

I starred him in his three best plays, "Mr. Potter of Texas," "Uncle Tom's Cabin," and "The Magistrate," by Pinero. For many years he had been able to insure success as Marks in "Uncle Tom," but I liked him best as Mr. Posket in "The Magistrate."

"It's your big characterization, Stocky," I assured him.

I was as sure of that play creating a furor in Oakland, as that I was alive. And it failed!

"Frank, why don't you take me out with your show?" suggested Stockwell.

It was the best thing I could do, although Jennie and I dreaded the road again. But Stocky knew his Coast, and his theatrical affiliations had always been of the very first order. So I put his illustrious name at the head of our little company and we deserted unlucky Oakland.

Everywhere, we secured the very best bookings. The tour promised well enough. Portland was our first stand, the dear old town where the Bacon Stock Company had first seen the light, and lived to make its record run of sixty shows. It had been kind to us then. It was kind now.

We played three weeks in Portland. Not only did we pay all our salaries during that time — which had seemed beyond hope itself — but we also paid up our printing bills and other debts. That three weeks was a happier period than any Elinor Glen would endorse later.

For closing week, we got up the comedy "Humbug." It had been played originally by Roland Reed. That went well, and we decided to keep "Humbug" with us on the road. From Portland we jumped to Seattle.

Again Jennie and I had trekked the coast line.

We played Seattle two weeks, changing the bill twice weekly. Our final week's bill there was to be our triumph. It was "Shadows of a Great City."

Stockwell had originated the part of Jimmie Farren in this play. It was one of his famous characters. On our first night the snow fell, but the house was filled just the same. It looked like a lucky ending for the last week.

The company left the theatre in groups of two or three, scuttling through the snow for the shelter of the hotel. Stocky came out alone, slipped in the white icy drift and fell headlong. His hip struck on a cleat in the wooden sidewalk. Somehow, we got him to the hotel.

"He won't be able to walk for two weeks," said the doctor we had called in. "His hip is badly sprained."

That was calamity to the company. But I put one of the boys in the Jimmie Farren part and we finished that week's engagement. The doctor we had brought in insisted that Stocky be left under his care, and anyhow, our little comedian could not go on. We hated leaving him in Seattle.

But we left without Stocky. We could not afford delay. We played through the smaller Washington towns, and everywhere we announced that the famous star, L. R. Stockwell, had been injured but a substitute would play. Sometimes this was well received — sometimes not. But we lived on the doctor's promise that Stocky would rejoin us in two weeks.

It was hard sledding without Stocky. Salaries became uncertain again. Our destiny looked gray as the Washington skies that winter.

We came into the little town of Coeur D'Alene, in the heavy dusk of a miserable winter's evening. The manager of the local theatre met us at the train. He wanted to speak personally with the manager of the Stockwell Company.

"I hear Stockwell himself is sick!—well, and what are you going to have for a trick tonight?" he demanded, almost hysterically.

He was a fussy little fellow, and was ready to burst into tears when I explained that without Stockwell, we could not play the promised "Mr. Potter of Texas."

"So we'll give them 'Humbug'," I added.

"No siree!" he fumed. "You can't humbug my people, no siree!"

"It's a play!" I said, with more emphasis than I ever gave three words in my life.

And in another Washington town we were all made up and ready for the curtain when the Constable came back stage. And he wanted to see me. I met him with dread, feeling he was going to demand the usual five or six dollar town license. And I had no money.

"Say, where is that Mr. Potter of Texas? I want to collect the license from him!"

"That's a play," I explained once again, wearily. "We're playing 'Humbug' instead, tonight."

He seemed disappointed in not meeting Mr. Potter, whom he had heard so much about! But he accepted the "Humbug" seats I timidly offered and forgot to mention the license again. Our days were growing sadder and our receipts shorter. We prayed for Stocky's return.

Stocky met us at last in Spokane.

We turned out en masse, every member of the Stockwell Company, to welcome our star back to the family. But our last hope died as he came bravely from the train. Stocky came to us wretchedly weak and on crutches—our star! And he was too weak from the journey to go on that night.

But we had announced him!

The manager of the Spokane theatre refused point blank to open his house that night unless the promised Stockwell played. Stocky could not play, and the manager coldly turned back several hundred dollars of reserved seat sales.

"Never mind, folks, I'll play tomorrow night," promised Stocky bravely.

And he did go on next night—brave little soldier that he was, for Stocky had been a drummer boy in the Civil War. Played the part on crutches, the long, strenuously funny role of the Magistrate, while on and off stage we watched him anxiously. I know all our hearts

161

ached for him as we would hear his full, comical voice falter and saw his face grow lined with pain through the make-up. But it was, "Sing, Pagliacci!" How our audience applauded! They did not know of the scene off stage when we carried Stocky to his dressing room after the last curtain.

This couldn't go on. I called the company together. Every one of us put every cent we had together for Stocky. Then we called in the leading surgeons of Spokane. Their verdict was dreadful.

"Not a sprain—but a fracture!"

Worst of all, the fracture had grown together during Stocky's short rest in Seattle, and one of his legs was left shorter than the other by several inches. That leg, the doctors said, would have to be rebroken if Stocky was ever to play his parts again as of old.

We gathered around his bed in the hotel room. He lay—our Stocky—propped on the pillows and trying to smile, a picture of sturdiness and woe. The Stockwell Company were there in judgment on his future and theirs—a jury of twelve actors.

"Well, we have to send Stocky back to San Francisco," said Jennie, firmly. "Treatment and rest…"

Stocky saved us, gave courage to the mournful group.

"Why don't you give me a benefit?" he suggested bravely from the pillows.

The idea took us by storm. Of course—a benefit! But what play should we give? In Stocky's trunk were many manuscripts and under his eye we read them over. One was the script for Romeo and Juliet, for Stocky had produced it once in San Francisco. And our leading lady, Kate Dalgleish, was born to play Juliet.

The manager of the Spokane Theatre proved to have a good heart, after all. He donated the theatre and its working crew. I chose the parts carefully, and really, that benefit was worth seeing. Spokane thought so, at any rate. The result was, we saw Stocky on his way to San Francisco and recovery.

But the momentum of the final grade had overtaken our poor little comedian. Stockwell was one of the finest on the Coast—his end was among the saddest. Fate wasn't content with taking away his theatre, his career. He never recovered from this accident. And a few years later he went totally blind.

Stocky did not go to San Francisco alone. My people were leaving the sinking ship. Without our star, what had we to hope for? I was up against a blank wall with twelve people looking to me for salvation. Within a few days, only seven were left of the company.

Norval McGregor, our leading man, went with Stocky to act as nurse. Two others went along—to act as substitute nurses, I suppose. They were wise. When might I again be able to give them return passage home?

And here Joe Muller left me; that was a severer blow than the loss of the leading man. Joe was later to return triumphantly to Spokane as manager of the Orpheum Theatre, where he is managing the Palace-Hippodrome today, but then he was glad to take what little money I could give him and escape.

I was left in Seattle with seven people on my hands, even as in barnstorming days.

That is the luck of the theatre. History, someone has said, is made by the clatter of wooden sabots going up the stairs, and the rustle of silken shoes coming down. The stage is like that. Many an actor has played at star and supe in the same season. I had started out gladly enough with Stockwell. Now I was lost in the cold northwest.

There was a temporary sort of structure in Spokane that called itself a theatre. One of its owners was John Considine, who later formed the Sullivan-Considine vaudeville circuit with "Big Tim" Sullivan, the political boss. Jennie and I were to play over his circuit, years later.

I took another toss with luck and opened in that theatre. A stock company had the house before me. I promised two bills a week. That meant hard work under any circumstances. It was slavery to us for—we were only seven!

But the seven members of the company, with one exception, were eager for this last chance to earn their passage home. The exception being our leading lady, for she held out for fifty dollars a week guarantee of salary. That was a dreadful obstacle, but I was helpless. Finally, I arranged to have the theatre take out her salary every night. The rest of us would share what was left. And believe me, usually there was very little left.

She had a friend, who had just closed as leading man for Madame Modjeska in San Francisco, and as business went from bad to worse with us, she suggested I send for him. He was willing to pay his own fare to Spokane. That settled it. We needed new blood in the company.

He arrived at last. And for his opening play, what did he select but "Romeo and Juliet!" The rest of us took stage fright at the thought. He was firm.

163

To play that historic love drama again in Spokane, and not as a benefit, took a mad courage. There was no kind management to donate the theatre now, nor a sympathetic public to attend. We were playing in a jinx house with a small band of desperate actors.

But fast in our hearts was the hunger for home. For that we would try anything once, even "Romeo and Juliet." And also, if by a miracle, the Shakespearean classic pleased Spokane, we might even take it on tour and in time work our way down the Coast. Also, how far it seemed from Washington to California, although only Oregon lay between!

I don't know how I scraped together enough money to rent our medieval costumes. We knew our parts from Stockwell's benefit, so opening night was not delayed. All that week we played "Romeo and Juliet" and did the best business in months.

On the strength of that week, solely, I managed to book our little company over the Oregon Short Line toward Portland. Once in Portland, I would breathe easily. That had always been a promised city to us. It was always our first lucky stop north of home.

Only, we would not play "Romeo and Juliet" on the road. That was too big an undertaking, considering the costumes we would have to purchase, for we could never rent them in the towns we were to make. Instead, we would offer "Humbug" and "Mr. Potter of Texas," in faithful rotation. They were easier, and were also "straight" plays, no costumes necessary for them.

But oh, how long the distance was to be between Spokane and San Jose!

Setting out on our zigzag route, we crossed the Idaho line long enough to play Moscow. I shall always remember Moscow as the dreariest town on earth. I never corrected this impression of mine as I was never to see the place again, but Jennie did. She returned to Moscow in 1907 with Bessie, grown and married, and Bessie's first husband, Wilfred Rogers. Wilfred's promising career was to be lost in his early and tragic death, but at this time he had just scored a great hit as Herod in "Salome," in San Francisco. He took the show on the road, where it was not appreciated by the small towns, being too sophisticated. Jennie, accompanying them, wrote back to me that Moscow had greatly improved and the State University was established there. I was playing at the Colonial in San Francisco during this short separation—one of the few Jennie and I have undergone in our careers.

164

Moscow was imbedded in a sort of trough formed by the Rockies, where the winds howled like wolves gone mad. The snows were melting, and we jolted up from the depot in the town carry-all, gazing out upon a dreary street fringed with single-story buildings. The wheels of the lumbering vehicle sank in black, cozy mud to the hubs.

"Looks like a no-business town," I remarked to Jennie, as we passed the town "Opr'y."

The opr'y was also a small, one-story affair. We stared at it from the hotel window, through a hazy slant of gray rain. This was a sad town to enter in dead of winter.

My "no-business" theory proved correct. The bitter hour came when I was obliged to draw our landlord aside and explain to him, with as much sangfroid as I could command, that he would have to send his bill on to our next town for collection. With his disapproval ringing in my ears, we escaped from Moscow and re-crossed the Oregon line.

Dayton, Oregon, was our next stand. There our leads went on strike.

"We do our best work in 'Romeo and Juliet'", protested they. "And we either play that—or nothing!"

"In that case," I returned with equal firmness, realizing that discipline must be maintained, "we play 'Romeo and Juliet!'"

The lights of home were growing fainter in my eyes!

"And where can we get our costumers?" demanded Jennie, scoffingly.

Aye, that was the rub! In Spokane there had been a costumer from whom we had rented the clothes. In Dayton there was not so much as a hauberk, and who had heard mention of a ruff!

"We can make our own costumes," replied the leading lady.

"We can not!" replied Jennie with much asperity.

Right there the ladies divided. Helen Hendry, our pretty little ingenue, sided with Jennie. They became the left wing, or radicals, who refused to take the creation of costumes seriously. And there was high temper in the company, for as our two leads demanded that "Romeo and Juliet" be played, there was nothing to do but sew.

And now we were no longer a theatrical company, but a sewing circle. Every man and woman in the cast found a needle and thread and perhaps a thimble, and how we sewed! We sat and stitched and fitted during the rehearsal. This of course, was kept a dark secret from Dayton! It would never do to let that town know we were making our own outfits.

The leading man, who was rather magnificent in the matter of apparel, was the possessor of five pair of tights! He divided these treasures among the men of the company. Juliet had a costume of her own. She helped the others design theirs, and contributed toward the costumes for Lady Capulet and the Nurse. Little Helen, who was essentially an ingenue, tiny and dainty and youthful, had to play Lady Capulet. And to tell the truth, she was years younger than her stage daughter.

But every other costume had to be made, and for twelve hours we were frantically busy. The trunks were rummaged, and every scrap of ribbon, lace and bead work was put to use. Helen, the ingenue, happened to possess a white broadcloth opera cape, and to top that, Mrs. Bacon reached down into her trunk and produced a gold lace cap studded with pearls.

We gathered eagerly around this little cap. Once, it had graced the lovely head of Kate Castleton — the Oakland girl who made her fame in New York. She had climaxed her career with the song, "For Goodness Sake, Don't Say I told You So," and died piteously young. While we were playing in Sacramento, word had rippled through the profession that Castleton's mother in Oakland was willing to sell her daughter's finery. Jennie bought all she could afford, forty dollars worth, and paid for it at length at the rate of five dollars a week from her own salary!

Kate Castleton had been noted for her magnificent dress. Jennie bought the first piece of silk crepe either of us had ever seen, two pieces of brocade, two beautiful caps and four pairs of silk stockings. Silk stockings were a luxury then, even to stage people. These were the first I had ever seen upon Jennie, and we simply had to create parts for her in our productions so she might have the glory of wearing them. They were European-made, one of heavily woven silk, embroidered with beaded lizards that ran from calf to toes, and one of the striped weave in pale blue, pink and garnet. Close your eyes one moment please, and recall those Kate Castleton stockings of Jennie's with me!

But then, ladies can always manage to be radiant with little or less, and we males fared less magnificently. I wonder now how we managed the costuming at all. But even the villain was displaying a rare talent for designing before our sewing bee had ended. Much

166

laughter and much competition went on in the little Dayton playhouse, behind locked doors.

Paris found for himself a British soldier coat and made that into a hauberk by adding slashes and pockets of white velvet.

I let Tybalt wear my padded silk smoking jacket and he cleverly covered up the embroidery with velvet.

Benvolio's costume was a blue soldier coat, betrimmed and decorated with what fragments of finery he could find, and the sleeves changed to Venetian style by inserting puffs and lace.

Capulet was tastefully robed in a long dressing gown that had served him well through this cold winter.

I, playing Peter, wore a smock that belonged to the leading man, and a pair of his tights. Friar Lawrence succeeded in unearthing an old Domino someone in the hotel had once worn to a masquerade.

E. J. Blunkall was playing Mercutio. He purchased a gray flannel hunting shirt, and with some scraps of yellow velvet for puffs and a few trimmings made himself the handsomest hauberk in the production. We awarded him the first prize. Let me tell you about Blunkall.

He had come to me when I was taking Stockwell out of Oakland and said he yearned to be an actor. I asked him what his occupation was then. He was driving a milk wagon in San Francisco and making more money than I could promise him. But he persisted in joining our show, and I've always maintained it was the ruin of a very good milkman.

Many years later, "Blunk" was to originate the role of Hammond, in *Lightnin'*.

After twelve hours, we wearily laid our needles down and straightened our sagging spines. Now let the worst happen in Dayton. We were ready to produce "Romeo and Juliet."

CHAPTER SIXTEEN

I JOINED THE ALCAZAR

With such lovely costumes of our own making, we were certain "Romeo and Juliet" would touch the heights that night in Dayton. I even wired on ahead to Walla Walla — we were to open there that Monday night — to announce our opening there would be with the Romeo production. And we gave our first Dayton performance.

Our finery was wasted on that Oregon town. All our hard hours of sewing had been thrown away. Not, of course, that the small audience we played to, knew the history of our "hand" costumes! That was our secret. But the first night was terrible.

Next morning arrived a communication from our last town, Moscow. It was the hotel bill I had been obliged to have sent on. Hopelessly I read the itemized account and put it away until that evening, our second and last in Dayton. That was Saturday night, and worse than the one before.

I reinforced the Moscow hotel bill with our Dayton hotel bill and sent them both on to Walla Walla. There was nothing else I could do. Walla Walla was our only hope. If it failed us, we were stranded again in a snowy land.

We left Dayton early that Sunday morning. The ground was frozen, and our poor faces were frost-bitten before we boarded the single passenger coach that, attached to a freight train, was to carry us to Walla Walla. It was an all day trip.

All day we jolted along between snowy gray drifts, behind those clamorous freights. No, not all of us. Jennie and little Helen — our left wing radicals — had remained over at Dayton for the day, for the landlord had invited them to be his guests. The rest of us went on from a sense of duty. But these two rebels stayed over for a glorious day and arrived late that evening in Walla Walla, without a cent, but perfectly contented, on the passenger train!

The rest of us, being of puritan conscience and willing to suffer, arrived in Walla Walla at seven thirty that night, only a trifle ahead of the two young scapegraces. We were a weary row of martyrs after that day's journey on the freight train, and I was in no forgiving mood, I remember, when Jennie came gaily into the hotel, happy as a child at the end of a successful holiday.

But we were all out by ten next morning, with revolt forgotten and new hope. We were not a crew to accept discouragement. And, at least, we still held possession of the company trunks, few though they were, that held the cherished costumes we ourselves had made. Scenery—we never carried that!

Every theatre we played had at least three standard sets. For "Romeo and Juliet" we fitted the scenes from these, built the balcony ourselves and even rented a small calcium for the moon! And we boldly held to our promise, to play "Romeo and Juliet" that Monday night in Walla Walla.

Back home in San Francisco, Blunkall had been a member of the California National Guards. He became our hero now. Directly after breakfast he hunted up the local military organization and became acquainted with them. He borrowed swords from the Walla Walla warriors for our gallants to use in the play. Surprising how little matters like that help advertise! For that night Tybalt killed Mercutio, and Romeo killed Tybalt, with local steel!

Walla Walla couldn't resist that. Then we proudly strutted our home-made costumes before filled and admiring rows, and even answered curtain calls, and learned that success is never so sweet as after failure. For after our money was counted that night, I had the exquisite pleasure of returning the hotel bills, with cash equivalent, to the hotel men of Moscow and Dayton.

We left Walla Walla with gladdened hearts, and played on through the smaller towns that lead to Portland. We played The Dalles, north of Mt. Hood, opening with Saturday matinee.

We had left our last town too early to eat breakfast, and the train proved to be late. So it was without lunch that our hungry company hurried from the depot to The Dalles show house. While rushing into our costumes for the matinee, we sent "Props" out to find us some sort of nourishment. We were ravenous.

"Props" returned with two pies, all he had been able to find on such short notice. We were in our costumes for the Romeo show by

169

that time, and stood eagerly around while Mercutio cut and served our slices of pie with the tip of his sword. With renewed will power, we were able to go on with the play.

We were willing to put up with anything to get to Portland. We struggled toward that promised city through an agony of small towns and uncomfortable jumps. In Portland, I promised my little group, there would be salvation for all. I smoothed our hard trail with soothing promises of Portland.

At last, wearily, we landed one night in that golden city. My old friend, John Cordray, booked us. We spread our posters, advertised in the papers for one week and opened with such glorious hope!

Within the week, our show closed.

The adventure north was ended. I was stranded as never before, with Jennie and all the company looking toward me to save them. And I was helpless. I hadn't enough money for one fare back to California.

"Try to get back to San Jose, mother," I urged Jennie when our last chance of hope had melted.

She hated to leave me. But she could be no help to me and she was hungry for a glimpse of her children. At last she telegraphed dear old Auntie Em.

And the others were leaving. Our leading man and lady were found missing right after the crash. Helen wired to her home for money and received it just as Jennie received her railroad fare from the Aunt that had never failed us. They left the same day. The others wired to New York for money, and at last went their ways.

But I was not left alone in Portland. Three men were left to me from my scattered company. One was Blunkall, one Eddie Crane, the other was George Osbourne Jr., and all were of San Francisco.

"Well," said Blunkall, gulping down all that was left of his pride, "I guess it's the pig train for us."

Either that, or become public charges in the city of Portland. Neither course appealed to me, but I couldn't worry very much, knowing the women were safe. Jennie was home safe in the little house behind the convent wall, and that was enough to content me.

I went to the manager of the steamship company. I had done much business with this line, carrying actors between San Francisco and Portland. I sat down before him by his prosperously wide desk and told him honestly all my Oregon misfortune.

"Mr. Bacon, I'll be delighted to give you transportation," he interrupted me to say kindly.

170

Lloyd and Bessie Bacon.

Bessie Bacon in costume, play unknown.

Lloyd Bacon in 1910, age 20.

"I'm not asking for it," I told him hurriedly. "And I'm not asking for myself alone. I can't go and leave my boys in Portland. But if you'll carry the four of us home to San Francisco, I'll pay you — with the first money I make."

That night four grateful actors stood on the deck of a south bound steamer and watched the lights of Portland fade into the dusk over the Willamette River. Eddie Crane stood next to me, leaning over the rail, and perhaps his feelings were strongest of all. For he had joined us in Spokane, having been left stranded there by another company. As the boat turned the first broad angle of the river, Eddie grasped my hand.

"Frank, accept my congratulations," he exclaimed feelingly. "You are the only manager who has been able to return me to San Francisco in four years."

But my thoughts were busy on the short trip down the coast. How was I to repay the manager of this line? Home held no prospects for me. Only the usual bitter returning. The usual family reception would be awarded the homecoming failure. I couldn't understand what shortcoming of mine made me encore my business mistakes. Only one thing was certain, I would have to find work immediately.

I had rescued George Osbourne, now he rescued me. When we left the ship and took the Market streetcar in dear old San Francisco, George led me to the Alcazar Theatre on O'Farrell Street.

The Alcazar holds a brilliantly lighted niche in California theatrical history. For many years it was the best stock show on the coast and great actors' names first saw print on the Alcazar programs.

George Osbourne Sr., was stage director at the Alcazar. The boy introduced us. I caught a late train to San Jose that night, but with no cringing state of mind did I enter the little house on Santa Teresa street. I could look anyone in the face — I had been promised work at the Alcazar.

In this year, 1898, I first played "bits" at the Alcazar.

My Alma Mater. It was a great school, from which I was not to graduate for many years, and in which I can truly say I learned to act.

There were several years of apprenticeship before I became truly a member of the Alcazar group. These years were busy ones, but rather lonely. Jennie remained in San Jose for a time, with the children. I made the forty mile trip, when I felt I could afford it, to see how pretty Bessie was growing in the years, and what a sturdy little bit of manhood Lloyd was getting to be.

171

It was during these Alcazar years that the old watch I carry today acquired most of its honorable scars. These are the scratches of many a San Francisco pawnbroker—I could lift the lid and show them to you now. It's a good watch, and with a fob Jennie had made for me once for Christmas, from a gold nugget her uncle had found in early days in Grass Valley. In the back is a very young picture of Jennie, so very young that folks always think it's of my daughter, and a snapshot of the children.

This watch was to carry me over many a bad period. I always got five dollars for it. Usually I had to borrow another five to redeem the watch. Then I would put it in soak again. In the meantime, I ate.

I played bits in old comedies until the Chinese Classic, "The First Born" was produced. In that I went on among a group of sightseers "doing" Chinatown, not a spectacular part. But the play was a great success, at least. It ran nine or ten weeks, and finally went to London under the management of Charles Frohman, and my friend George Osbourne Jr., with it.

While "The First Born" ran at the Alcazar it was preceded by one act comedies. I was given fair bits in some of these and became hopeful once more. Perhaps I was destined for the stage, after all!

Fred Belasco, brother of the famous David, was manager of the Alcazar then. There I met Mrs. F. M. Bates, mother of Blanche Bates. Once back in our pre-amateur days, we had seen Mrs. Bates in "The Octoroon" in San Jose. Now she was playing character parts.

I worked a year at small parts at the Alcazar and Jennie stayed on in the little house in San Jose. I could not support her in San Francisco. I could not support myself, at times. At the end of the year—mark my magic cycle of the year's end, again—Fred Belasco announced that he was planning to send another stock company to Los Angeles.

This new company would be headed by Juliet Crosby, in private life, Mrs. Belasco. It would play at the Burbank Theatre in Los Angeles.

Of course, there was much gossip in the company, wondering who would be selected. I didn't once think of myself, and I don't suppose anyone else did. But to my astonishment, I was sent with Juliet Crosby and her group to finish up the season in Los Angeles!

George Osbourne Sr., took us down and remained as our stage director for six weeks, just to get us started. Then he returned to San Francisco and the Alcazar. But before he left us, who should

172

arrive in our midst for a starring engagement but the famous Madame Helena Modjeska!

Modjeska is one of California's greatest memories. Auntie Em, I know, had seen her when in 1877 she played "Camille." From '77 on, in the San Jose home, we were doomed to hear of nothing but the beauty and rich acting of the actress from Poland.

She was like an inspiration to the rest of us. I for one, was immensely proud of playing with the great Modjeska. But her presence didn't keep me from indulging in a little of my nonsense when we put on "As You Like It," for charity, in the beautiful garden of the Childs' Home. I think the Los Angeles Examiner building stands there today.

I played William to the Phoebe of Georgie Woodthorpe. I wasn't so good and I knew it. Shakespearean actors are born and I am not marked with the purple. But to Georgie, Shakespeare was a religion, and I could not resist teasing her.

"Art wise, William?" she asked me seriously, and in old English form I was to answer, "Aye, I be wise."

Instead, I winked my eye at her and replied in the rankest vernacular:

"Sure, I'm wise."

Poor Georgie nearly fainted in my arms. I don't think anyone should take anything as seriously as that.

My small impudence was overlooked that afternoon, for the actor cast for the Shepherd arrived with all his lines adrift in a sea of alcoholic fumes. He had been celebrating our big event. Only one thought was left him, to get on the stage and remain there, smiling out vacantly over our large and classic-loving audience.

George Osbourne had not only stage managed the show, he was also playing the role of melancholy Jacques. Through all his lines he had to watch the Shepherd, hiss his words as he forgot them and steer him off and on the scenes. Of course George's own lines suffered — he was really playing two roles. At the end of the performance he was limp.

But George was always gallant, and as he helped the Madame into her carriage, she leaned out to pat his hand.

"Ah, Meester Osbourne, it has been ze hard day for you!" she purred with her fascinating little accent. "You were so verree fine — but, oh, Meester Osbourne, ze poor Shepherd! Vere did you get ze poor Shepherd?"

173

After Madame Modjeska, other stars came to us at the Burbank Theatre. George Webster came again, and we could laugh together over the days when he had been my leading man in Portland. I had been head of my own company then—I would not have returned to that shaky honor. My thirty—what salary then?—a week, steady and certain, was sweeter to me than the power and worry of managerial life.

Webster, just back from his Australian tour, came to us in the Brady play, "Under the Polar Star."

We played this all Fourth of July week, while America celebrated with double meaning, not only the day of Independence, but Dewey's victory in Manila Bay! Our men were battling still at Santiago, and only the week before, a little-known Lieutenant Colonel, known among his Rough Riders as "Teddy" Roosevelt, had led the storming of San Juan Hill. But not until December was the treaty of peace to be signed that ended our war with Spain. In this same memorable July of 1898, the United States annexed Hawaii, but we heard no mention of hulas and ukeleles then. Only, walking homeward from the Burbank Theatre after the show, nights, with Jennie we hummed together the plaintive and popular, "Farewell, my Bluebell."

Yes, Jennie had come down to spend a few summer weeks with me in Los Angeles. She was there when dear old Stockwell came to star with us.

Our comedian hero was limping still from the effects of his fall in Seattle that had wrecked our unlucky company and nearly ruined his career. Stocky was healthy enough, but he walked with a cane and wore a cork sole on one shoe. He was a game sport and willing to joke over our past bad fortunes.

We gave Stocky a tender welcome and Jennie played that week, I remember. Also, she "jobbed" in "Alabama," the play we put on after Stocky left us. Hugo Toland had been a member of the original star cast of this delightful Thomas play and staged our production.

I was given the part of Colonel Moberley in "Alabama." I was in love with the play, and every word came from my own heart. It was the best role I had been given, and again I felt myself creeping up the heights, when the downward slide began.

Jennie returned to San Jose before the final crash. Los Angeles had been kind to us, but destiny laid its firm hand upon the actors. Fred Belasco had sold his interests some months before to John

Fisher, who later was made famous by "Floradora," and Fisher, with the closing of the summer season, disbanded the company.

And there we were, jobless in the southland.

Nearly every emergency finds its hero. Someone had to lead us homeward, and only an actor knows how long a stretch four hundred miles can seem. It was George Webster who stepped forward now to commandeer the outcasts.

"I can organize a company out of this bunch and play it back to San Francisco," he declared. I joined him in the venture, and together we organized the Webster-Bacon Company.

Never have I seen assembled so many actors with a fondness for the flowing bowl. Sometimes it seemed to me I was the only sober man left on earth. It happens I don't drink myself, my mother's stern training never having lost its mark on my moral sense, but I certainly had splendid opportunity to study the drunkard's progress in all its phases on this wild tour home. Perhaps that is where I learned my skill as a stage drunkard. My interviewers seldom fail to mention that I have played more drinking roles than any other actor on the American stage.

At nearly every performance an actor would be missing, or turn up with a fit of the giggles, or a foolish orgy of tears, or perhaps he would refuse to rescue the heroine because he wanted "another li'l drink," until the curtain crashed desperately down.

We played Fresno a solid week. An old San Jose friend of mine, Lloyd Moultrie, our son Lloyd was named for him, had established himself there as an attorney. All that week I kept him busy, for every day at least one of my actors got into some sort of a scrape. Someone asked Moultrie how he was doing that week.

"Takes all my time keeping old friends and actors out of jail," he replied wearily.

Eddie Crane, who acted as property man and stage manager, painted the modest valley town of Fresno with one broad streak of red paint. One night, disgracefully late, I wakened to ribald singing. I got up and looked out of my hotel window down upon a street corner brightened by an old-style arc lamp that was misted around with night bugs. Directly under this lamp in the dusty street Eddie was lying and warbling to the stars.

On our final night, Eddie nearly wrecked the Fresno theatre. We were playing "Michael Strogoff," one of my old favorites. I had seen it on one of my first trips to San Francisco, featuring the famous George Wessels. In one scene Michael had been accused of

175

cowardice. He is in a little telegraph station, facing the enemies, when a bomb is tossed into the room. He takes it in his hands and flings the thing off stage, where it explodes. Then, facing his tormenters, he challenges them:

"Am I a coward now?"

Eddie had charge of the bomb explosion off stage, in a barrel. He wanted to give the audience something to remember, since it was our last Fresno night. He did, and lost his hair and eyebrows and a great deal of his facial appeal in the explosion and extinguished all the house lights as well.

These drinking companions of mine furnished great lessons for me, although I didn't know it at the time. Without realizing it, I noticed and remembered their ways and gestures when under the influence of alcohol. Years later, I would use these mannerisms in roles of my own. Just as I had years before unconsciously studied Uncle Morris and made his character my own in many a play.

The family in San Jose had been singularly silent on the subject of Uncle Morris for some time. I gathered he was in some disgrace, but didn't ask. Chance allowed me to find out for myself.

This was when we played Stockton, after Fresno. Stockton lies on the Sacramento River, north-east of San Francisco, and began as a "rag town" or tent city back in the days of gold. I had not been there since the old Higgins-Waldron days, and wandered down the Main Street to see the changes. In passing a little square, I was attracted to a figure lounging on one of the benches. Something was strangely familiar about it — I paused and looked into the bright eyes under those shaggy brows of Uncle Morris! He didn't seem surprised, nothing on earth could surprise Uncle Morris. Yet he hadn't seen me for years and I wondered that he knew me. There he sat, as I had so often seen him sit in my mother's kitchen in San Jose.

"Been here six months and hain't nobody asked me to carry a stick of kindling," he observed with a twinkle in his eye.

He had come down from Marysville, where he spent most of his time on the old ranch with his sister, to visit some "kin folk" as he called them.

That night I put Uncle Morris in a front row seat for our performance of "Alabama." You may remember my mentioning that I was abnormally proud of my work as Colonel Moberley.

I always spent a great deal of time making up for this part. I considered my small mustache and goatee positive works of art, and my Southern accent, only one generation removed from the real thing, par excellence. Although I don't know what anyone from Houston would have replied to that accent. But it was my favorite role, and somehow I wanted to impress Uncle Morris, who was never impressed by any deeds save those accomplished by his own glowing imagination.

After the show I took him out for a bite at one of the restaurants. It was the end of a full day for Uncle Morris, but he accepted it all with perfect calm. But he did look up with a twisted smile over his pie.

"Frank, you make a right good Frenchman," he admitted.

I was satisfied. That is the first hint of praise I had ever wrung from a relative of Jennie's or mine. Even if Uncle Morris had mistaken the goatee and the accent, I was pleased.

Again I was safely home, without an engagement. But I did not have to hang long around the stage entrance of the Alcazar. I went back to small parts again, playing jobbing engagements. The work was uncertain and without promise. Again my future was clouded.

After a time, Stockwell came back into San Francisco with a proposition. He was going to take Hoyt's play, "The Midnight Bell," on tour. He offered parts to Jennie and me.

Jennie was still down in San Jose. But the children were attending grammar school and Auntie Em could foster mother them, as she had Jennie before them. We didn't have to worry about the children. And Jennie, seeing the years pass while she still lived on in her childhood home, seeing my endless struggle against many odds, and longing to make what money she could, promised to tour with Stocky.

I was willing to go. Then the Alcazar promised that if I would remain, they would give me good parts. So I remained, but the promised roles were not given me. Just before "The Midnight Bell" went on tour, I went to Stocky.

"I'm coming with you," I said.

CHAPTER SEVENTEEN

TOURING WITH TROUBLE

Stockwell looked perfectly blank at my offer to join the "Midnight Bell," show. All the parts had been assigned. Jennie had the role of "Miss Lizzie," a comic old maid, for which she would never forgive Stocky as long as she lived. The only role left open was the heavy, and a wicked heavy at that!

"But can you play a heavy, Frank?" demanded Stocky, dubiously.

"Certainly," I informed him with professional dignity.

Jennie always said I was the worst heavy in the world. The last scene was laid in a church. There I had a sort of fit of remorse for my villainous deeds, confessed and fell as if dead.

The entire cast not on the stage in that act used to stand outside the scenes and have silent hysterics during that part. No matter how I tried, I couldn't help looking behind me for a soft spot before I fell. Then I would sort of droop over, like a melting candle. I never could see why they thought it so funny. Besides, I never did like a part where you have to fall down or do anything undignified.

We started out playing over the same territory we had once struggled over in our green night-hawking days with "Pop" Russell. It was the "paloosa" country again, and yet it seemed different. For we were making fifty dollars a week between us, Jennie and I, and we were reasonably certain of its being regular. Of course, out of this we paid expenses, and sent money home...Sometimes it didn't seem such a large amount, especially when we reached Seattle and Jennie became very ill.

On we played through the middle west, on the longest tour we had ever made to Kansas City. There Jennie was seriously ill. She could hardly speak her lines. Yet she struggled on and off gallantly, and would not give up. There was one scene where, with her old-maid curls flying and streaming bonnet strings, she had to come down a snow slide with Stocky. The audience would roar with laughter, but Jennie would stagger off with her face red and streaming with perspiration after the ordeal.

One afternoon in Kansas City she seemed better and I left her to go to a ball game. While I was gone she had a terrible attack. Stocky's sister put on the chloroform liniment, but it was too strong and seared her flesh. I returned to find Jennie screaming with pain.

"Get her back to California. She can't live three months in this climate," said the doctor we called in.

That night she played, blank with pain. I had to whisper every line to her. I was frightened, and begged her to go home.

She wouldn't. In the first place, there was no money for her fare, and although I knew Stocky would have sold the show for Jennie, she refused to let me borrow. And turning away from Kansas toward sun-warmed Mexico, Jennie grew better.

She recovered completely while we played the beautiful wastes of New Mexico and Arizona. But this taught me the horror of our day-to-day living, with never a cent ahead.

How well we knew the desert land! Every cholla seemed to shake its gray spines at us in recognition. We remembered our stranding in the desert, the hunger and the wretchedness, with the Russell show.

We played Yuma. Our advance man had plastered our square muslin banners all over the sun-baked town by the Colorado. We were proud of these banners. They were white with a blue bell in the center, and around this, red letters announced:

L. R. Stockwell Company
playing
"The Midnight Bell"

When we arrived in Yuma, we found the Indian women had appropriated all our gay banners and were wearing them over their backs, for shawls.

Jennie found herself unexpectedly popular on this Yuma trip. While in Denver, she had bought a bright red crash dress and a "dude" sailor hat. She wore this outfit on the Yuma streets and had a parade of squaws following her.

"Don't go near the hills in that dress," I warned her.

And the heat. Between appearances in that hot, crowded theatre, we dashed outdoors under the yellow desert stars for air.

179

And our big scene was a snow scene, and we appeared in knitted hats, fur coats, mufflers and mittens!

We came in at the end of a complete season. We had played from San Francisco up to Victoria and Vancouver, through Idaho — carefully avoiding Moscow — to Denver and Kansas City, through Colorado, New Mexico and Arizona to Los Angeles. We had come back from this same territory once in complete disgrace, having sent home ten dollars in seven months.

Now we had toured eight months, and not one single week had we missed sending money home!

One cannot live long on past records, not in San Jose, at least. I had to look about for another opportunity, and right away one showed its head. It came from my old friend, Joe Muller.

Joe had done many things since his property man days, and while we had toured with the Bell show, he had been managing a stock company in Oakland. His big success there had been with a comedy, "The Girl from Chili."

"Frank, it's a great comedy!" he assured me. "All we need is a small cast. It has wonderful paper."

"Let's take it on tour, Joe," I said, firing with his enthusiasm.

I didn't see how we could fail. But then, I never do.

We needed money to start the show, and I borrowed $500 from my lawyer friend in Fresno. Joe raised another $500 somewhere, and we were prepared. We made the cast up entirely of Coast Defenders.

At the last moment I got the shock of my career.

"I'm not going, Frank," said Jennie, sweetly, but with a firmness I knew.

She said she was tired of the road. She wanted to be with the children, after our long trip across the middle states. Jennie had learned to distrust the road.

But I suspect her real reason was her last role of old maid with the Bell show. Jennie was still young enough to resent character roles, and that Aunt Lizzie part had hurt!

So I went out alone with the "Girl from Chili." Jennie and I had rarely been separated before, and we were both sorry for the reason. We had seen many hardships together, and yet the time was to come on this tour when I was fiercely glad she was safe in the little house in San Jose. From the start, there was only trouble and financial despair.

Joe and I set out with that show without the faintest notion as to where we were going. Our route lay wherever the theatrical winds listed, and usually they proved evil pilots.

180

We played northward, farther and farther away from home. It was the playing of the gambler who loses and plays on. But Joe and I were both blessed with a sense of the ridiculous. And our hope lay always in the "next stand." All might go wrong in the town we were playing, but we were certain good fortune awaited us in the next. Yet often I felt my shoulders sinking under the task, as if our tribulations were like Job's, too heavy to be borne.

By the way, E. J. Blunkhall was with me again this trip, playing our juvenile lead.

Small and large annoyances turned out to meet "The Girl from Chili." There was Miles City, Montana.

Our Miles City manager had promised our agent an orchestra. We had to have music, for the leading lady and others, had songs. He had made our rehearsal call for three that afternoon and we were in full force at the show house at three.

An asthmatic old piano was standing in the pit, but there were no other instruments. Not even a pianist. We fumed around back stage for an hour and still no musician showed.

"We'll have to get hold of the manager," said Joe.

I went with him. We found the theatre's manager behind his counter, for he also owned the hardware store. We demanded he produce our orchestra.

"We haven't any orchestra!" he replied in complete astonishment. Then he thought it over. "Oh, yes, there's a fellow around here plays the piano, but he's in jail for beating up his wife."

"But don't you see we can't go on without music?" I burst in desperately. "Why, the leading lady has to sing . . ."

But the man's face had changed. He was looking at the Elk emblem Joe wore on his coat.

"Tell you what, the jailer here is an Elk," he informed us brightly. "Maybe if you'd talk to him he'd let the piano player out long enough to play for your show."

Joe and I hurried to the Miles City calaboose, where, sure enough, the jailor appeared with his keys and an Elk emblem.

"You see, someone has to play while the leading lady sings, so that Bacon here can get into the outfit he wears as a woman," explained Joe, with the deep respect one unconsciously gives to jail authorities.

Only because of that Elk tooth did the jailor reluctantly allow the pianist to play for the show. They came to the theatre that night and the leg of the pianist was shackled to the piano leg. Also the jailor sat directly behind him, armed to the teeth, so there seemed little danger of an escape.

After the first act, the jailor leaned over to the chained musician. "How do you like the show?" he demanded.

"Aw, hell," said the prisoner, wearily, "take me back to jail."

Of all the states that treated us harshly that season, Texas was worst. Texas was an endless area populated with the offspring of hardluck. We drifted through the small towns and villages, and I don't recall a single pleasant thing happening to us in all Texas.

In one little town down by the Mexican line, Joe was detained at the depot with the luggage, so I headed the company up the street into the first hotel and reached for the register.

The hardest-visaged Amazon I have met in all my travels was standing behind the desk. As I took the worn book, she covered the page with her outspread hand. Her voice was like a file.

"I don't allow no play actors in my hotel!"

I started to remonstrate with her.

"Young man," she interrupted wickedly, "Don't you multiply no words with me!"

I didn't, but as I led my disgraced crew out of the dingy place, I managed to pass a few casual words from the depths of my heart in regard to "Southern hospitality." There was one other hotel in the town and I marched the crowd in there.

At this hotel, Joe acquired indigestion. There was nothing in the place he could eat, or that any of us should have eaten for that matter. And we had to stay there two days!

Next morning Joe's wife timidly asked the landlady, who also acted as waitress in the shabby dining room, if Joe couldn't have some toast and a poached egg.

The landlady stood balancing the battered tray and thinking it over.

"Seems to me ah have got an egg, somewhere," she said at length.

"Perhaps you had better not disturb it!" suggested Mrs. Muller, hastily.

And we trailed over into Beaumont, Texas, hand in hand with old man Despair. We were booked there for a matinee and a one night performance. The extra matinee was Joe's idea. He rang it in on every one night stand as an extra expedient for keeping heads above water in "The Girl from Chili." And if we ever expected to see home again, we had to make those two shows.

We got to the theatre at noontime to find two stray horses

occupying the lobby. The lobby opened on the street and they had ambled in and taken possession many months before. The whole company, women and all, chased them out. They raced down the main street and back, and in a few moments were in the lobby again.

They seemed possessed. We whooped like cowboys, chasing them out over and over again. They would race between us gaily with flaunting tails and be back in the lobby. They seemed to enjoy being chased.

And what was worse, they had been in possession of the lobby so long that we had to call off the matinee to clean it out. This was a dreadful loss. But it was no time for niceties, and every member of the "Girl from Chili" worked at cleaning out that lobby. For without one show at least, we would not get out of Beaumont. We never did make up for the loss of that matinee.

We drifted back into San Francisco on the ebb tide of the worst run of bad luck any of us had ever seen. We had been gone many months, and Joe and I were each many hundreds of dollars in debt.

"Never mind, Jennie, we'll be sure to make some of it up in San Francisco," I encouraged her upon my homecoming into San Jose.

I really believed it. We arranged to wind up the season at the San Francisco Grand Opera House, and I was certain we would repair some of the damages.

Cheerfully, we prepared for the opening night. And it was a fair night, with such good returns that Joe and I were cheered.

That opening night, after the show, De Witt Clinton, our leading man, started out of the Opera House for his hotel. In the dark alley at the stage door he was shot down by a woman lurking in the shadows.

"I was jealous!" she said on the witness stand.

But that explanation did not save the "Girl form Chili" company. All our hopes were ruined. Joe and I were glad to quit. At least, we had succeeded in bringing our people home. Joe drifted to other fields, and I had to hunt up something right away.

Back in New York, Olga Nethersole had been putting on "Sapho", to the tune of much newspaper publicity. Florence Roberts had played it at the Alcazar. It was a sensational play.

Somehow I got hold of a non-royalty version of "Sapho", and gathered together my Coast Defenders. Jennie came up to San Francisco to play Aunt Divonne. I played her husband, Uncle Cesare. Fay Courtnay made a charming Irene, and Edith Lemmert was Sapho. And we all doubled for the masquerade scene.

183

For six weeeks we played up the coast and down, in the smaller California cities, to splendid business. It was very encouraging — too much so, perhaps. For when that six weeks was over, I conceived the idea of taking out the Bacon-Courtnay company, on "Sapho" money.

That tour was as pathetic as my tour with Muller. My company were all Coast Defenders, and we played along the coast again. Salinas and Watsonville and other towns I had known in my photographer days. On a Saturday night we played "The Estate of Hannibal Howe," at Monterey. The old play had been made to serve me often in these hard years.

We needed a bass drum in the Monterey house but the manager assured me he would be able to get it — because the drummer was out of town —

"He's gone over to Pacific Grove with a load of hay," was his explanation.

We played that repertoire season without one paying week! You must admit that record is almost as sensational as *Lightnin's* is today. I maintain few managers could have accomplished such complete failure. I was an exception.

We went north to Eureka, the shipping town on the upper coast. There I gave up. I sailed majestically back into San Francisco, with my company, aboard a lumber boat! This was in December.

Jennie went home to San Jose, while I sought some simple-hearted person willing to loan me the staggering sum of $250 to take the show out again for Christmas. While seeking, I received an offer from the Alcazar.

Would I return to them at $25 a week?

This was when I wrestled with my pride. Was I to give up my company for a miserable pittance? I wired Jennie. That same afternoon her wire came from San Jose:

"TAKE THE TWENTY FIVE."

It was a command from one who had never failed to know the best way. Meekly, I joined the Alcazar.

It was Christmas, 1900. I was to be with the Alcazar for several years. When I left them my salary was forty dollars, but for most of the time I played for thirty a week.

But it was the best move I ever made. I gave up forever the idea of carrying a successful show. I decided it wasn't in me. From then on, if I couldn't act, I was useless.

184

I opened in a small part in "Naughty Anthony." The naughtiness consisted of a girl changing her stocking on the stage. And if that wasn't considered daring, at the beginning of this century!

After I had been six months at the Alcazar, and for the first time my work with them seemed assured, Jennie came up to San Francisco. She brought with her the family, Bessie and Lloyd. Now we were quite a family, and the apartment we rented out on Larkin street was a large one. Too large in fact, Jennie said, after we were settled in it, and if she didn't take in boarders!

I don't know how she managed the time for it all. But then, I never did understand how Jennie found the time for all the things she did. Our boarders were all stage companions of mine from the Alcazar, and Jennie did the cooking for all of us, and attended to the house and saw the children off to school mornings, and occasionally played "jobbing" at the Alcazar.

One of our boarders was James Montgomery. "Jimmy" wasn't getting such a lot of attention those days, before he wrote the musical comedy "Irene" and became famous. I'd come into the kitchen often and find Jimmy pressing his trousers on mother's ironing board.

Sometimes we were short of money. Sometimes I'd look ahead and realize that twenty-five dollars a week wasn't carrying me very far. But there was something of security in the work at the Alcazar, and besides, it was fun. We were always playing jokes backstage.

The Alcazar Company was always lively, and at times brilliant. As play followed play, my parts became more noticeable, and in some vague artistic way I knew that I was improving. At the end of two years I was given a five dollar raise. Thirty a week!

To show you I wasn't as ambitionless as most people seemed to think, between shows, I was writing. I dramatized Helen Hunt Jackson's romance of old California, "Ramona." It had always appealed to me as a great love drama. All my ideas seem to have the California touch to them, perhaps because I had been first charmed by the west's romance as a boy. But after all my work and revising on the play, I was never able to raise the money necessary for an option on the dramatic rights of "Ramona." Just one more effort of my planting that never bore fruit.

I'll never forget one incident at the Alcazar during these early years. For a long time it was my pet horror, and I often woke up nights rehearsing again its awfulness. It happened when the Alcazar ran a week with "Romeo and Juliet." The management always put on the very best plays.

185

Florence Roberts was then at her loveliest, beautiful, blonde and young. She was an appealing Juliet. George Webster, who had once starred for me, although I often found that hard to believe, was playing Capulet. During that week, just before show time, George received a telegram. His mother was at the door of death. George left San Francisco on the next train.

I was playing the comic and not too difficult role of Peter. About seven-thirty, with just enough time to get into my make-up, I came ambling into the Alcazar. The stage manager dashed into the dressing room I shared with two other men. His face was working with excitement.

"Here, take this! You're playing Capulet tonight!"

He shouted this in my ear by way of gently breaking the news and shoved the fat Capulet script and costume into my paralyzed hands.

I cannot tell you the numb horror that squeezed my brain. I used to have nightmares resembling it, when a boy. Why, my greatest weakness had always been slowness of study. I simply could not memorize lines. Jennie always had to coach me for days. Before I knew a part, it had to be *mine*. I had to live it, realize every word's meaning. Then it would come over me with a rush, and I would paralyze the stage manager by knowing every syllable of a part of which I had seemed completely blank the day before.

I looked at Capulet's opening speech — one solid page of fine print! A week's study for me at my brightest. Like a man in a nightmare, I realized that the other men of the company were surrounding me, pulling on the pointed medieval shoes, sliding me into the stately robes worn by the father of Juliet.

Reading the lines over and over — yet what good was that! — I felt the boys steering me toward the wings. I felt like a man who has never learned to swim who is suddenly tossed off the deck into mid-ocean.

I was on the stage. I never will know what I said that night. Nothing, I know, such as ever came from the pen of Shakespeare. Probably my speeches sounded more like Uncle Morris than Capulet. I didn't budge a foot from the entrance and whenever the audience was distracted by someone else's speech, I slid myself offstage and feverishly read over the next few lines.

But this accidental part was my biggest in some time. After several seasons with the Alcazar, and after playing many roles, I was given my first real part.

This was in "Liberty Hall." I don't know how I happened to be given the part of the old man, Mr. Todman, the simple, kindly old book-lover of the play. But I loved the role and the morning after opening night I had the pleasure of sitting at breakfast in our apartment and reading aloud to Jennie my first big notice. All the papers noticed me in their reviews.

This press attention, I suppose, impressed the Alcazar, for soon afterward I was cast in a completely opposite role, that of the college man, Babberly, in "Charley's Aunt."

"Babbs" was completely different from anything I had ever done. Of late years I had found myself drifting into old man roles with a naturalness that sometimes had me worried. It was true my hair was greying over the temples, but then, I was only forty. But there were times, considering how little I had accomplished, when forty seemed pitifully old.

So it was encouraging to be given the Babberly role, and I gave it all my enthusiasm. I surprised myself and everyone else, masquerading as the maiden aunt, "from Brazil, where the nuts come from!" The play took San Francisco by storm and after that no Alcazar season was complete without a two week run of "Charley's Aunt."

When we of the Alcazar company learned that the management was putting on "Tennessee's Partner," I was the most interested one in the crowd. For I had heard much of that play. I knew there was an old man comedy role in it and I was willing to give my right arm for the part. My bent for old man roles was strong. Somehow Uncle Morris — or Bill Jones, as he was later to be known to the stage — would always be the most entrancing character I'd ever seen in or out of a play. I yearned to present Uncle Morris to the stage, show the worst and best sides of his droll, gentle soul.

They say every actor has his weakness. Bill Jones is mine.

At first it didn't look as if I were to get the chance in the Tennessee play. I begged the director to give me the part. I waylaid him behind the scenes and spent much time persuading him. I had heard many actors rave about this part and the opportunities it gave, until I wanted it worse than anything in the world.

I guess the director gave it to me at last to be rid of me. Triumphantly I carried the script home and Jennie and I began reading it over together. At the second page, she lifted startled eyes to mine.

"Why, Frank!" she exclaimed, "this is just like — this is! — your Uncle Morris!"

CHAPTER EIGHTEEN

I BUY BACONIA

My part in "Tennessee's Partner," as I played it, was Uncle Morris.

"Ad lib as much as you like," the director had told me.

And I did. I built my role around Uncle Morris as I remembered him, and when the part was finished I knew it was good.

As a result, after this, I was the established comedian of the Alcazar Theatre.

The play caused quite a sensation in San Francisco. I felt I deserved a raise. I had only had two during my years of faithful service at the O'Farrell Street Theatre, and I felt I deserved it. More than that, I needed it. The children were growing. Bess was a young lady now, asking for long skirts and flaps over her puffy sleeves, "just as Alice Roosevelt was wearing 'em." And aside from family cares, Jennie and I had crowds of friends. We loved bringing the whole crowd home after the show, and there would be Jennie's cooking and a bubbling pot of honest-to-goodness coffee on the kitchen stove and maybe some frosty bottles of beer in the ice chest. While it wasn't always easy managing, we managed to keep the home fire burning and have a great deal of fun besides, on my $40 per week.

Considering the good parts given me of late, I considered the Alcazar could spare me at least fifty a week. I told them so. But they couldn't see it my way at all. I was hurt.

Over across the bay, in Oakland, the Liberty Theatre was running a dandy stock company. This was the golden age of stock, the early 1900's. The Liberty made me an offer and I accepted.

It was a wrench, leaving the Alcazar. Many friends had come and gone there through the years as the company waxed and waned. Now that was another chapter in my life—finished.

188

But the Liberty offer held only through a short season. Suddenly I found myself again out of a job. It was startling, for I had been lapped in the security of a steady job so many years. Now I had to do something, immediately.

Jennie and I got out the old play Brusie had written for me in Sacramento, "The Estate of Hannibal Howe." It had helped me over many a close place in the past. We hadn't looked at it for years but now we read it over carefully and finally wrote it over.

We renamed the play, "The Hills of California."

And also I wrote another play, "The Girl from Dixie." We played this in a little repertoire company and also in vaudeville. For vaudeville had of late years held quite an enchantment for me, and once, during a lay-off at the Alcazar, Jennie, Bessie and I had played a two week vaudeville engagement in Portland.

But the "Hills of California" was our real hope. I was old man Hill himself, and I found myself clinging now to old man roles. "The Hills" as we called the play, served us loyally if not well. For two sesaons I carried that show around California and through the middle west and they were precarious years for me. It was sad to come back to this town-to-town existence after the ease of a stock company. Always hoping for luck in the next town. Always finding bad business lying in wait for us.

"Just wait until you come next year," the natives of every town assured me consolingly the first season.

Foolishly I believed them and replayed the route next season. It was worse than the first tour. We thought we had outlived the grief of our barnstorming past. Now we were in it again, adventuring through the country with "The Hills."

I realize now that it was a crude comedy drama. But my old man lead was sweet and wholesome, and I think perhaps some of the "artistry" attributed to "Lightnin' Bill" crept into the role of old Amos Hill.

The "Hills of California" owned a ranch and many farm creatures appeared on the stage. In the different scenes, particularly the realistic second act, appeared a few chickens, a duck, a cow and a horse named Blucher. We learned later how foolish we had been to write in all these beasts and fowl of the barnyard. Half our woes on the road came from them.

But the animals made a wild hit with our sparse audiences. They knew not the trouble it cost us to bring the creatures on the scene. I feel volumes will some day be written on the psychology of animals in stage life.

189

The chickens were the most troublesome. At the first town where we played for a week, we started in by renting a few from a butcher. We scattered grain on the stage to attract their attention and let them loose. The grain kept them amused, although the audience frightened them by wildly applauding the scene. We found them such an attraction and so attractive in themselves, that we bought the entire lot and carried them with us, as crazy an addition to a theatrical company as ever boarded a train.

At least, we had saved them from the butcher shop. Jennie, who is always mother first and actress by chance, cared for the flock with much affection. "Super-chickens," she still insists these were. Every feathered actor had a name and seemed to recognize it. They were on very friendly terms with the other members of the company.

There was Billy Waddles, the duck. This was before the days of quackless ducks, and Billy was often a great astonishment to brakemen. He was very loquacious, talked all the time, but had a heart of pure gold. When not in his crate, he followed Jennie around like a child.

When the audience clapped at Billy's appearance, he would stand looking out over the footlights and shaking his short white tail feathers in a perplexed fashion. People en masse alarmed Billy, but he adored his friends.

There was one big buff cochin rooster we named Jim Jeffries, and a large white leghorn named Edith. And the two little bantam chickens were known as Mr. and Mrs. Bantie. Mr. Bantie, like most little fellows, had an abnormal idea of his power over the opposite sex. He was very flirtatious, and developed one of those romantic attachments that upset the best of traveling theatrical companies, for Edith, the large white hen. She was three times his size. It was as ridiculous as such alliances usually are, but they were perfectly unconscious of being ridiculous.

When let out onto the stage, they always followed a certain routine. Bantie would strut up to Edith, scratching industriously and conversing with her about the merits of the cracked wheat that strewed the boards, coquetting with the vanity possible only in a bantam.

Then — and the audience was roaring so by this time that we often had to hold back our lines, Mrs. Bantie would step up to her coquettish husband and give an illustration of the verb to henpeck. This wounded Mr. Bantie's dignity mightily, and he ruffled his feathers and flew for poor Jim Jeffries, the most peaceable old rooster

190

that ever crowed. Bantie licked Jeffries to a stiff jell every performance and chased him off the stage, winning a curtain call for himself.

Upon our arriving in a new town it was my first duty to hunt up a cow and a horse. We did draw the line at carrying these. They added a great deal to our domestic life behind the scenes, for a sort of trained nurse with a large bucket would appear in our midst at regular hours to milk the cow.

In one of our Western towns I borrowed a cow — I think now it must have been half mule. A flight of stairs led back stage, and with the entire company pushing and pulling, we managed to get her to the wings. Once there, she refused to "go on" when her cue came. She stood off stage and bellowed wickedly, and finally refused either to go on the stage or to leave the theatre. She would not go down those stairs again and home.

When we left town that fool cow was still parked in the first entrance, right, and I hope she still stands there.

And the horses we found were just as likely to get stage struck as the cows. I got so I dreaded every new jump — it meant dealing with another temperamental horse. In Seattle the horse kicked our perfectly artistic stage well over into the orchestra pit. It wasn't really his fault, for he was very thirsty. I had to give him a bucket of water in the second act, and to make sure of his drinking it, we fed him salt fish before the show.

In this same scene, in another town, "Blucher" brought the show to grief. He was the only horse I had been able to find for that night. He was the horse the local Fire Department used to haul their hose cart to the fires.

I entered on the right as Amos Hill, driving the horse hitched to a plow. I unhitched him and led him to the well, gave him a brimming pail of water and stood patting him while he drank.

"Poor old Blucher!" I said to him gently. "If mankind drank more pure, good water we wouldn't have so many poor-houses and jails."

Then I tied him to the fence at the side of the property farmhouse, which occupied half the stage. Just as I was delivering the exit speech, the firegong rang down the street. I didn't hear it, but Blucher did, with his keen ear trained to the call for duty. Loyal to his trust, he made a wild dash off stage, carrying with him the farmhouse, the fence, and all the "orchard" attached to the fence.

We carried the "Hills" over into Colorado, and there another horse gave us an exciting night. As there was no runway or entrance by which we could get him into the theatre he had to climb the narrow and twisting stairs. Being fresh from the farm and suspicious as a yokel, he refused to make the climb. We had to start the show without him.

We went ahead with the first act. We didn't need the horse until the second. Then the house manager came back stage.

"Is that horse going on?" he demanded of me as I waited in the wings.

"We can't get him on," I replied.

"Either that horse goes on or you don't get any money," he replied viciously. "You advertised a horse on the stage and played it up in the advertising. Unless you make good I don't count up!"

It was a dreadful threat. As usual, my little group was living from show to show. I didn't have any money for fares to the next town. I ordered the two stage hands to brace themselves, one at the back and one at the front of the horse, who stood with feet squared in the dark entrance to the stariway. The actors surrounded the horse, coaxing with candy, hay, threatening, cursing, prodding, and even trying to lift the stubborn animal with planks for levers.

I don't know what the audience thought of our performance, for we all missed our cues and came dashing on stage at all points of the show, panting with exertion.

The second act commenced. I came on alone with my stage whiskers askew with excitement, dragging the plow myself! Far in back, over the heads of the audience, I could feel the weight of the manager's gloating eye. The act wound on without Blucher — he was only half way upstairs. The act ended.

The chickens and Billy Waddles were collected and stowed away in their crate. The great barnyard scene was over and our horse had not been on.

And the manager's verdict stood. "No horse, no money!"

The third act was a drawing room scene. It began just as the boys succeeded in bringing Blucher to the top of the stairs. By this time we were hot and out of temper and furious with the manager. Anyway, this was the only show we were putting on in this town and we could afford to take chances. And we took one.

The manager, gloating in back of the theatre, nearly dropped dead when he saw me appear for no reason at all in that drawing room scene, truimphantly leading the horse!

Well, the horse was "on," wasn't he, as advertised? No denying that, and we got our share of the money that night.

192

Jennie Bacon in costume, play unknown.

The Bacon family in front of the family home, Baconia. This structure still stands on Berry Avenue in what is now known as Los Altos.

Frank Bacon, 1907.

We were not sorry to escape from this tyranny of animals when we came back into San Francisco to close the show. But the feathered members of the company were different. Traveling around with a flock of hens and a duck endear them to your heart. After two years with us on the road, Billy Waddles and the Bantie pair and Edith and Jeffries seemed part of the Bacon family.

"How can we ever give them up? wailed Jennie, during this closing week with "The Hills of California."

We didn't even know how to provide for ourselves. We had weathered two years of the hardest theatrical vicissitudes. I had a wee bit of money, and that was the rebate on the season's railroad fare. I had nothing left to show for two — no, for many barnstorming years!

And yet the only real worry on our souls was how to provide for Billy Waddles and his companions.

During this final week, a friend of mine came up from Mountain View to see the show. We had started life together in that town when I had founded the *Mountain View Register* and he had ventured into real estate. He had fared better than I. Now he was one of the big business men of Santa Clara County. He knew all the possibilities of the beautiful valley and the best "buys."

"Frank, I'm advising you like a father," he urged me. "You ought to be providing in some way for Jennie and the youngsters, and real estate is the only safe buy. There's a little place down in Mountain View just made to order for you."

At last Jennie and I made the trip down to look at the place. Mountain View is about fifteen miles out of San Jose, on the road to San Francisco. I really didn't have much of an idea of buying. I went down to please my friend.

Made to order! The little ranch had ten acres of orchard land in full bearing. I knew enough about soil to see that this was rich and fine. Behind us and before us were the hills that guard the Santa Clara valley, with Mount Hamilton highest of all and crested as if with pearls by the white domes of Lick Observatory. My friend was steering me into a real bargain.

"And besides," added Jennie, enthusiastically, "it will be a home for Billy Waddles and the chickens."

I hadn't thought of this argument, although it seemed to settle matters. But there were other reasons. For I was forty years old and my many old-man parts made me seem older. The gray was heavy in my hair. And there was little enough for us against the future —

nothing but what work I could find. If anything happened — well, I wanted to know that Jennie and her children would have a place like this to call home.

And by birth I was a man of the soil, lover of the country and things that grow and turn green with summer. The prune trees on this place were like old friends. I had to have that place!

I began with my rebate money and collected a family jackpot. For once I had the support of all my family. Land was something they could appreciate. It could not be lost during a bad season or wasted in a run of bad luck. Auntie Em contributed the balance necessary for the first payment, and suddenly, the Bacons had a home.

It was the first we had been able to call our own during our entire married life. It made Jennie and me feel strangely settled. We moved into the little farmhouse at once.

Billy Waddles and the other feathered former actors arrived in their crate and were turned free under the prune trees. They took to the quiet life as naturally as we did. Mr. and Mrs. Bantie joyfully gave up public life forever and settled down to the business of raising a countless population of wee feathered puff balls that grew up into other bantams.

But Billy Waddles had the real career. One day he was found missing at roll call and Jennie wrote me tearfully. She was afraid he was lost. But the joke was on us for naming a duck without any idea of its sex. For when Billy was discovered at last under a rosebush "he" was sitting on a stolen nest of thirteen eggs!

I was not at Baconia, as my old friend, Clifford Dempsey, once a member of the " 4 Acts" Company, named our little ranch, when this important event took place. I would have been perfectly content to remain there always, hunting for eggs and picking prunes. I liked getting into overalls and cleaning out the coops, and nailing up an extra shelf in the kitchen for the cling peaches Jennie was "putting up" in steaming jars. For now Jennie was all wife and mother and tender of the ranch. No more grease paint for Jennie. Her career was with Baconia.

But Baconia was not paid for, and I was in debt as usual. If it had not been for that debt, I know I would be raising ducks and bantams on the ranch today in perfect contentment. But men must work, provided they can find employment, and I had to hunt a job.

Nothing doing in San Francisco. But the Liberty in Oakland made me a return offer and I went back to them.

I lived in Oakland, but got down to Mountain View once a week

194

to see the family. Bessie had gone on the stage and married her first leading man, a talented young chap, Wilfred Roger, and Lloyd was in school at Mountain View. The ranch was more than ever home, and during my weeks in Oakland, rooming with some other actor, I found I was lonely. It seemed as if all our lives before we bought Baconia we had been just camping out.

The same management that controlled the Liberty in Oakland owned the Majestic Theatre in San Francisco. I was alternated between the two companies, and some weeks would live on one side of the bay, and at other times on the opposite side. I was playing at the Majestic Theatre and sharing a hotel room in San Francisco with another actor, on April 18th, 1906.

An unforgettable date, as long as San Francisco stands.

Earthquake Day!

I woke to a trembling, as if my heart were pounding too fast for comfort. There was a dizziness in the air, and the bed seemed to sink into the floor and rise again. For a moment I felt seasick. The bed tilted to and fro like a cradle, then slid rapidly over the moving floor, while the walls seemed to be caving in.

Then I realized — this queerness was not of me. Something was wrong with the world.

Crash! An old picture in a horrible gilt frame just missed my head as I struggled to free myself from the gliding bed. All over the hotel things were falling. The hotel itself seemed falling through space.

I felt — death. Then this was lost in a wild personal rage. Why, I was forty — too young to be murdered like this in a cheap hotel room! Whatever this force was that I heard growling like a low thunder in the bowels of the earth, I hated it!

But that growling gave me a faint courage, for I knew it was an earthquake, and every Californian knows what to do in earthquake time. "Stand in a doorway." I had heard that formula many times, and now I staggered for the door. It was like walking across a deck during a storm. The floor lifted against my feet like something alive. I remember, as I staggered across that rocking floor that seemed miles long, growing panicky for terror of what might be happening at Baconia. Was Jennie in danger like this, and the children? And I couldn't help them! That was the horror of this hour, the powerlessness of it. I was like a mouse shaken between the jaws of a cat.

I stood in the doorway while slabs of plaster rained from the ceilings on each side. The real danger was always falling bricks, I

195

knew. The horrible trembling kept on, and from outside came a roaring sound as if the city were crashing into atoms. But I couldn't tell what was happening, and that was the horror of it, until the trembling grew fainter and died.

How we got into our clothes and out into the street, I cannot remember. Panic was upon the city. Men and women were running everywhere without any destination, simply running from fear. They were shouting and screaming. A man crashed into me. He wore bedroom slippers and a heavy, fuzzy blue bathrobe. On his head was a shiny high silk hat — the opera season was barely over in San Francisco, and Caruso had sung only a few nights before in the brazier-warmed patio of the Palace Hotel. A child sat huddled back from the sidewalk, crying for her mother. A woman came from a shattered doorway with her hand clutched to her head, and creeping between her fingers was a red stain.

Brick chimneys had catapulted into the street, brick buildings were down. What tragedies lay hidden forever under those ruined piles, I dared not guess. All my thoughts were in Mountain View.

Suddenly I thought of two young freinds of mine, married and with a baby, living not far away. They might need help. I found my way to their street through chasms of ruin. Houses lay cracked open like egg shells. Splintered roofs dripped loosened beams and shingles, like fringes, over the walls.

Everywhere people were carrying out what little furniture they could. Cabs, wagons, even scavengers' carts were being pressed into service, and families, piled upon what few household goods they had managed to save, were fleeing through the streets. Where! No one knew where safety lay, or whether or not the world lay in ruins. Through the streets ran the hideous cry:

"Fire!"

It was not six o'clock, but already the morning sun was a molten red globe gleaming through clouds of black smoke. The city was being blanketed with thick acrid smoke. It was like an eclipse, only ashes were falling through the streets like soft gray snow.

The sturdy new apartment house where my friends lived had not been damaged. But most of their chinaware had been broken. The young wife tossed a breakfast together somehow and we ate it on the remains of the dishes. Then we put their year-old baby in the buggy and started out. I was wild to get some sort of message to Jennie, if it were possible, or if Mountain View had not gone down.

Wild gossip filled the air. Everybody believed every rumor. The city was under martial law, troops from the Presidio were patrolling the streets, and there were mad stories of men being shot dead while trying to save their household goods. Vandalism was in the streets. It was said that entire blocks of boarding houses in the Mission district had been swallowed up in an enormous gap in the earth that opened and closed again. People who had fled to the beach for safety were returning again, driven back by rumors of a tidal wave that was to overwhelm the ruined city. Thousands were dead.

Out of all these rumors one thing was certain. All communication with the outside world was cut away. Everyone in San Francisco was frantic to send a telegram somewhere. I could get no word out to Mountain View.

"You'd better come home with us, Frank," said my friend, sympathetically.

As we pushed the baby buggy around the corner of their block, our way was stopped by police. In the wake of the earthquake had come rushing the Great Fire, and where their apartment house had stood lay a black area of smoldering ashes. From other blocks came the loud dynamite as houses were blown up in an effort to fight back the fire.

And past us swarmed the endless flood of refugees, homeless and bound for nowhere. Some fled into Golden Gate Park and lived there many days. Many were fed by the Salvation Army and other charitable organizations. Some camped out on the beach.

The fire was roaring on through the city and the sky was whipped to a red hell. We stood there on the corner, juggling the buggy to keep the baby from crying. Down the street a man and woman stood hand in hand, looking at the ashes that had been their home. The woman was crying, and I saw the man put his arm across her shoulder to comfort her in their homelessness. And we also were homeless.

"Come home with me," I invited, turning to my two young friends earnestly. "We can walk to Mountain View . . . it's not far . . . very!"

My dears, I don't suppose it is very short of thirty miles, and with steep grades in some places. We started down Mission Street, taking turns pushing the baby buggy. It was still quite early in the morning.

We tried to lay in a stock of provisions before our journey but all we could get was a box of crackers and a bottle of Syphon Water.

197

We pushed the buggy over the lower slope of Twin Peaks and down into Colma, and then, like poor Mary, Queen of Scots, we walked and walked and walked.

Even at San Mateo the fire still seemed to be scorching our backs. The sky behind us toward the bay was like an open furnace. Our feet blistered from the hard, hot highway. We put our lips in turn to the syphon bottle and squirted its fizzy water down our grateful throats. The baby woke, wept, munched its way through a cracker and slept again. We trudged on.

Refugees in strange costumes passed us, driving in stranger vehicles. They were like people seen in a nightmare to our hot and reddened eyes.

We reached Palo Alto at evening. Beautiful Stanford University that Mrs. Stanford had poured her money and soul into, and that I had seen founded, lay in ruins, we learned at the railway station. Memorial Arch had cracked down like an egg shell. That news made me shudder for Mountain View, not many miles from Palo Alto.

We did not stop to look at the University, for it lies a mile south of Palo Alto. We pushed our baby cart and marched on after it, to Mountain View.

CHAPTER NINETEEN

THREE A DAY—ALSO FIVE!

Our walk from the village of Mountain View to my ranch nearby was the longest part of our trip from burning San Francisco. At midnight on this day of quake and terror, three weary people, pushing a go-cart containing a sleeping baby, arrived at last at Baconia.

Inside the ranchhouse living room an oil lamp was burning and Jennie was pacing the floor. She screamed when I called to her from the porch. She had thought me dead.

I don't know how the house sheltered all the people who fled to it during the days that followed. The Ingraham's baby had arrived with nothing but the little nightie it wore, and a kind Mountain View neighbor brought over clothing from her own children's wardrobe.

Lloyd Ingraham and his wife were there. Elmer Booth, who had played with me at the Majestic and shared the room with me, came down two days later from the still burning city. With thousands of other refugees, he had been sleeping out in Golden Gate Park and existing by the largess of the Salvation Army. Then his fiancee was found, Irene Outrim, and she also came to Baconia for shelter.

Everybody helped keep house and I'll never forget Jennie's honest country suppers—baked beans with fat sweet pork in the center, and biscuits that melted with lightness before they reached your mouth. Not that there was much house to be kept in those days. This was before we built over the old house. It had been built originally for a barn, with a quaint peaked roof and bare rafters. When we bought it there were divisions making three rooms, and we papered the ribby ceilings ourselves, with colorful Sunset magazine covers, and hung them with Indian rugs.

But the outdoors at Baconia! Permanente Creek gurgled through

199

an end of our small estate and our guests caught trout therein for the family larder! During these trying days Elmer caught one a foot long. Overhead oak trees interlaced with sycamore, so that the little river slid down an archway of green. And such redness of toyon berries, the holly of California, and such fullhearted singing of every variety of western bird!

"We'll never leave this place again!" declared Jennie, after the first horror of the earthquake was over.

But our little ranch was not paid for. I knew these flurried holidays were only temporary and that I must find work as soon as the theatres opened again in the ash-strewn city. At any rate, we swore never again to be separated. Alas for vows — within the month I was playing at Ye Liberty Theatre in Oakland, and Jennie was running a company of her own, in my name, in San Jose.

I went up to Oakland when the theatre opened there, lured by the promised fifty dollars a week. Jennie said she would remain at the ranch with Bessie who had joined us that spring, fresh from the triumph of her first season in the East. She was perfectly content there in the shelter of the prune and apricot trees, and had great plans for building a glass porch, two stories high, in the front. This porch was to include the big oak tree that towered over our cottage. So Jennie remained in Mountain View when I joined the ranks of the Liberty.

It was the usual grind for me, learning new parts barely in time for the next week's shows. But I indulged in a business venture on the side, with Jennie supplying the business. Over in San Jose, fifteen miles from the ranch at Mountain View, the old Jose Theatre on South Second Street stood "in the dark." Ed Redmond's traveling players had last occupied the stage. It came to me like an inspiration to start a stock company there.

My ventures always began, and usually ended, with a loan. I started this stock company with forty borrowed dollars.

Jennie was manager. I dared not yield up my fifty dollars at Ye Liberty for the uncertain fortunes of the new company. But I supplied the actors. San Francisco and Oakland were populated with stranded actors in those days before the ruined streets were rebuilt and theatres rose again. I couldn't resist their pleas for work, for had I not stood in the thin-soled shoes of uncertainty many a time?

"Go down to Jennie in San Jose," I told every actor who met me with a story of hunger and despair. "She'll give you work."

200

Finally Jennie wrote me a hysterical letter. She had twenty-three actors working for her and only forty dollars to start proceedings! Even then I found it hard to keep from sending more actors down to San Jose.

Her adventures with that company! Jennie was manager, director, press agent and character artist. Aside from learning her own roles, life was made miserable by calls for "data" to supply the two town papers. Bess played the ingenue and Lloyd took tickets at the door. They lived at a side-street boarding house, with the rest of the company, for the modest sum of fifteen dollars a week for the three of them. That included meals.

The other actors occasionally paid the landlord five dollars on account and borrowed it back the next day. Also, they borrowed his carryall that met all the trains, and went driving in it. Sometimes they met the trains themselves at the broad gauge station.

The San Jose company opened with my old barnstorming favorite, "The Hills", and reached the summit of glory in "Hearts of Tennessee," played with a cast of twenty-three souls! The opening matinee Jennie looked out over the house with awe. It was packed to the walls. Fortune at last, she thought, had come to the Bacons, but Lloyd counted up that night to only thirty dollars. Three hundred people had filled the small house at ten cents a seat. The week passed and there was no money for salaries. Jennie called her big family together on the stage.

"I can't pay you, but I'll be glad to have you keep on playing on the commonwealth," she told them, as I had many another company, in many another gloomy hour.

They were glad to stay. There was no work in the "city" for them, as we of the west call San Francisco. So she paid them what she could, five dollars to the leading man one Saturday night, and smaller sums to the others, and one man quit because she wouldn't raise a salary he knew he never would receive! But he came back to her.

Our company lived seven weeks in San Jose. At the end of that time what was known as the "Tent Theatre" had been completed in San Francisco. This was a big tent erected on the site of the old Central Theatre at Market and Ninth Streets.

This was the first theatre to open in San Francisco after the earthquake that took place in April, 1906. Most of the San Jose company secured engagements with this management, and they opened the shattered city's first playhouse with "Hearts of Tennessee."

Meanwhile I was playing at Ye Liberty in Oakland and Jennie joined me there every night after the performance. I knew what a dreary ride that was for her, on a street car that ran through miles of ruined streets, in a cemetery of a black, unlighted city, reeking with the wet ashes of ruined buildings.

I stayed with Ye Liberty until the first theatre opened in San Francisco and I was offered the management. This was the Colonial Theatre. It had been in the course of construction before the disaster. The owners asked me to bring a company to the new theatre. Actually, it was an invitation to start theatricals again in San Francisco. As this was the most important thing that had ever happened to me, I left the Liberty overnight.

I was going to New York! San Francisco and the bay cities were haunted with the sad faces of the jobless coast defenders, but the Colonial demanded importations, real stars from the big time areas. That's how I happened to pay my first duties to Broadway.

I have no memories of this first trip to New York. I didn't get off Broadway. I didn't see Coney Island or the Brooklyn Bridge or the Statue of Liberty. I rummaged the theatrical agencies. I collected the best group of actors I could find and shooed them home with me, like startled chickens, to the Coast. I came in weary but triumphant and we opened the Colonial.

One of my prizes from Broadway was Izetta Jewel, who later stepped from stardom to become merely Mrs. Brown and had a stirring political career. She made one of the striking speeches at the Democratic Convention in San Francisco in 1920.

Izetta Jewell did not disappoint me. This was her first starring engagement. In San Francisco they still talk of her work in Oscar Wilde's "Salome." In fact, the astonishing success of this daring play stirred the souls of Jennie and Bessie and Bessie's young husband, Wilfred Rogers, and the three of them took to the road with "Salome." Oh, what a time they had! Trouble from the day they deserted Market street for the paloosa trails of long ago. I was glad to see them return, disillusioned but not discouraged.

My work at the Colonial was received with the applause only San Francisco could give, in spite of her woes of that tragic April. Here is a clipping in the old scrapbook again, from the *San Francisco News Letter* of October, 1906:

"Frank Bacon has achieved almost instantaneous popular success in the opening of the Colonial Theatre. Bacon is well-beloved of theatre goers. He is possessed of splendid ability as an actor and also as a manager. There are few men so well known in the theatrical profession who count so few enemies. In fact, it would be difficult to find anyone to say he did not like Bacon. As an evidence of all the above, while most of the city theatres have suffered from the fact that people preferred to stay at home during the recent carnival of crime, the Colonial saw no diminuation of its patronage."

Sounds like victory, doesn't it! Nothing of the sort. The dramatic world has no yesterday, and success lives only through the hour. I ran the Colonial for twenty-three weeks. At the end of that time I shed the glory of management and returned meekly across the bay as an actor again at Ye Liberty. Such are the ups and downs of my chosen trade.

It was sad work, disbanding that company. We had been like one big happy family. But we scattered, for the Colonial closed.

We had been playing into our seventh month when another calamity struck San Francisco. This was the great streetcar strike.

Again our poor city was bossed by terror. People were afraid to walk by night through the shattered streets. The "scab" was born. Men were found at lonely, ash-heaped corners, shot dead. Nothing could lure the public from their homes at evening. The theatres closed. The Colonial held out bravely but at last "went dark." And that is why I returned to the Oakland Liberty.

I fretted at the life. For one thing, I needed more money than the theatre seemed to think I was worth. Remember, our little home down in the country was not wholly paid for. And Bessie and Jennie and my son-in-law came home just then, broke from their paloosa tour with "Salome."

This was in the infancy of popular three-a-day vaudeville. I wrote a one act play, "An Easy Liar," for Jennie, Bessie and myself. But when the time came to try it out, Bess was playing stock in the east with her husband, and we had to find another girl.

We first appeared in vaudeville in the Bell Theatre in Oakland. This was in 1907. For the second week I found another playlet "Going Home," and for an added attraction that week the Bell found a little-known comedian who was later to be the riot of Broadway — Al Jolson. Al followed our act and had a lot of fun "ragging" it.

"That fellow that just left here — he's not 'Going Home', he would inform the audience. "He's going down the street to get something to eat!"

Next week we were booked by Archie Levy to play San Jose. Jolson played there with us, also. It was a terrific frost — we played to less than our own salaries!

We realized, having exhausted the local theatres, that we would have to leave California. Baconia was all we had in the world, and I wanted its title clear. But it was particularly hard for Jennie to say a definite farewell to the little ranch and set off with me on a vaudeville tour. The place had grown very dear to both of us, but it was Jennie who had cared for its house and orchard since the day we bought it, and I knew how much she hated to leave. But she did, hung up the kitchen apron and turned back to the make-up box. Archie Levy booked us to play over his circuit, the old Sullivan-Considine, into Denver.

My recollections of that tour are the mere drudgery of vaudeville, and yet, it is a light-hearted life and I liked it. The lives of the three-a-day players criss-cross like drops of rain on a window, to vanish at last and be forgotten. There is something ephemeral about vaudeville. Friendships are made in a week, to be renewed, perhaps, at other ends of the continent, years later, while playing another "time."

Our first week in Denver was such a success we were offered a second week in a theatre across the street — a very different sort of house. It ran continuous, lively vaudeville and I hesitated at offering it our quiet, refined skit, "Going Home." But we needed the money and decided to take a chance. We gave "Going Home" for that week, five times daily! And it was a riot.

That you cannot prophecy to the public's taste, is a truth that is known from Main Street to Broadway. But I have never faced the audience that does not respond to straight sincere human appeal. There was a tenderness about that quiet little act of ours that appealed even to an audience that liked acrobats, gymnastic dancers and soft-shoe artists served up five times a day.

From Denver we hurried to Chicago to get more bookings. Instead, I met Fred Lincoln, general auditor of the Considine time, and he had just taken over the Burwood Theatre in Omaha. He knew I had put in most of my life with stock companies.

"I'd like you to go as general supervisor for the new company I'm putting into Omaha, Frank," he offered.

That was safer than the uncertainty of vaudeville, and in February, 1908, we opened in Omaha in "Young Mrs. Winthrop." It was a play I had seen and revered in my earliest youth in the old Baldwin Theatre, San Francisco.

This was the time when the first faint stirrings of revolt were turning the actors against the theatrical trust. Sarah Bernhardt and

Mrs. Fiske, pioneers in the movement that was to result at last in the great Actors' Strike and the victories of Equity, were touring the country and playing in any tents and halls that could be rented, rather than bow to the Simon Legrees of the dramatic world. And when David Warfield came to Omaha in "The Music Master," he found he could not obtain a theatre. I gave up the Burwood to him.

We met in the box office the morning he got into town. It was not our first meeting but he didn't know that, of course, until I reminded him. The famous Warfield could not be expected to remember the gaunt young fellow who had played with him in the small town of Napa, California, as mere "local talent." Yet in those days Warfield had been unknown. I told him of Jennie's scrapbook, and the old notices and playbills pasted therein.

"I'd like to see it," he said eagerly. "In fact, I'd like to have it. Always interested in collecting old theatrical scrapbooks. . . ."

"I'll get it for you," I promised, with that rare generosity one shows with valuables not our own.

I was quite grieved when Jennie refused to part with that scrap book.

The next season I again yielded up the Burwood, this time to Frank Keenan and Emma Dunn in "The Warrens of Virginia." Also, we daringly produced "The Devil," the first Molnar play to create a sensation in America, I believe. It created such a sensation in Omaha it made the unprecedented run of three weeks! Encouraged by this, I put on the equally daring "Salome" that had shocked and edified San Francisco only a few years ago. It was completely lost upon the honest Nebraskans. In other words, a "flop."

Between these two Omaha seasons, much happened of family importance. Jennie fell ill — very ill. Through days of high fever she raved her way through every part she had ever played. The doctors kindly told me that, in case she did live, she would never again revert to normal, mentally. This nearly lost me what intelligence I had left after the long worry of her sickness, but I could depend upon Jennie. Six weeks later she opened dazed eyes and stared out upon the counterpane, a white, quilted affair.

"I think I'll eat that cracker," she remarked, taking up the nearest corner. But it wasn't delirium, it was honest but dazed hunger, and from that hour on she was safe. I had to leave her — finances again — for work.

I went to Denver and there in the Majestic Theatre made my first and only appearance as a monologist. How terrible I must have been!

There was one line of my invention, "One large Bermuda onion eaten slowly, will entirely destroy the odor of vanilla ice cream."

The line was expected to roll the audience off their seats. It was met with shrieks of silence.

Bess and her husband had been playing in stock in Jersey, and they came West now. Jennie returned with them to the little ranch in California. There, at Baconia, our first little granddaughter, Jean, was born. Our three grandchildren have first seen the light at Baconia, I'm glad to say. I can't think of a better birthplace. Bess's second little daughter, Betty, was not to appear on the scene for another four years. And Lloyd's little girl arrived later and was not as much of a disappointment as she might have been, for they named her Frances in my honor, after all.

When Jean, the baby, was four weeks old, she was left at Baconia in the charge of Auntie Em, who had never failed us. The entire family rejoined me in Omaha, and I shined up the company at the Burwood and got it into better working order than during the first season. How we would ever have weathered the leaner years of our existence without Auntie Em, I hate to contemplate. I'm glad that the last years she spent with us were brimming with every bit of happiness she could hold.

At the end of the second season came the usual upheaval. I left the Burwood when that house closed, and hurried to Denver to get a place in vaudeville. In March, 1910, we entered that swift life again, Jennie and Bess and I, in our little old favorite, "Going Home." We opened in Winnipeg, and played the circuit through.

It was in one of those towns, somewhere about this time, that I received a shock that was to jolt me into sudden activity. For a good many years, an obsession — they say every actor has one — had been growing upon me. I was afraid of becoming a back door man! All my years in the theatre, the back door man appeared to be one and the same man. Usually he was an actor who had outlived his day. He was broken, bent, snowy of hair. He had outdreamed all his hopes. A forgotten Bill Jones of the world of props and scenes, sitting in the background watching other men, who in turn might become as he. And one day, in the crowded dressing room of a small vaudeville house in the east, I stared at myself in the mirror with new eyes.

My hair was white!

I had noticed it before, but never with terror. Why, I was nearly fifty, and playing three wretched little shows a day! Was it because I'd never had a chance? or — because I'd never taken one?

206

I think most men, no matter how bravely they usually face life, have these moments of pure scare.

"Let's try for the big time!" I suggested to Jennie a few days later.

Bessie was the most enthusiastic. She saw no reason against our securing the best New York had to offer. I confess I was shaky, but we worked our way over the Winnipeg time to the big town. I had not seen Broadway since I had been sent to buy up talent for the San Francisco Colonial Company. Then I had been supplied with plenty of money, even if it hadn't been mine. Now I came on my knees, a mendicant, to the gods of the Big Time.

We found an air-tight little apartment way over on Eighth Avenue and I began a desperate round of the theatrical agencies. Of course I ran into swarms of actors I had met on my travels and among them was James Montgomery, who had been our star boarder back in San Francisco, during Alcazar days. Jim had always been able to turn his hand at anything. He could write a play and act it and I've often admired his blase professional way in the days when we had all laughed at poverty together, at the rate of thirty dollars a week.

Now Jim was playing in "The Fortune Hunter" at the Gaiety Theatre and was a real New York actor. I hailed him as a brother, but he welcomed me for a very different reason.

"I've been telling Winchell Smith I knew a *real* Daddy Graham, and now I can show you to him," he declared.

Smith had written "The Fortune Hunter." Daddy Graham was a character of the show. It had been a hit in New York. Now they were opening up with a second company, in Chicago, and Smith needed a Daddy Graham for that city.

Jim insisted upon my going with him to meet Smith. I didn't think I made much of a first impression upon the man who was later to rewrite the finishing touches in *Lightnin'*. But he said quietly to Montgomery after looking me over:

"You're right, Jim. He IS Daddy Graham!"

It didn't occur to me that anything would come of this conversation. I was worrying around trying to get bookings. I got them of course, the very day Jennie and Bessie were inspired to put every bit of clothing we possessed in the wash. They had been going in for New York with a vengeance and neglecting the domestic side of life in the tiny apartment. We had been in New York six weeks before I received an offer from the Keith Circuit. We were to open in Lawrence, Massachusetts, the next day!

And all the wash was hanging on twine around the tiny rooms, and had to be taken down and packed — wet. And how cross my women folk were, as if I could help our falling into such sudden good fortune. We left on the next train and awoke in Lawrence.

Now just before the Keith offer came, and solely to please Montgomery, I had gone to the Gaiety to see him in "The Fortune Hunter." The play was a revelation. I felt as though I had written the lines! Montgomery was right. The old druggist part had been written for me. But I forgot it in the excitement of opening in Lawrence and playing twice that Sunday. Someday, we hoped, we would play New York.

Next day, Monday, I found myself casually opening a telegram. It was from Sam Harris. It offered me the Daddy Graham part in "The Fortune Hunter."

It was Bessie, suddenly becoming the practical member of the family, who urged me to accept. It would mean my first Eastern showing, although it would be with a Chicago company.

"Because New York will come later, father," she prophesied.

I didn't exactly believe her but I allowed my child to have her will. I wired Harris I was returning to New York to rehearse. That was the part I dreaded. I knew, once I was in the swing of the play, I could carry that role. But I've always been a bad student and the worst hand at rehearsals I've ever seen. Can't seem to remember any of my lines until opening night, when they all run together smooth as velvet, as if I'd always known them. Workings of the subconscious, I suppose the weightier minds would call it.

There was only a week left. Then the "Fortune Hunter" would open in Chicago. I doubted if I could learn the role, or rather, that anyone would believe I could learn it.

It was like the night I had played Capulet without knowing the lines, years ago at the Alcazar. Daily, Mother and Bessie heard my lines, coaching me patiently, until we were all three racked with headache and discouragement. The rehearsals were terrible. Mr. Smith was patient with me, but he was the only one. Long afterward, I learned that after our arrival in Chicago, my trunk was pulled off the truck. Harris insisted that I be fired — sent back to New York.

"Give him a chance," urged Smith, tolerantly, "He'll improve."

Probably feeling no human being could continue to be as bad as I was, Smith persuaded the others to let me open with the show in Chicago. It was a desperate night and I was the dead albatross hung around the neck of the company's hopes. The curtain rose and I was the only calm person in the company. That is, I appeared to be calm, but in reality I was shuddering inside. I feel other people that way, but not myself. When troubles are swamping me and I seem calm and self-sufficient, in reality I am running on raw nerve.

I didn't stumble over a syllable that night. The play slid through like silk. And "Daddy Graham" established me as an actor, east of the Rockies.

Years before in San Francisco the critic Ashton Stevens had referred to me slightingly as a "gum-shoe comedian." During the years he had been moved to Chicago. When he saw my work in "The Fortune Hunter" he apologized.

"The Fortune Hunter" ran on and on. It brought security. It brought, what seemed to me prosperity. I made the final payments on Baconia. I built additions on the ranchhouse that had been our shelter during earthquake days and welcomed us now between seasons.

A second successful season followed the first, and through it all I was not idle. Seems to me I couldn't take things easily after the hardness of my less successful days. I had to find some work for my hands.

I invented a burglar alarm. It's a good burglar alarm, and I'm going to patent it someday. And when that was as perfect as I could make it, I turned my odd moments into literary endeavor. Through those long Chicago days, I was writing a play.

CHAPTER TWENTY

"LIGHTNIN'"

I was rewriting the play that had laid in the bottom of my old wardrobe trunk for thirty years!

I had begun it as a young photographer in the little town of Salinas, in California. I had thought about it since, worked it over in my mind and wondered about it. No one had ever been impressed by it. But the leading character in the play was a man whose whimsey permeated every character role I had taken in these years between.

That character was *Lightnin'*.

But while I was playing in "The Fortune Hunter" in Chicago, I named this play "The House Divided." Doubtfully, I got up enough courage to show it to Jim Montgomery. He liked it! I was astonished.

Yet it had occurred to me that the play must have something in it to have haunted me for thirty years.

Montgomery rewrote my play and renamed it, "Me and Grant." For many years I had fallen into the habit of saying I had "Bill Jonesed" a part, and this was pure Bill Jones stuff. While this iron was warming in the fire, Cohan and Harris followed up their long success with "The Fortune Hunter" with "Stop Thief!" George Cohan was to do the directing and he offered me the part of Mr. Carr. My rehearsals, as usual, were awful. The stage manager couldn't forgive my stupidity, and kept harrassing me. Like the dolt in school who is belabored by the hard-hearted teacher, I merely grew stupider.

"Let Bacon alone, he'll come through with the part all right," Cohen ordered, and after that I was let alone and figured the part out to please myself. He perhaps remembered how hopeless I had seemed during rehearsals for "The Fortune Hunter."

It wasn't that I was stupid. It was because I was feeling my way through the lines, stumbling over them because I was thinking them over, making them all mine. Cohan won my everlasting gratitude for this kindness. I tried to repay him with my work as Mr. Carr, and whether I did or not, "Stop Thief" was a success and gave me two seasons.

And after that I originated Higgins, the Hotel Keeper, for him in "The Miracle Man."

And after that — the Shuberts offered to produce my play — Jim's and mine.

The Shuberts had no real faith in "Me and Grant" nor in me, but they had a great deal of respect for James Montgomery. I put all the hope I had left in myself into that play. It ran for one week in Newark . . . failed.

And yet, that play was *Lightnin'* in another form. Why one version should fail and another bring in millions, I do not know, and neither does anyone else. That is Broadway's own secret that her worshipers try in vain to discover. But I had added another failure to my long, sad list.

After this, I went over to Brooklyn for a few weeks and played there in a stock company. It was a shock to me to find that once familiar life utterly strange and hard. I couldn't get used to the rapidity of it, the learning of new parts, the swift changes of character. The others changed their personalities with the week's change of bill as carelessly as they did their make-up and costumes. Playing with them, I felt old!

I couldn't believe this life had once been mine. I had grown to crave a part that, once learned, lasted at least through a season. Stock was a torrent that swept past me, leaving me old and subdued on the banks.

And yet stock was foster mother to my acting and I had played it thirty-four years! I like to think that sometime, out beyond space and time, all the members of all the stock shows I have played with will meet once more, one shining company, beyond the eternal footlights.

After this experience, the east seemed suddenly too rapidly driven. And as suddenly, I went home.

I might have changed, but the Santa Clara valley was the same as when I was a boy. Jennie and Auntie Em had wrought miracles with Baconia. The ranch had been improved in an effort to make it self-supporting, the house was a real hacienda with a glass porch and there was a dam stemming the lovely little creek. The barnyard was populated with the descendants of the duck, Billy Waddles, and the

211

Bantie chicken family who had barnstormed with us in rural roles years before.

"I'm never going to leave the ranch again!" I vowed, and there was no regret in my words.

I felt I was too old to fight the past. I'd failed enough. One thing would not fail me, and that was the marigold seed with which I showered Baconia. I've always loved marigolds. Also, I planted lettuce, after a method of my own. Instead of digging a trough to hold the straggly little plants, I went along the earth puncturing it with a pencil. Into this pencil hole I angled the string-like lettuce root, and tamped it down. My more experienced neighbors used to follow me down my lettuce rows, and by their countenances I read no respect for my agricultural discoveries.

However, our family lunched on salad that summer. Also, I joined the Masons and learned the ritual from my fellow worker while I was picking prunes. You see my time was not wasted.

I might be at Mountain View now, chewing on a mustard stalk and wearing the hat mother had thrown away three times, and just "tinkering" around the place. I love to "tinker," trying all my surgery on a broken chair leg, or the alarm clock that refused to alarm — usually because I've been "tinkering" with it. And I like cobbling my own shoes. Ever since I was a kid in San Jose, I've liked watching cobblers at their work. I'll bet you never saw an unhappy one!

But Oliver Morosco knew I had retired to country life and made me an offer. Asked me to come down to Los Angeles and play there at his Burbank Theatre. I had to go, for the customary economic reason, but with little enthusiasm. My life as an actor had seemed fairly ended and all my mind was taken up with the pruners we had hired to trim the trees — funny how few men there are who can prune a tree properly! But I left the family and the ranch, regretfully, for the south.

The motion picture industry was at its height in Los Angeles. Hollywood was a name gone into the language, and tales of fabulous wealth among the stars had swept the world like news of a second Gold Rush. It was another '49, and I fell for it as my grandfather had for golden tales of wealth. In other words, I left Oliver Morosco's company to play in Pictures.

Oh, yes, I've been in the movies! It was in "The Silent Voice," and I supported Francis X. Bushman.

About this time the all-star cast of "The Henrietta" played Los Angeles. Winchell Smith came with them. I heard he was in town and looked him up. I wanted to tell him about my play. Smith, always polite, said he would like to see it, and I rushed back to the lot and rescued it from the hands of Bushman's secretary — Bushman had thought it might make a picture. "Bring it to New York and we'll see what can be done with it," Smith invited.

"I am going there, anyway, with the Metro folks," I told him.

This was not a Bill Jones fiction, but the truth. But no sooner was I east again than I deserted the motion pictures forever to play once more for Oliver Morosco. This time I was Jerry Primrose in "The Cinderella Man."

Smith was practising the surgery of the stage on my play, amputating chunks of it and grafting on other parts. He is a master at that sort of thing. At last he read it to me. I thought it was fine, and said so. I may have been prejudiced.

On my fifty-third birthday I stepped into a telegraph office on Broadway and wrote a wire to Jennie with a hand that would shake a little. Far off on our California homestead, she read this word from me:

"Smith has accepted play — paid five hundred dollars
deposit — some little birthday present — Frank."

There are more slips between the cup and the lip in the theatrical profession than any other I know. Time passed. To all my anxiety Smith replied that he was working on the play. It seemed like hopeless waiting and I went home again. And here once more I might have settled down but for another telegram. This wanted me east at once, he was "producing a play."

"*Lightnin'*"! I told the family gathering at the ranch.

We were electrified into action. This time I raced east, but not alone. The entire family emigrated with me to New York. Jennie came with me. I had written the "Mother Jones" part for her, but she would not be able to play it. She had not been well since our last tour in vaudeville. Bessie came, a young widow now, and with her the two little girls. And blessed Auntie Em, our pillar of strength always, for her first glimpse of the big American town.

I found them a nice cool place in New Jersey that came up to all traditions in the matter of mosquitos. But the time we spent out there was worth it, for the sight of our feminine neighbors slapping their ankles gave me one of the biggest line hits in *Lightnin'*. It's where "Mother" comes out in the flamboyant evening gown and the silver-headed *Lightnin'*, badly shocked but game, tells her, "The mosquitos will give you hell in that this summer."

213

But Smith was not producing *Lightnin'*. After all our hopes, we found out that the play to be produced was one called "Toby's Bow," and he wanted me to play blackface! And I had moved the family east to receive this blow. I was stunned.

I took the blackface offer. "Toby's Bow" played one week "on the dog" in Wilmington, and was shelved.

I wonder how many playwrights have died waiting for their plays to go on. Smith kept assuring me he was working on ours. During the long wait, he produced — and I played in, "The Jackknife Man." We played Asbury Park and Long Branch but it never got "into town." Then Smith and Golden loaned me to Arthur Hopkins to play with Marie Doro in the Plymouth Theatre in New York. I felt more lost than ever. Especially so, when that play, "Barbara," also failed.

I'll never forget Thanksgiving, 1917. The streets were gay with color, but in all the horror of war. My family had moved back into New York and were living in an apartment that made us all homesick for Baconia. Lloyd had enlisted and Jennie was sick — the bottom had fallen out of my world.

There always is a surprise waiting around the corner, no matter how dark life may seem. For, by the time Christmas came, *Lightnin'* was in rehearsal in New York!

Of course I was in the Bill Jones part, playing it with the image before me of Uncle Morris, dead and gone these many years. For once I had found a part ready to my mind, for was it not my own? No stumbling at rehearsals now. The character I played was as much mine as if I had been living it — as I had — for more years than I care to remember. I just drifted off-stage and on and rambled away at my speeches as if I'd never said them before.

My costume was one I had seen the boys wear in the Old Soldiers' Home, a faded suit of army blue, and a battered blue hat of the G.A.R. with a gold cord about its crown. The sight of that pathetic hat, the memories it gave me of the old fellows in the Home near Yountville, California, the stories they had told me and their memories of heroisms forgotten, often brought tears to my eyes. I know now it affected many another person the same way.

Lightnin' was produced for the first time on any stage, January 25, 1918, in Washington, D.C.

It was wartime. The life and secrets of America were centered in this lovely city by the Potomac. It was a scene of moving regiments and anxious diplomacy, and upon this stirring scene, silver-headed and willful and old-fashioned, came the wistful figure of *Lightnin'*.

214

Jennie Bacon, 1910.

Frank Bacon, December 1910.

Best Wishes all the ways
Frank Bacon
Dec. 1910

Moffett
Chicago

Frank Bacon in character of Lightnin' Bill Jones.

From the first moment, when Bill comes on the stage, slightly tipsy but bearing a sheaf of honeysuckle "slips" for the grave of his young friend's mother, applause followed him. I seemed very calm and my voice didn't flutter on a syllable. But under my calmness I felt my life racing away, panting for breath, with nervousness. I had met with too many failures to take this moment calmly.

After the second act I was called before the curtain for a speech. I made it calmly enough, not dreaming that I would be called upon to make that speech again, over a thousand times!

There was war in Europe, men were being shuffled by the thousands overseas, our lads were in training in field and barracks throughout America. Here, before me in box and stall, sat the leaders of America, the men whose steady hands played behind the pawns. Here in one box sat the man whose reputation would be divided among men before the war ended, who would die ignominiously for some, and live to others, in glory. He sat with his family in a box nearest the stage, and I was glad to see that even in wartime, the long, intellectual face of Woodrow Wilson could wrinkle with laughter. I've admired Wilson. As Bill Jones might have said, "I've been a dreamer myself!"

About Wilson were clustered members of his Cabinet, men whose movements were followed by all America. And they could all laugh, even while the world was draped in misery. I went to my hotel with a sense of exaltation. It was good to make men forget for an hour, in wartime.

That week *Lightnin'* closed in Washington.

We brought it back to New York, but it was too late in the season to put it on.

During the interim, Bessie and I were placed in the cantonment company of "Turn to the Right." But I would not have missed that experience for anything in life.

We played the war camps out of New York, down through the southern states and back. I shall never forget those living panoramas tinted in khaki. In the southern camps I saw frightened mountaineers from the Blue Ridge districts or the Ozarks. Some had been brought into camp wearing Mother Hubbards! They had never seen a school book. War was a word that burst upon them like rifle fire. They were brought down like frightened wild things, and I have seen them walk across fields at dusk, holding hands out of sheer terror. How many went back to the mountains, I wonder, and what tales did they carry there!

215

In May, 1918, we were back in New York and Smith began assembling the *Lightnin'* cast for the new season. By June rehearsals were in full swing and late in July we put on the first show, over in Atlantic City. It was here Jennie saw it for the first time. And yet Bill Jones had been a member of the family for thirty years!

I stole glances at her during the acts, and saw her face working, but with what emotion I could not fathom. Afterwards, she came backstage and I found her weeping on Matthew Allen's shoulder. Matt — he was our manager taken over from the cantonment company where he and Bess had met for the first time. Later they were married. Now Jennie was clinging to him in uncontrollable grief.

"Is — is this what we've been planning for, so long?" she managed to ask me.

I felt terrible. Of course, the play had gone rather badly that first performance, and some inhuman person had walked out during the courtroom scene. But I wasn't prepared for Jennie's disappointment. We went home together, miserable.

"Frank, it never will go in the world!" she told me flatly after we were home.

Then I turned to her, fighting to control my own doubts.

"Jennie, you're committing murder!" I told her. "Don't kill my faith in this play — it's all I have!"

She was braver after that, but I knew what she was thinking. The entire family had come to New York on the strength of a hope this play had given. It would be back to the prune orchards for all the Bacons when this play failed.

Next we took it to Stamford, Connecticut. And there the ticket brokers saw it, and bought a block of seats. The barometer of our hopes went up to the bursting point. To have the brokers buy up your tickets is a certain sign of popularity. But, would our quiet little tale of life on the California-Nevada line bear the withering criticism of sophisticated New York? Bess and I believed it would. We opened at the Gaity Theatre in New York on the night of August 26th, a night of sweltering heat.

Broadway! No matter how soon it ended, I was playing Broadway in my own play! It was the pinnacle I had hunted from my first part as a stripling "supe" in San Jose, near half a century before.

Of all the "guessers" in New York that night, no one could have guessed at the reception that would be awarded *Lightnin'*. I didn't, not even after the curtain fell on the last act and Bess and I started for home, as we called our apartment. Jennie had not come backstage to join us, but with her theatre guests, Auntie Em and Nina Gleason, who once had been a leading lady of ours, had drifted off with the rest of the crowd. Bess and I waited in the living room until Jennie and Auntie Em came home.

"This is nice work — deserting a Broadway star on his opening night," I scolded Jennie.

"We just went out for some ice cream," she explained placidly.

I hemmed around and finally asked her what she had thought of it!

"Frank, I've seen you do much better in stock," she replied, and to this very day she holds to that conclusion.

We sat round and talked and fell into short naps and were to chat again, but nobody admitted we were actually waiting for the morning papers. At daybreak, we were all looking rather pallid and had run out of conversation, and I went down to the cigar stand on the corner to buy every morning paper published in New York. On the way home I opened to the dramatic pages and read just the headings. They all read to the same harmony. I came back to the family and was able to flush their weary faces with the statement:

"Folks, I've arrived!"

The next night we tried to buy tickets for some friends. The Gaiety was sold out.

I was not elated. Pleasantly happy, but the wild thrill of victory I had dreamed about was not there. Still, I knew the success of this play I had helped to write and was starred in, was sweeter to me for my many failures! There can't be much fun in easy victories, although perhaps I have no right to judge, never having been an easy victor. *Lightnin'* was a success from the first night, but I was old!

The news is forever press-agenting me — "He succeeded at seventy!" Well, I'm not seventy, although I feel so at times. But I had played aging parts. My movements had dulled to the parts I had played in, until I was living always in a perpetual old-man role. My movements were slow. My voice sounded rather tired. And worse, I was tired.

But how I loved the role of "Lightnin' " Bill! It had grown to be part of me through the years, until I was Bill. And one night I came out and found Jennie in the wings sniffling with emotion. For the first time, I knew I had made good!

And still, we couldn't believe it. The weeks were swollen into months and there was no thought of closing the show. We ran to our

217

hundredth and first night — passing Edwin Booth's record in "Hamlet."

On and on ran the nights, and every night from out front came the joyous refrain, "Sold out." Steadily we crept up and passed the records of plays that had made history for their famous runs. "The Two Orphans," "The Old Homestead" — we left them behind us.

The critics began referring to me as "the second Joe Jefferson." It is strange that of all my early heroes, he is the one I never saw play. But I have always revered the memory of Jefferson. He, it was who said, speaking of his play and his public:

"I'm not shooting over their heads. I'm aiming at their hearts."

Came the night of September 9th, in 1919. General Pershing was home from overseas, home from war. The Armistice was at last a matter of history. After a day of parades that paid him honor, Pershing and his staff spent their first evening of return to American soil at *Lightnin'*.

When I came out in my old G.A.R. uniform for the curtain speech, I put my hand to my hat:

"General, I salute you!"

He rose in the box and stood at attention until I left the stage. And once he, the Nation's idol, had been a young Lieutenant on the New Mexican desert and I a young night-hawking actor, and we had been friendly then. Yes, life could still hold surprises glad as a Christmas stocking is to childhood, even to a man whose hair was a shock of snow and who was beginning to feel strangely tired.

"The first five hundred nights are the hardest," I told John Golden, our producer, after we had broken the record of David Warfield in "The Music Master" with our 541st show.

"Peg of My Heart", "A Trip to Chinatown", a dozen more flashing successes — we left them all behind. Life became routine. At the end of the first year's run in 1919, I bought a Long Island home at Bayside. It was charmingly like the country, and Jennie and the three little girls were there, and Auntie Em to mother and scold us as in less luxurious days. We had a car and someone to drive it. I commuted and became an expert at making the theatre train into town at the last possible moment. Mornings and Sundays I fooled around the place with a paint brush and can, wearing my ancient duck trousers and a navy sweater mother declared was the disgrace of Bayside. But I didn't have to worry about that, or anything else. When our actor friends came to visit us I put them to work. Only we never seemed to get much work done.

218

Frank and Jennie Bacon in Bayside, Long Island, where they lived during the run of Lightnin' in New York.

Frank Bacon with his granddaughters at home in Bayside, Long Island.

Frank Bacon in Bayside, Long Island.

Along about this time I bought Jennie her first real diamond. We felt we could afford it even if the house wasn't paid for. It was a grand diamond, one of the biggest and clearest I could find. I remembered her first stone, how I had bought it — on time, on a salary of five dollars a week, and she had nobly sold it for $100 that I might found another stock company! Jennie deserved the best I could find for her and she got it that Christmas.

After a while I bought her another one. And then I sort of think she hinted for another, and got it. When her birthday came and I asked her what she wanted for a present, her eyes sparkled.

"Oh, Frank!" she gasped. "Could I have a diamond ring?"

"Great Snakes, Jennie, you have three of them already," I rebuked her. "And, anyway, diamonds are hopelessly vulgar."

All the smoldering resentment against our long years of poverty flamed in her answer:

"I don't care. Bring on all the vulgarity you can, and I'll wear it!"

Lightnin' ran on and another year passed our heads and still another. Every night and matinee we played to crowded houses — it seemed New York could not get tired. The newspapers had another name for me now, "the most feted man in New York." I'll swear that I attended five thousand luncheons during this period and at all but one we were served chicken a la king.

Success has its delights but it often brings on dyspepsia. Sometimes I was reminded of something that happened when I was playing at the San Francisco Alcazar at thirty a week.

Then Jennie was her busiest, playing character bits the Alcazar found for her, keeping boarders and attending to the housework and cooking. At the time I recall, my father decided to come up from San Jose to pay us a visit.

"I'm going to make his trip a wonderful one if it kills me," vowed Jennie, for it was the first time father had made the forty mile trip to the "city."

I'll have to let you into a family secret to explain this. Father had been at sword points with Jennie ever since she had first encouraged me, a young husband and father, to desert the calling of photographer and go on the stage. Jennie was not one to apologize, and domestic relations had been a bit strained between them for many years. Now she decided to atone, and atonement for Jennie meant complete surrender.

Every morning she was up early, for father was a country riser, whipping together the light southern biscuits he loved. Every

219

morning after breakfast she allotted him a quarter from the family reserve fund and told him to be sure and be home in time for dinner. And what a day father would have! He would walk Market Street till his feet hurt, staring at the crowds and buildings. Then he sat down to rest on the large green municipal garbage can that used to adorn Powell and Market. And there, I, passing with the dandies of the Alcazar company on our way to matinee, would find father sitting at ease and contemplating life as it passed on wheels and hurrying feet.

Father was a man of few words. On the day he returned to San Jose, he made this speech to me, and they held the apology of a lifetime:

"No matter what may be said about Jennie encouraging you in this play-acting business, Frank, I've always said she was the very finest girl in the world!"

So you see how any successful experiment makes people forget the rockier roads you have traveled.

Lightnin' crept up to its third year and critics who once had jeered at me as a barnstormer now wrote of me in a way I would blush to rewrite for you.

And then, just as Triumph and I were sharing the throne together, came the Actors' Strike.

I was nearing sixty.

After a lifetime of failure, for the first time I was free. Free to indulge in any little luxury I had ever desired. I could step into a taxi without a twinge of conscience. I could shower presents upon the children, keep two cars if I liked and a driver for both of them. Life was easy — when the Actors' Strike came like a blow in the face.

I had joined the Actor's Equity Association a few years previous to the *Lightnin'* run, without thinking much about it either way.

The trouble began just as *Lightnin'* was setting out on its second year's run. If any man could sympathize with the actor, that man was I. Didn't I know what it was to be left in strange towns without friends, money or carfare home? Actors had been piling up grievances for a long time — the injustice of long weeks rehearsing with perhaps one week's salary if the play failed — actresses had to defray the cost of an expensive wardrobe — lay-offs and extra performances, these and other causes piled up fuel for the fires of discontent. I don't think anyone realized the seriousness of the issue — nor the bitterness it caused. We believed the managers would grant the demands. All we asked was a small amount of protection such as any employer grants his men. Yet this was refused.

220

Personally, I had many friends among the managers — Winchell Smith had given me my first big part in the East — he and John Golden had produced *Lightnin'* — George Cohan had been a friend when I needed him. One of the keenest joys I've ever felt, I experienced recently when our hands met again in a strong friendly grasp! Conditions were going on happily in our theatre — I was in the midst of rehearsals of "Five O'clock", a new play I had done with Freeman Tilden — but loyalty to Equity was paramount, and I followed the banner of the A.E.A.

There was trouble in the air, and I sensed it one evening when Bessie and I were dining with friends at the Hotel Astor. Surely, in such gilded surroundings, there was nothing to worry over!

About eight o'clock we left together for the Gaiety. I never troubled about getting to the theatre early as my make-up took only a few minutes.

The theatre was dark!

"Something must be wrong with the electric sign," I said, as we went through the alley to the stage door.

Not a soul was stirring in the house. One of the stagehands lunged past. He was not working.

"The strike's been called — didn't you know?" he explained.

It came as a shock to me. I had firmly expected some sort of arbitration. We went up to Equity headquarters and received instructions, and then rode home to Bayside. Jennie, startled to see us home so early and fearing the reason, turned rather pale.

There would be an Equity meeting the next morning at ten o'clock. Jennie and I went out on the porch and sat there until close to morning, talking things over. It was not as if I had any personal quarrel with the management. Remember, I was part owner of *Lightnin'* and if I chose to present that excuse I could continue to play.

"I'll leave it all to you, Jennie," I said. "All we have in the bank is $5,000 and this house isn't paid for. If Equity doesn't win, and the management closes me out of *Lightnin'* — you know what it will mean to us."

She sat very quietly for a moment, and in the first gray paller of dawn I saw the lines in her face. We weren't young any more. And what we had in life had come so late. She got up suddenly.

"Let's sleep on it," she said.

Before I left for the meeting next morning, mother gave me her ultimatum. She was fresh and serene again and spoke in her own high-spirited way:

221

"Frank, you and I never did have things easy and perhaps all this isn't natural for us, but this struggle isn't for us — it's for the rank and file! Think what an Equity victory would mean to all the struggling actors in America! Think of the boys and girls who stood by us in the old lean days! I could never look one of them in the face again if we left the ship now!"

And then she added, cheerfully:

"No, I've kept house in a furnished room and cooked on a coal oil stove, and I'll do it again if I have to. We'll stick!"

I wish you could have heard those Equity members cheer when I gave them Jennie's words in my speech that day!

And that was when I headed my first Broadway parade. I've led two parades down that glittering street, but this first was the Actors' strike parade, and I'll tell you we felt we were making history. I stumped around making speeches for Equity and helped raise funds, and the struggle lasted four entire weeks. At the end of that time, the managers gave in and the theatres blossomed again in lights and we were all called back to work. That was my only vacation in three New York years, and I spent most of the hours working for Equity.

I'm proud of the success *Lightnin'* has been. I'm prouder still of that Equity victory "for those that follow after."

About this time, Jennie and I celebrated our thirty-fifth wedding anniversary. Dear old Auntie Em baked another wedding cake and Lloyd brought his wife from Hollywood to join the family party. Many changes had come to us through the years, but the sight of our children, and the happy little grandgirls was compensation.

I might be playing *Lightnin'* now in New York, only our contract with the Gaiety ran out and called us to the Blackstone Theatre in Chicago. The show broke the last of all dramatic records and ran on into three years and a day!

"The show of One Thousand One Nights," the press named it. Wilson, Taft and Harding, three Presidents saw the play in turn. Governor Al Smith and Mayor Hylan saw it many times. People returned to it over and over, bringing their friends. Admiral Glennon broke the record. He attended thirty performances.

The time allotted in our contract was passing and every minute was precious to me. The Lambs Club and Equity promised me a "turn-out" when I left the big town for Chicago. Then the Green Room, not to be outdone, also offered me an escort to the station, and the Friars added their promise. Oh! How I hated leaving New York!

222

Closing night came. With the 1,291st performance we dropped the Gaiety curtain on *Lightnin'*. People were turned from the doors. The Mayor made a speech, Admiral Glennon made a speech, all the notables in the boxes were called upon for speeches and were cheered wildly.

In the faded suit of army blue, I made the same old *Lightnin'* speech I had made so many times during the New York run.

"Lightnin'" Bill had remarked, and the remark had been held against him in court in the play, that he had once driven a swarm of bees across the plains and not lost a single bee.

"When you're chasin' a bee," I told the audience again on this final night, "let it be. Well, once during the Civil War I had General Grant with me on Lookout Mountain. I was the only man he would let look out. In the midst of the war he comes over to me and says, 'Bill', says he — (He always called me Bill) — 'Willie', says he, 'How long can ye hold out?' 'All summer', says I, glancing down at my wrist watch.' 'Then', says Grant, 'We'll fight it out if it takes all winter.'"

Just nonsense, and afterward I tried to tell that big audience something of the friendliness I felt toward them. I couldn't — but they guessed, because still they kept swarming down to the footlights and refusing to leave.

"I hope it rains tomorrow," I said miserably to Jennie on Sunday evening, the day before we were to leave New York.

She seemed surprised.

"Because . . . oh, you know what a parade is, and I'd hate to see a handful of people straggling after me to the station," I said, with the dread of being ridiculous only a comedian can feel.

But Jennie refused to waste sympathy upon such a wish and the morning dawned cloudless as crystal. I went into town early, on the nine o'clock train. Jennie and Bessie drove in later. At Broadway a traffic policeman halted their automobile.

"Street closed," he explained. "Parade in honor of Frank Bacon, the actor."

Jennie had a hard time explaining and getting to the Pennsylvania Station on time for the train. But she stood on the running board of the car, little as she is, and managed to see the parade.

Broadway was solid with human beings. Never before had a crowd like that been seen in New York, they tell me — not even for a President. In our three years run over one million people had seen *Lightnin'*. It seemed to me they were all there that gala afternoon; parading to the tune of bands and a chant that swelled from the throats of one hundred thousand marching men:

223

"Good-bye, Frank, don't forget to bring home the Bacon!"

The watchers along the sidewalks took it up, until all New York seemed chanting luck in my wake. Three thousand of the marchers were Equity members, fellow actors I had fought beside during the Equity Strike. As they marched they waved flags and sang, "Auld Lang Syne." The crowd took that up, too, as they came tramping down Broadway.

Mayor Hylan and I walked side by side at the head. We decided to walk instead of ride, although the day was warm. And there was Winchell Smith and John Golden and Grant Stuart, and other friends. And in our wake marched the hundred thousand. We wore satin badges and mine is pasted in my scrapbook now:

"FRANK BACON ... LIGHTNIN' "

"GOODBYE NEW YORK ... GOOD LUCK CHICAGO"

"August 29, 1921."

I was out of the habit of making theatrical jumps and I might never have caught this train without that crowd behind me. But we turned away from Broadway into Thirty Third Street and marched into the great vault of the Pennsylvania Station. There was Jennie, pressing through the crowd behind an excited porter. And there came the hundred thousand, or as many of them as that station could hold.

The bands played and all that crowd began singing, like the voices of friends heard long ago:

> "Should auld acquaintance be forgot
> And the days of auld lang syne?"

They were singing still as I yielded up our tickets to the gateman and followed the porter down the length of that Chicago destined train. The voices died as we found our plush bottomed chairs in the drawing room car. We sat very quietly, silenced by the memory of that warm hearted Broadway we were leaving. And up above us ran the pointed streets of New York, a city that would always be to me the last lap of the long paloosa trail I had followed so long.

I leaned back on the soft chair cushions and stared out of the window, suddenly tired with the heat and the marching and happiness.

The train was pulling down the gray corridor of tracks, slowly and easily, away from Broadway. Outside, two baggage men were sitting on a truck, and I'll never forget their wonderful, friendly grins as they waved and shouted through the car window:

"Goodbye, Frank, Don't forget to bring home the Bacon!"

Jennie and I smiled at each other through tears of happiness, as I said — "I wonder what father would have said to this?"

She replied — "Just what he always did."

"What was that?"

"Frank, the whole town's talking about you."

Frank Bacon, 1922.

FOOTNOTES

1. BROHASKA OPERA HOUSE: The Old Armory Hall, located on Santa Clara Street near 3rd Street. Became Brohaska's San Jose Opera House in 1870, under the management of Gustav Brohaska. Burned to the ground on July 5, 1881.

2. WRIGHT'S PHOTOGRAPHY STUDIO: Operated by Wilbur Wright and located at 1st and Santa Clara Streets above the First National Bank.

3. SAM W. PIERCY: One of the foremost American actors of his age. His family home was for many years at Julian Street near Sixth, in San Jose. In 1878 Piercy took over management of the San Jose Opera House as an enlarged and improved theater. He died of small pox in 1882 at the age of 33.

4. EDWARD MC LAUGHLIN: Listed in the 1881-82 San Jose Directory as Manager of the Commercial and Savings Bank. Lived on McLaughlin Avenue which bears his family name.

5. ELMER CHASE: (1874-1939) Active in the canning industry for 60 years. Served as President of the Golden Gate Packing Company, and as Vice-President of the Richmond-Chase Packing Company for 22 years. He was also President of the California Canner's Association from 1915 till his death, with the exception of the year 1926 when he was President of the National Canner's Association. Chase was also very active in San Jose civic affairs, serving on the city council and as President of the Chamber of Commerce from 1913-1914.

6. HUGH DE LACY: Publisher of the *City Item* in 1883. This paper became the *San Jose Evening News*. A member of many amateur theatrical groups in San Jose in the 1880s, he also served as Chief of Police from 1892-1894.

   STEVE DE LACY: Brother of Hugh. He became publisher of the *Daily Morning Times* in 1879 in partnership with Francis B. Murdoch, John G. Murdoch, and Francis W. Murdoch.

7. UNIVERSITY OF THE PACIFIC: UOP, now located in Stockton, California, was an important educational and cultural institution in San Jose from 1850 until 1925. It was affiliated with the Methodist Church. Bellarmine College Preparatory now occupies the site of the original UOP campus.

8. LOUIS LIEBER: (1862-1932) A sign painter with David Renaldo until he went into business for himself in the mid-1880s at 61 East Santa Clara Street. He later moved to 63 S. Second Street. Lieber owned the Lyric Theater on North Second Street, according to Eugene T. Sawyer's *History of Santa Clara County* published in 1922.

9. CALIFORNIA THEATER: Located at 81 S. Second Street from 1879-1892. Destroyed by fire.

10. JOHN W. DUNNE: Joined the San Jose Amateur Club in 1866 and then moved on to the professional stage. He managed the career of his first wife, Patti Rosa, and after her death the career of his second wife, Mary Marble. According to Sawyer's *History of Santa Clara County*, he played in Hoyt's comedies from one end of the country to the other until vaudeville became the rage.

11. EUGENE T. SAWYER: (1846-1924) Newspaper reporter, play-wright, and actor. A member of the first amateur dramatic company in San Jose, organized in 1865. In 1922 Sawyer wrote a *History of Santa Clara County*.

12. HOBSON: A tailor; T. W. Hobson & Co. was located at 44-54 W. Santa Clara Street and listed in the July 1885 City Directory as clothiers and merchant tailors.

13. CHARLES SHORTRIDGE: (1857-1918) Editor and manager of the *San Jose Daily Mercury* from 1884 to 1898. Served as a state senator from 1899 to 1906 and edited the *Daily Morning Times* from 1907-1909. Thereafter he was listed in the San Jose City Directory as Attorney at Law.

14. HORACE KEESLING: (1855-1940) Married Annie Bacon in 1880. He worked as orchardist at the Hayes estate in Edenvale in the early 1900s, and later owned his own cherry orchard in Willow Glen. Credited with planting rows of walnut trees along the old Monterey Highway. Farm editor of the *San Jose Mercury Herald* for 28 years.

15. JOHN MC NAUGHT: Native of Newport, Florida and well-known figure in American newspaper life. Editor of the *San Jose Mercury* in 1890s and later managing editor of the old *San Francisco Call* and *New York Morning World*. Married Margaret Schallenberger of San Jose and died here on March 12, 1938 at the age of 89.

16. LENZEN: Jacob, Theodore, and Michael Lenzen, German immigrant brothers, arrived in San Jose in the 1860s. Jacob and Theodore became architects and Michael the founder of the Lenzen Paint Company. Theodore W. Lenzen, son of Jacob, was also a member of his father's architectural firm from 1884 to 1900. Among the buildings designed by the Lenzen family were the 1887 San Jose City Hall, the old O'Connor Hospital, and the Hall of Records in San Jose.